PRAI
From Kuan Yin

"*From Kuan Yin to Chairman Mao* is a must-read book for anyone who is interested in China. Xueting Christine Ni has woven history, society, religion, beliefs, and most importantly a perspective into the Chinese mind-set. A fascinating book that gives all of us a better understanding of today's China."

—**Ken Hom**, OBE, chef, BBC presenter, author of
My Stir-fried Life and numerous other books

"I have yet to be as pleased or as excited as I am at the opportunity to join in the celebration of Xueting Christine Ni's debut, *From Kuan Yin to Chairman Mao*. If you seek a primer text on the Chinese pantheon of divinities, then look no further. Luminous and detailed, this is an encyclopedic treasure trove that now renders the gods and goddesses of Eastern lore accessible to the West. Edifying, scholarly, and yet a sparkling, mesmerizing read, *From Kuan Yin to Chairman Mao* is a personal favorite in my library."

—**Benebell Wen**, author of *The Tao of Craft: Fu Talismans
and Casting Sigils in the Eastern Esoteric Tradition*

"What a marvelous book! *From Kuan Yin to Chairman Mao* is essential reading for anyone who has stood in bewildered delight in the midst of a Chinese temple wondering at the meaning and importance of the statuary that surrounds the visitor. Xueting Christine Ni's beautifully written guide to the Chinese pantheon is the sort of book that should be in the hands of any visitor to Hong Kong or Mainland China, explaining as it does the history, meaning, and continued relevance of the various deities the traveler encounters. And not just in temples. Ni explains how for the most part these figures are all a part of a living tradition that have significant afterlives in popular culture, from movies and TV shows to video games and comics. Part of what makes this book so interesting—and so important—is her incredible knowledge, not just of the mystical past but the very vibrant present in which Chinese populations all over the world continue to practice and expand their rich spiritual traditions.

"*From Kuan Yin to Chairman Mao* opens up the full complexity of Chinese religious life, explaining not just the three religious traditions usually attributed to the Chinese (Buddhism, Taoism, and Confucianism) but also the next level of popular religion which embraces a whole cast of generals, courtesans, and wise governors who have all been elevated to important positions in the Chinese hierarchy of gods and spirits. Constantly fascinating, always surprising, and immensely helpful, this is the book many travelers, occultists, and pilgrims have been waiting for."

—**Walter Mason**, author of *Destination Saigon* and *Destination Cambodia*

"Xueting Christine Ni has created some enthralling profiles of China's sprawling cast of deities, from their mythical origins to their manifestations in 21st-century pop culture. If you want to learn about China's rambunctious spiritual life, *From Kuan Yin to Chairman Mao* is a first-class guide."

—**Ben Chu**, economics editor of *The Independent* and author of *Chinese Whispers*

"I used to think *Chinese mythology is extremely complicated—who would be crazy enough to write a book trying to explain it?* Despite common misconceptions, China is not a monolithic entity with a singular belief system across the vast country, let alone the diaspora. Depending on who you ask, the stories, mythology, even the gods themselves can vary across regions and even families. Explaining the Chinese gods has always been difficult for Chinese people and even more difficult for Westerners to understand. Xueting Christine Ni has accomplished what very few have done for the common English-speaking audience, providing enough depth to bring insight and deep understanding into the gods, but not so much that the information is bogged down amidst potentially conflicting legends. Moreover, she is not afraid to present information that is controversial, that would create heated friction between Chinese people themselves. *From Kuan Yin to Chairman Mao* is perhaps the best book for unfamiliar readers to begin gaining familiarity with the spiritual complexities of the Chinese gods."

—**David Borji Shi**, author of *North Asian Magic: Spellcraft from Manchuria, Mongolia, and Siberia*

FROM KUAN YIN TO
CHAIRMAN MAO

FROM KUAN YIN TO CHAIRMAN MAO

THE ESSENTIAL GUIDE TO CHINESE DEITIES

Xueting Christine Ni

WEISER BOOKS

This edition first published in 2018 by Weiser Books, an imprint of
Red Wheel/Weiser, LLC
With offices at:
65 Parker Street, Suite 7
Newburyport, MA 01950
www.redwheelweiser.com

ISBN: 978-1-57863-625-9
Library of Congress Cataloging-in-Publication Data available upon request.

Interior photos/images: While the images reproduced in this book are believed to be in the public domain,
there are a few images for which provenance is unknown. In these cases, every effort has been made to
research and trace the copyright holders and obtain permission to reproduce them in an editorial manner.
The publisher apologizes for any errors or omissions and would appreciate any information
regarding the copyright holder for these images.

Typeset in Centaur

Printed in Canada
MAR
10 9 8 7 6 5 4 3 2 1

For Joseph, my soul mate
For Siu-Zun (婆婆), my Cantonese grandma
with love and gratitude

TABLE OF CONTENTS

Acknowledgments

I WANT TO THANK MY PARTNER, Joseph, for his steadfast and unwavering belief in my work, and for his boundless support through the years. It was he who first recognized the value of my unique perspective and encouraged me to pursue what has now become a lifelong mission in writing about China, and translating its culture and literature for the West.

I'd also like to thank my editor, Judika, for her belief in my work and my writing. She has provided me with excellent guidance and advice, and her openness and support through difficult times have been greatly appreciated.

I am grateful to the British Library, where I spent many happy hours researching this book, for providing a well-rounded collection of materials on Chinese religion and mythology, as well as elegant spaces in which to browse them.

I'm indebted to Ma Shutian's comprehensive "Hua Xia Zhu Shen," which I relied on as the main basis for my research. It enabled me to focus my limited time and resources building on previous research, interpreting the existing strands of histories, and investigating how these have evolved in the modern day. Apart from my interpretation of the origins and history of the deities featured in this book, I have also explored contemporary beliefs and customs surrounding their worship. For this, the Internet has proved invaluable. It is truly a great resource for learning about popular culture because it is composed by the people. While it is virtually impossible to record every image and source I came across in this sprawling and interconnected space, all of them have, in their own way, contributed to this work.

And, of course, I must give thanks to Wen Chang and Huang Di, who have guided this book from its conception in my mind to the volume in your hands.

INTRODUCTION

CHINA IS A COUNTRY OF PARADOX. Some in the West perceive it as an ancient land of mysticism that still caters to the whims of dragons and spirits. Others, influenced by modern interactions with China, see it as a land where capitalist communism reigns, its relentless citizens operating with varying degrees of recklessness for personal gain. In other words, they see it as a reflection of the tension between the Qi Gong (the work of the spirit) and the Ren Gong (the labor of men).

The truth, as with so many things, lies somewhere between these two extremes.

The Chinese are a stoic race who have built a civilization that began by weathering the floods and droughts along the banks of the Yellow River. The rise and fall of dynasties, the upheavals of revolution, and the impact of historical tragedies have made the Chinese pragmatic survivors. But none of these have diminished our excitable, whimsical, and highly emotional nature, which constantly seeks to entrust hopes and fears to some greater being or higher spirit.

I was born and raised in the city of Guang Zhou (Canton). Back then, my family still lived with my paternal grandfather in the labyrinthine alleyways that made up the old city's residential areas. Here, I was taken care of by a circle of *Po Po*—the Cantonese word for "grannies"— who were a living embodiment of traditional Cantonese culture. One made mouth-watering Shunde[1] cuisine at her coal-heated stove, while another loved to listen to *Yue Ju* (Cantonese opera) on the radio amongst the traditional carved wooden furniture. They all shared their homes with an array of porcelain gods, like Kuan Yin, Goddess of Universal Mercy, and Cai Shen, the gods of wealth.

I remember Siu Zun, the Po Po who practically raised me while my parents pursued their dreams of the New Prosperity. In one corner of her living room sat a small wooden altar where there were invariably

offerings of fruit throughout the year. The altar featured the usual collection of household deities—Tu Di Ye, the earth god; Men Shen, the
door guardians; and Fu Shen, Lu Shen, and Shou Xing, the gods of
happiness. The framed picture in the middle of the altar, however, was
not of a deity. It was of her late husband. On Qing Ming (the Chinese
festival of the dead), after sweeping his grave and burning offerings of
paper money, Siu Zun placed roast meats before the altar, accompanied
by incense and prayers. Alongside the deities, she prayed to his spirit to
keep her family safe and bring them prosperity. This was a scene repeated
throughout the tenement building, the sweet smell of sandalwood smoke
filling the corridors and stairwells.

Later still, when my parents moved out of the alleys and into modern high-rise apartments, I still visited the old lady at least once a week,
until my family moved to England. As an adult, I rediscovered my fascination with these earthy spiritual icons and rituals, which had never really
left me. On my visits to Canton, I seek out those winding back alleyways
of my youth, and am delighted to find that the traditional threshold
offerings of oranges and apples, stuck through with incense, still adorn
doorways. This native spirituality is still very much alive in China.

The Western concept of a Judeo-Christian god, or even a Greco-
Roman father god, is fundamentally different from the Chinese idea of
deities. In Chinese religion, there is no concept of a single omniscient
being. Rather, there are many gods in the pantheon and, while they are
supposedly divided among the three religions that co-exist in China—
Confucianism, Daoism, and Buddhism, or *Ru* (儒), *Dao* (道), and *Fo*
(佛)—the boundaries between them are not at all clear-cut.

Confucianism developed out of the teachings of the philosopher
Confucius, who lived in 500 BCE, during a war-torn era (see chapter
13). During his lifetime, Confucius was revered as an advocate for an
ordered society. Upon his death, his family and students worshipped him
in the traditional manner in which the deceased were honored. The sheer
number of his followers raised Confucius to the status of a protective
deity who watched over his local community. When this was brought
to the attention of the emperor, he knighted Confucius's family and
elevated him to a patron god of the bureaucracy tasked with ensuring

social harmony in the emperor's household—which was, of course, the entire state.

China's indigenous religion, Daoism—which literally means "The Way"—is primarily concerned with the state of existence itself. Daoist philosophers and alchemists explored their unity with nature and searched for the elixir that granted immortality. For the majority of Chinese, however, this faith is intimately connected with everyday life, initially through shamans or sorcerers of local communities who communed with spirits to divine the future, invoke rain, and cure diseases. Later, the Dao Shi, priests who lived in villages as well as temples, attended to the needs of the people, dispensing talismans, treating ailments, and performing funeral rites. A Daoist pantheon emerged when the ambitious Zhang Dao Ling (34–156 CE), an enterprising Daoist scholar widely recognized as the founder of Daoism as a religion originally known as Tian Shi Dao (Cult of the Heavenly Master), turned this native faith into a religion by instating Lao Zi (sometimes called Lao-Tzu) as its mystical founder (see chapter 13).

Buddhism, on the other hand, came to China from outside its borders and traditions. It traveled from India to China, where it adapted and diversified into branches of Chinese Buddhism like Zen. Because the development of any Chinese deity is inseparable from the land and the people, however, it was inevitable that the Buddhist deities introduced into China would develop a distinct identity over hundreds of years of evolution.

Yet even those who clearly identified themselves as Buddhist, or Daoist, or Confucian had very little problem visiting a temple of another discipline. Chinese practices within these three separate religions are very much linked and mutually reinforcing.

There is also a fourth aspect to China's religious identity—a folk religion whose gods grew from myths, folklore, and legends. This tradition capriciously took whatever stories it liked from the more established faiths, dropped the less favored parts, and twisted the disparate strands together to form new and wonderfully diverse narratives. Buddhism and Daoism, in their heavy competition for followers and spiritual power, have both been adept at adopting new deities who rose out of folklore and took root in popular thought.

For this reason, the subjects of Chinese worship are a haphazard and eclectic variety of personages—gods, real people, ancestors, and sometimes even animals—who are considered divine simply because their followers and worshippers have made them so. There are gods of the elements and terrain (in fact multiple versions of each), deities of agriculture, and dozens of household gods and goddesses. Industries and trades each have their own gods. Even silkworms and toilets have their patron goddesses. There are patron gods of culture, crafts, and writing. There's a god for tea, as well as one for wine. And as if that weren't enough, there are a couple of dozen gods of medicine and healing and some sixteen gods of fortune to look after the welfare of the people. There is even a god of gods, the Jade Emperor, who presides over the Immortals.

The old adage that men made gods before gods made men is writ large here, as is the truism that belief empowers. During the infamous years of the Cultural Revolution, many temples in mainland China were sacked and destroyed, leaving an unfathomable void for researchers delving into long-held beliefs and indigenous deities. In the last thirty years, however, many Chinese have rediscovered their faith in the old gods. Incense sticks are burning bright, donations are pouring into temples— both those that survived the purge and new ones now being built. People are gathering their family clans to perform ancester worship around renovated tombs, and it has become fashionable to re-enact the ancient traditions and ceremonies on festive occasions.

In this book, I bring you the stories of sixty Chinese gods, goddesses, spirits, and sages. Sixty is a significant number in Chinese culture, being related to the full sexagenary calendar cycle, created by Dao Rao Shi around 2700 BCE under Huang Di. This calendar is still in use today. Sixty also represents the twelve zodiac animals multiplied by the five elements. These sixty deities have been selected across a broad spectrum of mythical beings, deified heroes, gods, goddesses, and Immortals from Buddhism, Daoism, and folklore. Confucianism is also represented, although this tradition is less apt to create new gods. This is by no means a definitive list. Nor are these necessarily the most important deities—although I have included many of the most significant and popular gods.

I have chosen to present these particular gods to show how varied and rich the Chinese religious experience can be. Indeed, I have deliberately included both the sublime and the ridiculous. You'll find that Chinese gods cater to diverse devotees in diverse walks of life. In a society that so highly values conformity, the Chinese people are surprisingly drawn to rebels, outcasts, and misfits.

The book presents not only the traditional depiction and worship of each of these deities, but also their contemporary representation and their place in modern China. Even in modern custom, the Chinese people have a deep and passionate reverence for statues and icons. This is reflected in their customs of worship, which are rooted in the traditional belief that statues are actual vessels for the gods. They give them physical form and, in some cases, ground them in a locality.

Many of these myths and origin stories appear in different, often contradictory, versions. I have examined multiple sources—official interpretations, folklore, academic references, and historical records—to bring you an authentic, but uniform and understandable, story. In my retelling, I hope to give you an experience more akin to teahouse storytelling than to an academic lecture.

Shen Ming (神明) is the proper name for Chinese deities or gods. *Shen* refers to a deity, a spirit, or the mysterious; *ming* means "bright," "to understand," and "to be wise or clear of meaning." So to the Chinese, a deity can be a supernatural being who is wise, or one who brings light to the dark, or one who enlightens. I've always felt it a pity that when, over the last century, elements of Chinese culture entered the English language, these deities left their names behind and so no longer stood as unique concepts. This was partly because of historical trends in language use and because of the way Western culture received and absorbed foreign ideas. Now, the popular trend in English literature on China is to use the proper Chinese names, whether speaking of a dish, a custom, or an expression. I have done so in this book as well, as I think it adds value and promotes the deities as unique beings. All Chinese names in this book are presented in the traditional way, with surname preceding given names. The one exception, done with the intent of avoiding confusion, is the romanization of Guan Yin as "Kuan

Yin" as that is the name by which this immensely popular goddess is currently best known to her many devotees in the West.

The Chinese religious tradition is more than just a collection of whimsical beliefs and fancies. China's veneration of its deities is inseparable from its local and national history. The origins of many deities can be found in the Han Dynasty, a golden age of Chinese art and culture, or during the Spring and Autumn, Warring States period, a time of immense change and social disorder when new gods rose to respond to the needs of the people (see appendix B). Their veneration often matured during the Tang and Song Dynasties, reaching its height during the Yuan, Ming, and Qing eras. During the Song Dynasty, when the capital city and much of the Han Chinese population moved south, mobility and migration took many Chinese deities out of their local territories and encouraged the formation of popular pantheons that catered to the needs of both the rural and urban populations. Many of these colorful beings are still worshipped today.

Chinese gods evolve. They move about or come into being along with socio-economic trends and changing social roles. The new gods of our age are being born as we speak—pop stars, screen icons, literary giants, and athletes. And the old gods are evolving to support the needs of modern society; their young devotees are creating new forms of worship. There is a wonderfully egalitarian quality to Chinese deities—who represent a meritocratic pantheon in which anyone can become a god. And these deities can give us a fascinating insight into China's national psyche.

THE
ESSENTIAL GUIDE
TO
CHINESE DEITIES

Pan Gu, the Origin (c. 1607)

Chapter 1

Creator Gods

Creation myths are a fundamental part of any people's belief system, anywhere in the world. Apart from making the world and its inhabitants, these gods had the responsibility of protecting their creations from cataclysmic destruction during primeval times. In the Chinese pantheon, these roles were fulfilled by two gods, the giant Pan Gu, who fashioned the world, and the goddess Nü Wa, creator and savior of humanity.

PAN GU, THE ORIGIN
盘古

The Daoist religion, which grew out of China's earliest folk religions and shamanism, believes that the universe and all things in it originate from a single primeval force or element called Yuan Qi (元气). This force or element originated from a perfect, original, incorruptible being named Yuan Shi (元始), who existed before the birth of the universe and was regarded as the supreme god in the Daoist pantheon. Long after the inception of this myth, during the time of the Three Kingdoms (220–280 CE), the creation myth of Pan Gu appeared in the work of the Wu Kingdom historian Xu Zheng (220–265 CE).

The myth of Pan Gu tells of creation coming forth from the splitting open of a cosmic egg, within which resided the deity. Xu Zheng describes it thus in his *San Wu Li Ji*:

> Heaven and earth were opaque as an egg, and Pan Gu lay within. After 18,000 years had passed, the egg split open. All that was light and clear became the sky. All that was heavy and murky became the ground. And Pan Gu stood between them. . . . He gave his spirit to the sky. He gave his wisdom to the earth. The sky grew ten feet higher each day. The ground grew ten feet thicker each day. The sky became very high. The ground, very deep.

Daoist practitioners adopted the mythical giant Pan Gu as their Yuan Shi—the elemental original force—then various other creation myths arose to fill in the rest of the story. One told how, when Pan Gu died, his left eye became the sun and his right eye the moon. His hair and beard became the night sky and the stars; his body and limbs became the four corners of the earth. His teeth formed the huge mountain ranges that ringed the states; his bones and marrow became the minerals in the ground. Pan Gu's skin and hair became the earth and the grass, while his sweat and blood fell as rain and flowed as rivers, which eventually merged to form the seas. Thus the body of Pan Gu was the origin, and provided for the distribution of Yuan Qi throughout the world.

When Pan Gu became a god, his legend became more detailed and elaborate. In another work, Xu Zheng describes him as having a dragon's head and a snake's body. His breath summoned the wind, rain, thunder, and lighting. When he opened his eyes, it was day; when he closed them, it was night. The legend of Pan Gu was carried through the ages by works like the novel *Accounts of Strange Things* (*Shu Yi Ji*) by Liang Ren Fang (508–460 BCE). By the Ming era, the tale had evolved even more. In the Ming Dynasty compilation *Deities Through the Ages* (*Li Dai Shen Xian Tong Jian* or *San Jiao Tong Yuan Lu*), Pan Gu splits the world open with an axe. This work and *How the World Began and Continued* (*Kai Pi Yan Yi*) by 17th-century novelist Zhou You extended the legend again, presenting Pan Gu as the ultimate ancestor of humankind. After his mortal existence, the spirit of

Pan Gu traveled the skies and encountered Tai Yuan Sheng Nü, the primeval female being. He dived into her mouth and came out through her spine as an Immortal. With her, he sired three major gods, two of whom in turn spawned the five great ancestors of humanity.

Pan Gu is an important deity, not so much because he is the head of the Daoist pantheon, but because he is a timeless mythical hero who is deeply imprinted in the nation's consciousness. As the world's creator, he is China's ideal type of hero—one who built the world through complete self-sacrifice. The Chinese national anthem, *March of the Volunteers*, expresses similar sentiments in its lyrics: "Let our flesh and blood construct our new Great Wall." Today, the Pan Gu creation myth is studied as part of the national curriculum in China, and retold by generation after generation with the aid of colorful and enticing children's books and cartoons.

Pan Gu is usually drawn as a muscular, powerfully built, hirsute giant (his hair being a part of the creation story). Sometimes, he is curled up inside the primeval egg. When in the act of separating the sky and the ground, his body is tactfully covered by either a loincloth or a particularly well-placed curling cloud. The Ming version of the myth seems to have stuck, however, and Pan Gu is often shown carrying his world-splitting axe. This is especially true with the popularity in China of Western fantasy narratives like *Lord of the Rings*, *World of Warcraft*, and *Thor*. In older paintings and Daoist icons, Pan Gu is shown with horns on his head, holding heaven and earth in his hands.

You can find old temples to Pan Gu all over China and in Chinese-speaking regions around the world, with as many as 220 in some provinces. The major temples are in Xin Zhu, Taiwan, and Cang Zhou in He Bei, where a village has been named after the god, as well as the local port. Devotees visiting from abroad later added a grave for Pan Gu, where they could pay their respects and give thanks for his sacrifice.

On the borders between Yu Nan and Mi Yang, in He Nan, is Tong Bai Pan Gu Temple, which marks the spot where the giant is said to have stood when he first pried heaven and earth apart. The temple was heavily damaged during the Cultural Revolution, but in the 1970s and 1980s, local villagers formed the Pan Gu Society and expressed their love for this mythical ancestor by rebuilding the temple themselves. Incense was lit again and the temple fairs resumed. In 2006, a giant statue of Pan Gu was commissioned that was shipped 400 miles from the Nan Jing studio of the sculptor, Wu Xian Lin.

Temples to Pan Gu are still being built today, like the one in Shen Zhen, a relatively new city. You can also visit the Seed of Pan Gu in Shao Guan, Guang Dong—a giant, entirely natural phallic stone that is part of the region's protected red stone national heritage site. Thousands flock each year to pray for fertility from the seed of the world's procreator. The custom of holding festive temple fairs with re-enactments and lion dances has recently been revived, with events in some regions supported by the local councils that present the god very much as a symbol of their indigenous culture.

Contemporary devotees in many fields have adopted Pan Gu's name, including fantasy writers and the makers of jail-breaking software. The spirit of Pan Gu is also represented by the eponymous punk band from Jiang Xi, rather boringly known as Punk God in English.

NÜ WA, MOTHER OF HUMANKIND

女娲

If there is one deity that comes immediately to mind for the Chinese, it is Nü Wa. While Pan Gu is the formidable giant who created the world, Nü Wa saved it from destruction. She also created humankind. Here is her story as generations of Chinese have heard it told through the magic of bedtime stories.

A long, long time ago, just after the world was first created, a mythical being with the upper body of a woman, the horns of an ox, and the lower body of a serpent wandered the earth. She found it a beautiful place. But she felt alone and longed for the company of beings like herself to share all the wondrous things in the world. One day, as she mused by the banks of a river, she scooped up some mud with her hands and, glancing at her reflection in the water, fashioned it into images of herself. She decided to give the images legs instead of a serpent's tail so they could walk.

Nü Wa, Mother of Humankind

When Nü Wa placed the figures on the riverbank, they came to life and their prancing made the goddess laugh and filled her heart with joy. She worked day and night trying to create enough of these delightful little beings to fill the world, but she was soon exhausted. So she took a length of vine, dipped it in mud, and whirled it in the air. Droplets of mud fell from the vine and transformed into more dancing figures as they touched the ground. The goddess was content. Little did she know that, soon, she would have her hands full.

The god of water, Gong Gong, was fighting with the god of fire, Zhu Rong, in a contest for control of their realm. Having lost the battle, Gong Gong was so ashamed that he struck his head continuously against Mount Bu Zhou, the Pillar of Heaven. It came crashing down, tearing a great hole in the sky. Fire and water spewed from the heavens, flooding some parts of the earth and setting other parts on fire. Nü Wa's creations fled in desperation from destroyed homes and farms. Unable to bear their suffering and the destruction of the exquisite world she loved, she resolved to save them.

Nü Wa gathered stones of five colors from riverbeds and melted them into a viscous substance with which she patched up the gaping hole in the heavens and repaired the broken firmament. To give the skies extra support, she took the legs of a giant turtle and placed them on the four points of the compass. Gathering ashes from the burning reeds, she built dams to stop the flooding waters. Although Nü Wa had saved the earth and humankind, traces of this upheaval left its mark on the landscape, for it had caused the heavens to tilt to the northwest, leaving a void in the southeast. This is why all the rivers in China flow to the east.

Nü Wa and Fu Xi

Even in the children's stories of today, Nü Wa is presented as sensible, wise, and benevolent. In these tales, Gong Gong is one of her subjects in charge of administering punishments. His violent temper eventually turned him into a rebel, and he challenged the minister Zhu Rong to a fight that ended up irrevocably damaging the world.

The earliest renditions of the Nü Wa myth present her as a mystical ruler of the Chinese people who succeeded her brother, Fu Xi, as sovereign around 2900 BCE. Traditionally, Fu Xi has been associated with Nü Wa during the Han Dynasty, when the pair frequently appeared on funeral stone bas-reliefs with human upper bodies and intertwined serpentine lower bodies. Fu Xi holds the sun or the compass and Nü Wa holds the moon or the carpenter's square. The image symbolizes the harmony of the universe, between the Yin and Yang, with Fu Xi as Nü Wa's husband and Nü Wa his assistant. In this book however, I focus on Nü Wa, the creator of human beings, as the far more interesting story and to bring a major female goddess, too long overshadowed by her male counterpart, to the forefront. Variations of her appearance include her having the head of an ox. Despite her only partly human physique, however, she possessed all the virtues of a divine sage, according to China's first great historian, Si Ma Qian (145–87 BCE), in his famous 8th-century *Shi Ji* (*Historical Records*).[2]

While Pan Gu was a giant of great strength who sacrificed every fiber of himself, Nü Wa was a brave, intelligent, and kind matriarch. In children's tales, her serpentine lower body is often glossed over and she is rarely illustrated with horns on her head, as these features are considered inconsistent with her motherly image. In fact, these elements of her appearance are a reflection of prehistoric animal and totem worship. While her appearance may share some commonalities with spirits in Greek mythology—like the *lamia*—creatures like spiders, toads, and bats, which typically connote dark and evil forces in Western culture, are often auspicious and powerful symbols in traditional Chinese beliefs.

Although Nü Wa is full of love for humankind, she is not a deity to be trifled with. She watches over the human world and has powerful sway in the course of history. The widely influential Ming fantasy novel *Feng Shen Yan Yi* (*Investiture of the Gods*) by Xu Zhong Lin (circa 1560–1630), which molded the images of many Chinese deities in the popular consciousness, starts with the premise that Zhou Wang, the last ruler of Shang, incurred the wrath of this goddess.

In the novel, after succeeding to the throne, Zhou Wang rules peacefully for six years. In the seventh year, however, news comes of rebellion. At the instigation of the imperial tutor, Zhou Wang visits the temple of Nü Wa on her feast day to ask the goddess for help. When he approaches the statue of the goddess, he is mesmerized by her beauty, so much so that he impetuously leaves a love poem on the temple wall, refusing to rectify his behavior even when reminded by ministers that he should be praying for the prosperity of his country, the well-being of his people, and their protection from natural and man-made disasters.

On this day, the goddess descends from heaven and is furious to see the poem on the wall. She summons all the demons under her sovereignty and chooses three of the most deadly—a 1,000-year-old fox spirit, a nine-headed bird spirit, and a scorpion spirit—and charges them with the task of misleading Zhou Wang and aiding his rival's efforts to take his place. Thus begins a story of battles and quests of gods, men, and demons. Eventually, the Shang Dynasty was toppled, just as surely as the tyrant had been 600 years before—with the aid of the same goddess.

My first memories of Nü Wa in children's tales are of a strong-armed goddess with flowing black hair and skin the color of the earth from which she had created humankind. In our contemporary search for relatable, yet authentic, representations of the goddess, her upper body—including her head—is pretty consistently depicted as human, rather than bovine. Her serpent's tail, however, is displayed in its full glory in a lot of contemporary artwork.

In depictions today, she stands strong amid a landscape of falling giant rocks, chaotic lights, and raging torrents—like a steady ray of light in the collapsing darkness. Her arms open wide, sending huge rocks up toward the firmament, the one thing standing in the way of the destruction of the world. She usually wears very little, yet the exposure of her breasts and voluptuous figure never appears lewd. Rather it supplements her power and glory. This is unusual in traditional Chinese culture, which prefers willowy femininity and favors a subtle, discrete appreciation of the body, which is usually covered up.

Countless artists have posted their own interpretations of Nü Wa mending the sky on the Internet. Sculptures and statues of the goddess in variations of this image adorn memorials around the country, where Nü Wa cultural festivals are often celebrated with re-enactment dances and ritual ceremonies on the goddess's feast day, the fifteenth day of the third lunar month. You can visit the biggest statue, a bronze figure that stands sixteen meters high on the Nü Wa Mountains in Zhu Shan county, Hubei, the location where she is said to have repaired the heavens. May is the best time to visit. Thanks to recent legislation, all women can enter free of charge during the week that begins with the Chinese Mother's Day as part of Veneration of Motherhood Week.

Today, the Chinese are coming to realize the importance of preserving their heritage and take pride in their indigenous culture. So, like Pan Gu, Nü Wa enjoys great fame. Domestic online role-playing games (RPGs) like Wang Zhe Rong Yao (King Pro League) feature her as a major character with powerful attack capabilities that include remote assault as well as the ability to use magic. Online poetry journals that focus on China's literary heritage have borrowed her name. Ping Li County in Shaan Xi, one of the eight major tea-producing regions in the Tang Dynasty and provider of imperial tribute teas, has named their entire range of green tea after the goddess. The range includes high-quality and rare varieties like Long Jing, Mao Feng, Yun Wu, and Yin Feng.

Nü Wa recently appeared in Cheang Pou-soi's 2014 movie *Monkey King*, yet another retelling of a famous episode in the *Journey to the West*[3] (1592) in which Sun Wu Kong, the Monkey King, wreaks havoc in heaven (see chapter 10). The film follows the original novel, in which the chaotic monkey spirit is born from a 1,000-year-old stone—one of the very stones the goddess had used to repair the heavens and thus imbued with her magic. Today, an Internet series based on *The Nü Wa Diaries* net novel by Ling Wu Shui Xiu, which tells a comic story of young gods transplanted into contemporary China, is being filmed in Shanghai. The animated series has already been released.

Xi Wang Mu, the Supreme Goddess
(Alamy Stock Photo)

Chapter 2

Xi Wang Mu

THE SUPREME GODDESS

西王母

Prehistoric Chinese societies were matriarchal. Even today, we can still see the remnants of this in native Chinese spirituality. One of the most powerful goddesses is Xi Wang Mu, Great Mother of the West. She may have been the leader or shamaness of a tribe in the western regions of China, hence her title. The first appearances of Xi Wang Mu differed greatly from the dignified and matronly image she possesses today. The *Book of Mountains and Seas*[4] describes her as a female monster that is half human and half tiger, with tiger's fangs, leopard's tail, and a head of long, wild hair. She dwells on Yu Shan (Jade Mountain) and likes to roar. A punisher goddess, she also reigns over natural calamities. This kind of portrayal was based on the totems of her tribe, the tiger and leopard, and talismans made from tiger teeth.

The image of Xi Wang Mu underwent a dramatic change in *The Travels of Zhou Mu Wang*, written by the king of Zhou about his travels through the strange lands of the west during the Warring States period. To reinforce his own public image as a well-informed, well-traveled ruler, it was important that he record his meetings with key figures in each region.

Writing about a half-beast, half-woman monster was simply not appropriate for his purposes. So he wrote instead of a graceful, sophisticated lady who welcomed him at her residence of Kun Lun by the Jade Lake, introducing herself as Xi Wang Mu, the daughter of the Jade Emperor. During the following era, works like *Stories of Han Wu* immortalized Xi Wang Mu as she had been depicted in Zhou Mu Wang's *Travels.*

By the Han Dynasty, Xi Wang Mu was appearing in literature with full immortal powers. Si Ma Xiang Ru's *Poetic Essays on Immortals* feature her as a silver-haired celestial who ascends to the skies. This indicates that she has left her roles as controller of pestilence and punishment behind, along with her feral image, and taken on the role of granter of happiness, longevity, and sons.

Xi Wang Mu's endorsement by royalty and literati prompted Daoism to rank her at the top of its pantheon, as the daughter of Yuan Shi, the supreme god. She is wedded to the Jade Emperor and considered the ancestor of all female celestial beings. She bore him seven daughters, also spawning one of the most famous love stories in Chinese mythology. Xi Wang Mu's seventh child falls in love with a cowherd in the living world and stays on earth as a weaver before she is recalled to heaven. The goddess takes pity on her child and permits her to meet her husband once a year on the seventh day of the seventh lunar month, on Qi Xi, the Chinese Valentine's Day. On this day, sympathetic magpies form a bridge for the lovers across the stars.[5]

The tale of the cowherd and the weaver first appeared in poetry during the Three Kingdoms, and has been featured since then in major literary works like Gan Bao's *In Search of Supernaturals,*[6] and Ming legends like *Tale of the Weaver* and *An Immortal Match.* It was also adapted for the Huang Mei opera. As contemporary Chinese are reconnecting with their heritage, many couples are choosing to be married on the seventh day of the seventh month in traditional ceremonies. Occasionally, even foreigners living in China, attracted by the beauty of the story and traditional Chinese wedding clothes, have joined in this renewed custom.

Xi Wang Mu is known for her Pan Tao, the celestial peach that can make you immortal and bring the dead back to life. The magical tree that provides these peaches only bears fruit once every 3,000 years. The Pan

Tao first appeared in the *Book of Mountains and Seas*, but it was not until the Qing Dynasty that the goddess is linked to it through the poem *Pan Tao Palace*. You can still visit the temple in Beijing that inspired this poem. On the third day of the third lunar month, a lively fair is held at Pan Tao Temple that is a pale imitation of the goddess's heavenly banquet, which Sun Wu Kong famously gatecrashes in *Journey to the West*. In Tai Shan, Shan Dong, elaborate ceremonies involving Daoist rites, lanterns, dance, song, and crafts are held on the same day around Wang Mu Lake, an earthly representation of Xi Wang Mu's Yao Chi (Lake of Jade) in Kun Lun.

Today, devotion to Xi Wang Mu has remained strong and she is poised to become a major goddess of the East. Conventions on Asian traditions and customs have been held at Jing Chuan, Gan Su, where one of the earliest temples dedicated to the goddess was built. Donations have flooded in from Chinese around the world to support this project.

Xi Wang Mu's representation in pop culture is somewhat varied. She is largely depicted in human form, dressed in full regal robes complete with stole and jade pendants hung around her waist, accessories that symbolize power. She is always shown wearing an elaborate headdress, and sometimes carries a staff, a gourd of elixirs, or her flute of white jade that can control the weather. She appears in computer games as a major and supreme goddess. Occasionally, devotees have even created drawings and digital artwork that hark back to her prehistoric form and portray her as a beautiful and ferocious cat lady.

Xi Wang Mu's presence continues to grace modern editions of classic and contemporary fantasy works, from TV series and films of *Journey to the West* and *The Lotus Lantern*, to Hollywood movies like *The Forbidden Kingdom*. She features as a major character in Xu Lei's 2007–2011 novel series *The Grave Robber's Chronicles*, which imagines her as a zombie queen who finds a rather gruesome way to live in eternity. She also appears in a 1,000-year-old love story with Zhou Mu Wang. These novels were soon turned into a comic-book series, then formed the basis for a highly popular domestic TV series and for the 2016 international movie *Time Raiders*. You can find six of the novels translated into English from Things Asian Press, and an eight-issue comic-book mini-series based on the novels was especially adapted for English readers by Image Comics.

Kuan Yin, Goddess of Universal Mercy
(anonymous, Tang-Yuan Dynasties Yulin Caves, Gansu, China)

Chapter 3

Kuan Yin

GODDESS OF UNIVERSAL MERCY

观世音

The Goddess of Mercy may be the goddess most associated with Chinese religion, both in China and around the world. Even during times when worship of other deities was deemed a superstition to be quashed, Kuan Yin often appeared immune to these efforts.

Kuan Yin has many origin myths, but perhaps the most important and distinct comes from her Buddhist heritage. According to Indian mythology, Avalokitesvara, whose Sanskrit name means "regarder of the world's cries," was one of a pair of brother monks who took vows to deliver the world from all distress. They became attendants of the Amida Buddha. Avalokitesvara evolved to become a Bodhisattva of great mercy and compassion. The many tales of the miracles he performed—breaking shackles, shattering weapons, and subduing man-eating demons—appear, not only as Chinese legend, but also in some historical records of the Northern Dynasties.

In an earlier incarnation, Avalokitesvara existed as early as the 7th century BCE in the form of Hindu deities called the Ashvins, a pair of twin colts that were joined at the shoulders. These gods were portrayed with stars on their heads and wearing crowns of lotus. They were beings of mercy and benevolence who healed the sick, bestowed sight on the blind, provided limbs to the handicapped, granted children to the infertile, and made flowers grow in rotted trees. The colts were adopted into Chinese Buddhism, where they evolved into a Bodhisattva with a human body and a four-sided head—one equine, one benevolent, one beaming, and one furious. This portrayal has been popular with Chinese minority faiths like the Zang.

In Chinese, the name Avalokitesvara translates as Guan Shi Yin, which was shortened to Guan Yin. In the United States, she is popularly known as Kuan Yin. Although Bodhisattvas are supposed to be asexual, early incarnations of Kuan Yin tended to be male. When the deity was formally introduced into the Chinese pantheon during the Three Kingdoms, the god's gender changed to female. By the time of the Tang Dynasty (618–907 CE), Buddhism had become widespread in China, and Guan Shi Yin has been completely localized over the past 400 years, evolving into an identity completely separate from his first moustached appearance in the Mo Gao Grottoes.

Leading Chinese Buddhists believed that there needed to be an intermediary between the Amida Buddha and the Chinese—a sacred being who understood their language, lived among them, and could report on the sufferings and good deeds of the people. From the Northern and Southern Dynasties (420–589 CE), many women from the upper classes began to join Buddhist monasteries to lead lives of devotion. They needed a representative female figure to balance the exclusively male *arhats* (guardian gods), so a female representative of royal descent emerged. The story of this princess is recorded in *A Short History of the Bodhisattva Guan Shi Yin* (*Guan Shi Yin Pu Sa Zhuan Lue*) by Guan Dao Sheng (1262–1319 CE), a female poet and painter of the Yuan Dynasty who based her creation on her research into folklore.

The tale Guan Dao Shen drew on is set in the Spring and Autumn period. King Zhuang of Chu was a tyrant who, after usurping power, wished for healthy sons to complete his triumph and ensure his legacy. Instead of sons, his wife gave birth to three daughters, Miao Yan, Miao Yin, and Miao Shan, who grew up to be beautiful and talented. The king wanted to marry them off to men who were suited to running the kingdom. If he couldn't have sons, then he'd have sons-in-law. The third daughter, Miao Shan, stood apart from the other two because of her devoutness and charity. She refused to acquiesce to her father's demands unless the "three woes of the world" (aging, sickness, and bereavement) were removed from human life. She chose, instead, a life of devotion in a nunnery.

Her parents tried to foil her plans by ordering the abbess and other nuns to mistreat her and foist on her the most unpleasant, menial tasks. The mountain gods and earth gods came to her aid, and Miao Shan did not give in. Running out of patience, her tyrant father ordered her execution. The gods intervened, however, breaking the executioners' swords and dissolving their spears. In the end, Miao Shan was finally killed by strangulation. The gods preserved her body with elixirs and brought her back to life with the peach of immortality. Miao Shan was then guided to the mystical Pu Tuo Mountains, where she spent years perfecting her wisdom. During her sojourn there, she gained two disciples, who are usually portrayed flanking her on either side—the hermit monk Shan Zai and Lung Nü, the grateful daughter of the Dragon King, whom the goddess had saved from capture. As a token of his gratitude, the Dragon King gave Miao Shan a most luminescent pearl, whose light enables her to read in the dark of night.

In the meantime, King Zhuang fell gravely ill and was desperate to find a cure. He consulted a monk who told him that the only remedy was an eye and an arm sacrificed by someone who was without anger. Having heard of the wisdom of the seeress who dwelt in the Pu Tuo Mountains, but unaware that she was his daughter, the king's servants came to the mountains seeking advice. Miao Shan voluntarily gouged out one of her own eyes and cut off an arm. These were brought back to the king, who took them and was miraculously cured. After recovering, the king and his wife went to give thanks to his benefactor and, to their astonishment, realized that the mutilated woman was, in fact, their own daughter. They pledged themselves to lives of devotion thereafter. The world shook and multi-colored radiance broke through the clouds. Flowers rained down and, when the clouds lifted, Miao Shan was reborn in the form of Qian Shou Qian Yan Guan Shi Yin, Thousand Hands and Thousand Eyes Kuan Yin.

There are various explanations for why Kuan Yin ended up with 1,000 arms and 1,000 eyes, including one version in which carpenters misheard a king's instructions as he commissioned a statue of the Bodhisattva. Another explanation suggests that, in order to heal all the distress of everyone in the world, the goddess needed as many arms and eyes as she could get. She could observe the cries for help with her many eyes, and then administer suitable remedies with her many arms. Kuan Yin does indeed hold a different treasure in each of her hands: her golden pestle in one, her lotus branch in another, her granting staff in one, and her book of sutras in yet another. Many hands make light work.

According to the scriptures, Kuan Yin has thirty-three forms and thirty-three different representations that feature the goddess in varying robes, holding different objects symbolizing different kinds of remedies, and surrounded by different scenery. Devotees who seek her assistance vary from those desperate for offspring to prisoners on the execution block, and from people who failed in their dreams to those in danger, in great pain, or on their deathbeds. Clearly this goddess needs to be extremely versatile. She must adapt to all kinds of environments and be prepared wherever she is needed, whatever the situation.

Popular forms of the goddess include Yang Liu Guan Yin, who holds a willow branch that drips sweet dew with healing powers. Yu Lan Guan Yin, another form, holds a fishing net that symbolizes abundance and prosperity as well as community, friendship, and marriage. Shui Yue Kuan Yin, yet another, is portayed surrounded by water and illuminated by the moon, representing the mastery of emotions.

The largest and most spectacular Kuan Yin statues are in He Bei. The wooden sculpture in Pu Ning Temple, Cheng De, and the copper statue at Long Xing Temple, Zheng Ding, both stand approximately twenty-three meters tall. The wooden sculpture has many arms and multiple hands on each arm, making up 1,000. Or you can visit the 108-meter-tall Kuan Yin statue on the tropical Chinese island of Hai Nan. This figure, which features three faces of the goddess and is China's largest

Bai Yi Guan Yin, portrays her in her "white-robed" form, in which she symbolizes purity.

Kuan Yin is one of the most practical deities and possibly the most efficacious. You can find small porcelain sculptures of her virtually anywhere in the world. Any devotee of Chinese gods, in China as well as around the world, is more likely to have a statuette of Kuan Yin in their home than one of any other deity, along with one of Fu Lu Shou, the gods of happiness (see chapter 11). Her enduring popularity as a goddess in modern times is self-evident. In June 1989, following the death of deposed liberal Communist leader Hu Yao Bang, China's youth gathered in thousands across 400 or more cities to protest for full political rights. One of the figures the young people in Beijing erected as patron was this 1,000-year-old goddess.

Although it is always good to give thanks and show your appreciation, Kuan Yin is not demanding of offerings and will assist anyone regardless of their social status, history, gender, sexuality, ethnicity, religion, or race. If you're moving to a new home or relocating, be sure to take your Kuan Yin with you. She will protect you.

Throughout history, Kuan Yin has graced fictional works in many genres, and famously appears many times in *Journey to the West*. She is represented in the many Chinese mythical and fantasy films inspired by this epic. Her predominant image is serene, demure, and dignified, but even in her traditional Chinese forms, slightly different representations exist—like that of Yu Xi Guan Yin, who is laughing and playful. Recent characterizations of the goddess in comic books have shown this, some even returning the goddess to her much older roots and portraying her as a hermaphrodite, or giving her an updated identity as a mature den mother who looks after four young pilgrims. The very recent illustration of her story by Gene Luen Yang in his graphic novels *Boxers and Saints* (2013) testifies to both Kuan Yin's importance to the populace in Chinese history and to her current popularity in the U.S. as the Chinese deity that English readers are most likely to recognize.

Hou Tu, Lady Earth (source: quora.com)

Chapter 4

Nature Deities

Early civilizations' vulnerability and dependence on nature were driving forces in the evolution of religions. Like other peoples of the world, the ancient Chinese were in awe of the elements. The forces of nature seemed to be imbued, not only with magic, but with fickle personalities whose whims had great power over mere mortal destinies. Over the centuries, the veneration of these deities has evolved to give them human shape, behavior, and even office! While science and study can now explain the workings of these forces, they still remain uncontrollable. To this day, to some extent, the Chinese still see them with a certain sense of wonder and try to sway the fickle deities that control them.

HOU TU, LADY EARTH

后土

The earth, from which all manner of things grow and on which all manner of things live, is a fundamental subject of early Chinese beliefs. The Chinese have venerated an earth deity since antiquity, whose earliest form was She (社, pronounced "shurgh"), not to be confused with the female pronoun. The way in which this primitive deity was worshipped is reflected in the character for its name—the left radical referring to Zhuo Shi or Ling Shi, a stone construction formed to resemble the earth deity, and the right half of the character representing earth and the veneration of natural earth mounds. This type of worship, which was practiced by the common people as well as in royal rituals involving animal sacrifice, was well documented in the Shang and Zhou eras. During the Eastern Han period, the vast realms of She were defined into Wu Tu, the Five Earths—the mountains and forests, the plains, the hills, cemeteries and graveyards, and lowlands and marshes. The earth deity has also been a prominent force in minority faiths in China.

The earth deity was thus a very powerful one. People were thankful for what the earth brought them, and fearful of the destruction caused by She's wrath. They considered the deity to be the Emperor Earth Spirit, the equal of the Jade Emperor on earth. Her name, Hou Tu Huang Di Qi, was shortened to Hou Tu.

In the beginning, Hou Tu may have been a male spirit, whom some believed to be the son of Gong Gong, god of water and floods who tamed all the land. Others thought he was the offspring of the five legendary kings that descended from the gods. According to Shan Hai Jing, Hou Tu was the grandfather of Kua Fu, the snake charmer who chased the shadow of the sun.

The change in the gender of this deity may be related to the creation of the concept of Yin and Yang, which holds that the entire cosmos was filled with and balanced by opposing energies. The sky was considered Yang, which is associated with the male; the earth was seen as Yin, associated with the female. In the Sui Dynasty (581–618 CE), rulers may have re-envisioned the earth deity as a goddess in response to this belief. At this time, female effigies began to appear in ancestral temples and people began to refer to the goddess as Hou Tu Niang Niang, Lady Earth (后土娘娘).

It is more likely, however, that Hou Tu was female to begin with. In both Jia Gu Wen (tortoise shell carvings) and Jin Wen (the oldest form of writing), the character for "Hou" resembles the female form. The original meaning of this character was a term of power and respect for the leader of the tribe in matriarchal societies. Research also shows that veneration of Hou Tu derived from early traditional worship of Di Mu, or Mother Earth (地母). Indeed, the fertility of the earth makes the concept of Mother Earth a very natural and almost universal one. Hou Tu is also one of the twelve ancestral wizards in ancient mythology, along with the likes of Tian Wu, the wind god, and Xuan Mo, the water god.

Since the Zhou Dynasty, Hou Tu has received imperial tributes. In the 12th century, the Song emperor Hui Zong granted her an official title that put her on a par with the Jade Emperor, assigning her the same level of honorific rituals. She was made one of the Four Imperials, the highest rank within the Daoist pantheon.

While Hou Tu does not have quite the global or national recognition that Pan Gu or Tian Hou (Empress of Heaven) do, incense still burns bright for her across the backwaters of China in smaller towns and more inland regions where livelihoods remain dependent on the soil and people still live relatively close to the earth. Investment companies in Shan Xi take their names from the goddess, and all their staff participate in ceremonial rituals on special occasions. Traditional temple fairs are held on the fifteenth day of the first lunar month or on the eighteenth day of the third lunar month. On these days, whole families and groups of worshippers set out for the temples bearing offerings of paper for burning, whole pigs and sheep, cakes, and fruit.

This goddess is venerated with the customary rituals of planting trees and flowers. In China, planting is permitted in temples dedicated to Hou Tu. Sometimes flowers or plants that symbolize safety are plucked from devotees' own gardens and offered to her. Donations for the maintenance of her temples are also customary to purchase earthen tiles for the walls or roofs. And if you can't make it to a temple, simply plant some bulbs or a sprig of grass in your own garden to serve as offerings.

Hou Tu's contemporary popularity is evident from the amount of content and artwork produced on individual blogs and social media sites—even in primary school essays uploaded to the Web. Her traditional image remains popular as well, as seen in the huge variety of designs and made-to-order fiberglass statues currently available. In her traditional form, the deity is a regally clad middle-aged lady, sometimes dressed all in gold and yellow, often very colorfully dressed with ornaments of peacock motifs and jade accessories. She is sometimes seen surrounded by dragons, and often holds a representation of the world in her hand. On some modern statues, she is portrayed with one foot on a globe.

In her contemporary incarnation, Hou Tu is featured as a major and playable character in computer games, where she generally appears in a younger guise. The game Invincible League of Gods (Feng Shen Wu Di) depicts her as a graceful young woman with a soft kind of beauty. Bai Du, one of the largest Internet service providers in the world and China's answer to Google, hosts a game called Uproar in Heaven OL (Da Nao Tian Gong OL) that is based on the Daoist concept of seventy-two transformations and inspired by Pokemon and Avatar. In it, Hou Tu is a powerful earth-type character who is reincarnated from the legendary phoenix. She is clad in a bikini of feathers and tall flame-shaped boots, and sports an iridescent fantail. She wields a staff that can open mountains and split stones. Her powers, a real exhibition of the powers of earth, include remote strikes like "giant stone bursts," "quake waves," and "subterranean assaults," as well as the "heaven and earth shatter" move that can deal damage to entire groups of players.

TU DI YE, GRANDFATHER EARTH

土地爷

With the expansion of agriculture and industry, and the growth of villages, Hou Tu became distanced from the Chinese people as her devotees developed a need for approachable deities who were closer at hand—deities like her far more popular male counterpart Tu Di Ye, Lord Earth or Grandfather Earth. These regional beings of far lower rank were the original earth gods who lent their names to local Chinese deities whose powers were governed by the local terrain.

Through the ages, local heroes, scholars, and warriors have all been nominated by the people as local earth gods—figures like Confucius and Wen Chang, as well as courtiers like Han Yu (768–824 CE), a Tang official and writer and an early proponent of neo-Confucianism, and warriors like Yue Fei (1103–1142 CE), a Song Dynasty general who is one of China's most treasured heroes. There are earth god temples all over the country. In some cities, even streets and alleyways contain a communal Tu Di Ye shrine. And it seems that every city likes to think of itself as the earth-god headquarters.

The most impressive temples are in Beijing, where a Yuan Dynasty structure stands three stories high, and in Chong Qing in Si Chuan, where thirty pairs of earth gods are found. Supposedly, this temple housed off-duty, retired earth gods from all over the country, along with gods sent there to be "re-educated." These shrines can also be very simple, however—just a representative tablet or a paper sign from a god shop with the deity's name, decorated by the offerings brought to them.

The veneration of Tu Di Ye takes place on the spring and autumn equinoxes. Originally, worship of this god consisted of offerings and large celebratory meals, but these rituals have developed into the She Hui, a gathering that features the performance of plays and acrobatics. These festivals are predecessors of the temple fairs we hear so much about today, where farmers traditionally purchase their farming tools for next year. Today, in cities like Guang Zhou, there are still whole alleyways and streets in which each household has a small, permanent shrine just outside the front door for Tu Di Ye (or Tu Di Dong, as his name may vary between regions), usually with an offering of incense.

Tu Di Ye comes in the guise of a stubby, smiley, silver-haired old man not unlike your elderly relative or your neighbor. In fact, people have felt so close to this god that he has been granted a wife, and comical instances of his match-making are documented in various Tang, Song, and Ming texts. He not only looks after the fertility of the earth and its produce in his region, but comes to the aid of the locals when they call, as made evident in *Journey to the West*. Wherever travelers pass, they can call upon the aid of the local Tu Di Ye and the old chap will dutifully appear. Sometimes, he may seem rather put-upon, but he is always good-natured and offers useful guidance or information.

As the lowest ranking god, Tu Di Ye is generally perceived as amiable, pliable, and obliging to all. The one exception occurs in his portrayal in the fictional *Du Ti Bao Juan* (*Treasure Scroll of Tu Di Ye*), which was in wide circulation during the Ming and Qing eras. In this work, the earth god wreaks havoc in heaven and takes on the Jade Emperor himself—a remnant of his grand origins, perhaps. It is interesting that this side of Tu Di Ye manifests itself in the recently released animation by Light Chaser (Beijing) called *Little Door Gods*, which was released in 2016 in English as *The Guardian Brothers*.

LEI GONG, LORD OF THUNDER
雷公

The awesome powers of nature have fascinated humankind for its entire existence, and have informed its ideas of the divine. The might and beauty of natural phenomena are often personified as deities, and storms in particular have spawned a slew of gods. The most common of these weather gods seems to be the personification of the roaring thunder, leading to some of the wildest gods all over the world.

The very early Chinese believed thunder to be the manifestation of a higher, invisible power that controlled their fate. Unknowable and terrifying, it was first seen as a beast. Early myths collected in the *Shan Hai Jing* show a menagerie of monsters, including Thunder Beasts. To the west of Wu (now roughly the areas of west China near the desert) dwells a creature with the head of a man and the body of a dragon, its belly a thunderous drum. By the East Sea, there is another with a dark green bull-like body that glows as brightly as the sun. The legendary emperor Huang Di caught this beast and made a drum from its skin and bones that could be heard hundreds of miles away.

Over time, these Thunder Beasts took on more elaborate forms, gaining scales and horns, and taking on the forms of both domestic and wild animals. But as society grew more human-centric, talismans of stuffed humanoid puppets in bright embroidered cloth appeared to represent the deity, who was depicted with a large demonic head and a bull's nose, wielding axes and hammers or drumming furiously. By the time of the Ming and Qing eras, Lei Gong or Lei Shen (雷神)—lord of thunder or thunder god—had gained a gladiator's torso and arms, and the wings

Lei Shen, the eagle-faced Thunder God (from Myths of China and Japan, *by Donald A. Mackenzie. Published 1923, by Gresham Publishing Co. London)*

and claws of a hawk, all in a deep green hue. These contrasted with his crimson ape-like face, which boasted three eyes and a sharp pointed beak. He is seen with five drums slung from his waist and another at his left foot and is variously referred to as Lei Shen Ye (雷神爷), Lord Thunder or Grand Thunder, and even as Old Devil Thunder (雷公鬼).

The belief in a thunder deity seems universal in ancient civilizations, and it is interesting to see the similarities between them. In both Chinese and high Western Norse mythos, we see thunder personified as an axe-wielding warrior who is very powerful and ranked highly in the pantheon. He both administers and represents justice, but is also prone to acts of chaos.

Lei Gong eventually evolved into a totally human form through a legend set in Lei Zhou that is a curious amalgam of reality, belief, and fantasy. This tropical peninsula, built up during the Tang Dynasty in Guang Dong, is inseparable from thunderstorms. Stone axes excavated there (now known to be relics of the Li civilization) were thought to have belonged to Lei Gong. Where these relics were found, temples soon followed.

An alternative origin myth for Lei Gong says that, one day, a local hunter named Chen was guided by his nine-eared hound to a strange ball of flesh in the forests of Lei Zhou. When he took it home, it opened to reveal a baby inside, with "Lei Zhou" written on one palm and the name "Chen Wen Yu" on the other. The hunter raised this child, aided by a string of Immortals who came to nurture and teach him. Chen Wen Yu grew up to become governor of Lei Zhou, implementing many reforms to improve the lives of the locals. After his death, he was granted official status as the presiding ruler of the gods of thunder, wind, and rain.

Now a figure in the bureaucracy of heaven, Chen Wen Yu was elevated by the Daoists to even higher status as the ruler of Thunder City. There, he reigned with thirty-six drumming underlings managing the five types of thunder in the world, following the lead of Lei Gong himself, drumming on his own instrument. These gods of thunder were worshipped, not only by the Han people of China, but also by many minorities. Despite now having what we can only assume is quite a cushy desk job, with probably quite a lot of paperwork, Lei Gong is still seen as one of the wilder gods. Apart from his spectacular manifestation as thunder, he also plays a role as punisher and executioner, bringing down the wrath of heaven, a belief that inspired the popular proverb "may the Five Thunders strike you down." Lei Gong was chosen by secret Qing Dynasty societies like the Hong Men as a protector god charged with deterring any would-be betrayers of the organization—a strong indicator of the degree to which people put their faith in him.

Lei Gong makes frequent appearances in computer games, is used as a mascot for some Chinese energy producers, and appears as a protagonist in the 2015 Chinese film *League of Gods*, which was based on *Investiture of the Gods*. He has even inspired characters in the Marvel Comics universe. Iron Fist, the martial arts hero, trains with an Immortal master in the celestial city of K'un-Lun. Looking like a combination of a gladiator and a Luchador wrestler, with an I-ching pattern on his chest plate, this master Lei-Kung the Thunderer is, like his namesake Lei Gong, a formidable warrior—rigorous and harsh, but just.

The day to make offerings to Lei Gong is on his birthday, the twenty-fourth day of the sixth lunar month. Traditionally, the people of Lei Zhou made linen drums that were placed on large carts along with statues of Lei Gong for processions. Because Lei Gong is also connected to agriculture, small portions of the harvest were devoted to him as thanks for favorable weather. For contemporary devotees, the preparation of a meal using locally raised meat, local farm vegetables, and a regional staple is a good way to show thanks.

Whereas past celebrations of Lei Gong have been accompanied by Daoist sutras and operas, he is probably equally happy with some of the heavy-metal music coming out of China, much of which really tunes in to the aesthetics of the ancient warrior god and has drums that would impress even Lei Gong. Many bands devote songs to ancient deities, and Lei Gong seems to be one of their favorites, inspiring a few tracks on one of the earliest compilations of Chinese metal—which is, significantly, titled *The Resurrection of the Gods (Zhong Shen Fu Huo)*.

The pantheon of Daoist Immortals, which was mirrored not only by earthly bureaucracy but by society as well, tended to assign family members to its members. Thus, in southern China, it is customary to make Lei Gong godfather to baby boys so that he can watch over them and bestow courage on them in later life. Wooden tablets are made and painted silver, then inscribed with the child's name and a request to Lei Gong. Bundles of gold paper are burned in tribute to the god and the tablet is dipped into the ashes so he will acknowledge his new godson.

While, historically, Lei Gong has never had ties to health or longevity, in recent years many have begun to incorporate devotion to him into a spiritual approach to cancer treatment. This practice is based on claims made about the anti-carcinogenic properties of Lei Gong Teng (thunder god vine), an herb native to Asia whose roots and vine are used in Traditional Chinese Medicine to treat a variety of conditions.[7] As I write, this claim is still being investigated.

Lei Gong and Dian Mu: Lord of Thunder and Mother Lightning

电母

As Lei Gong evolved from an animalistic storm deity to a thunder god of human appearance, the deputy god in charge of lightning—Dian Mu, Mother Lightning, or Shan Dian Niang Niang (闪电娘娘), Lady Lightning—gradually evolved into his mate and companion. First documented during the Tang Dynasty, Dian Mu makes a fitting partner for Lei Gong. Like him, she was striking rather than attractive. She was described during the Song Dynasty as being of only vaguely human shape, with a head of wild crimson hair and three fingers on each hand. *Liu Yi the Messenger* (*Liu Yi Chuan Shu*), the famous play from the Yuan Dynasty (1279–1368 CE), features the appearance of both Lei Gong and Dian Mu, the latter carrying a pair of large mirrors to produce lightning by reflecting the sun's rays. This portrayal helped to define her iconic image. By the 14th century, she had become a well-dressed, handsome female deity known for her power. She was even adopted by the Yuan military as a mascot, and appeared on their flags and battle banners.

Some believe that, when thunder rolls and lightning strikes, it is Lei Gong having a fight with his wife. More significantly, the two appear as joint agents of justice. Dian Mu is described as the one who illuminates unjust happenings, while Lei Gong administers his corrective measures. She is also worshiped in conjunction with other deities of nature and her statues are found among those of other storm deities at Jin Tian Guan, the major Daoist temple in Lan Zhou. Here, she appears alongside Lei Gong, but also with the gods of wind and rain.

In traditional worship, Dian Mu is more of an accessory and companion deity to Lei Gong. However, in contemporary pop culture, she has gained a powerful standing in her own right in the award-winning computer game Xuan Yuan Sword. Here, she is a very independent, strong fighter, although her romance with Lei Gong is one of her few character developments.

FENG BO, UNCLE WIND
风伯

Feng Bo, god of the wind, has conjured up different sacred images for people across China. Because the wind is not a visible phenomenon, many regional cultures have associated it with the totems of their tribes, or with visible parts of nature that harness the power of the wind, like birds. The ancient Chinese pictured the god of the wind (风神) or master of the wind (风师) as a mythical bird. This is why the character for phoenix (凤) is practically identical to that for wind (风), in written form as well as in pronunciation. In fact, during the Shang and Zhou Dynasties, 凤 (phoenix) was used to denote wind, as the phoenix dancing was synonymous with the wind blowing.

The *Book of Mountains and Seas* refers to the northern god of the wind as Yuan, an auspicious bird very similar to the phoenix. From this book, we can see that other elements of nature—like certain mountain valleys—were venerated because they "gave voice" to the wind and were thus considered bringers of the wind. People of the Qin Dynasty attributed the force of the wind to the stars, specifically four stars in the Sagittarius constellation that form the shape of a Bo Ji, a shallow bamboo woven pan used for winnowing and other purposes that can be waved to generate a breeze.

Around the same period, southerners believed that the god of the wind was a strange beast, Feng Lian, who was portrayed with the head of a peacock. He had horns, the body of a stag, leopard spots on his skin, and the tail of a snake. The great poet Qu Yuan describes Feng Lian as the force that powers the carriage of the god of the moon in the sky.

Feng Lian apparently trained under the same master as the legendary tribal leader Chi You. In the mountains during his training, he found a Ling Shi (spirit stone)—a very old stone that contained mystical powers, having gathered the essence of heaven and earth. (There are, in fact, five types of Ling Shi, corresponding to the five elements.) The stone transformed into Feng Mu, the mystical sack. Feng Lian caught the sack, and it allowed him to further control the wind. Later, he fought alongside Chi You against Huang Di with Yu Shi, the god of rain (see below). Their skills helped to confuse the enemy, but Huang Di regained the advantage with his great invention, the compass (see chapter 9). After their defeat, Feng Lian and Yu Shi surrendered to Huang Di and took on the responsibility of managing the weather.

It is said that, during the Han era, images of the wind god in his fierce beast form were part of burial rites; he was portrayed as a guardian of the grave. As with so many gods, after the Tang Dynasty, this one was anthropomorphized and sometimes venerated in folklore as a female called Feng Yi (Aunty Wind), but more predominantly as Feng Bo (Uncle Wind). Drawings found along eastern coastal areas depict Feng Bo as a gladiator puffing out his cheeks and preparing for a mighty blow. Later, during the Qing Dynasty, he took the form of an old man with a long beard who carried a wheel in one hand and a fan in the other.

The wind can be a destructive force. When it damaged houses and ruined crops, it was sometimes considered to be the work of a malevolent god who required appeasement through ritual sacrifices. At other times, people believed that Feng Bo worked together with the gods of thunder and rain to nurture all things in the land. Because he conjures up images of speed and movement, Feng Bo was believed to be a messenger of the Jade Emperor.

Feng Bo has survived in modern China mainly through computer games set in a mythological fantasy universe. These games present this deity in pretty much every form he has taken—as a white-haired old man with wheel and fan, as the muscled gladiator or warrior seen in tribal interpretations, as a raging beast, and as a winged goddess. Even when he assumes human form, he has a distinctly hybrid appearance as both man and monster. Sometimes he is seen carrying Feng Mu, the mystical sack.

The game Kai Tian Bi Di depicts him as half monster and half shaman, rendered in crooked lines and a jagged style very reminiscent of the *Hellboy* comics, in particular *Sword of Storms*. The game Mythology features a very dangerous hybrid boss mode combining the gods of wind and rain.

You can visit Feng Bo Mountain in Qi Yang, Hu Nan, where the god allegedly trained and acquired his mystical sack. Sadly, not all temples to Feng Bo have been well maintained. Xuan Ren Temple in Beijing is in good condition, but Feng Bo Temple in Chao Zhou has fallen into disrepair. This is the region where Feng Bo used to enjoy immense popularity, being on the southeastern-most coast of China and relying heavily on the sea. Today, the Chinese god of the wind has taken on new forms and remains a powerful deity in the global consciousness, thanks to world-famous works like Wing Shing Ma's mythical Wuxia manhua *Storm Riders*. One of the major heroes in this series is named after the element Wind, and is portrayed as one of the strongest warriors under heaven, alongside Cloud and Frost. Wind possesses magic and divinatory powers, as well as skills in hand-to-hand combat and weaponry. His signature techniques include the "Ice Heart" and "Deity of the Wind Kick."

Yu Shi, Master of Rain

雨师

Veneration of rain developed as part of a primitive awe for the natural elements. Rain was a particularly important element because it affected all outdoor activity—hunting and, most importantly, the growing of crops. Rain-making was, therefore, a key part of the shaman's role, especially once China's civilization entered the agricultural phase. During the Zhou and Spring and Autumn periods, sacrifices for rain were part of state ceremonial rituals and hundreds of temples dedicated to the god of rain were built across the country.

As in their worship of the wind, the Chinese first looked to the stars, associating eight stars in the Taurus constellation with rain. They called these stars Bi Xing, the rain stars. According to Han scholar Cai Yong (133–192 CE) and *Shang Shu*, an early collection of historical documents, when Bi Xing is visible in the sky, rain will come. According to a poem from the *Book of Songs* (*Shi Jing*), an early poetry collection from between 1000 and 700 BCE that is a great record of customs and beliefs, when the moon is seen near Bi Xing, it will rain.

Other early forms of the rain god include the primeval being called Xuan Mo, whose shape was very vague, and Yu Shi Qie, the rain master's concubine from the *Book of Mountains and Seas*. Coming from "the land of the ten suns," Yu Shi Qie had black skin and wielded a green snake in one hand and a crimson snake in the other. She also sported two smaller snakes, one through each of her ears. Another mythical being, a bird called Shang Yang, could forecast rain, supposedly by hopping on one leg among the crops whenever rain was imminent. Shang Yang was considered more of a messenger spirit than a deity, however.

It is perhaps not surprising that the deity who outlasted these as the summoner of rain was Chi Song Zi (赤松子), who reflects the social transition from matriarchy to patriarchy and the development of a human-centric society. Chi Song Zi started off as a wild savage. *Deities Throughout the Ages* describes him as a feral man with tousled hair wearing a cape of rice straw and a kilt of animal hide that barely covered the yellow fur all over his body. His nails were as sharp as claws and he went about barefoot. His speech was deranged and he carried a branch of willow that he waved about in a frantic dance.

The savage Chi Song Zi trained under a Daoist master for many years and eventually learned the art of transforming himself into a crimson dragon that could command the rain—hence the word *Chi*, or crimson, in his name. He ate a mystical crystal that made him immortal. He was appointed Yu Shi, Master of Rain, a sub-deity to the dragon king, by the highest of Daoist gods. Later works depict him in a more dignified form, as a strongly

Yu Shi as Chi Song Zi

built man with a black beard who carries a basin in one hand in which a dragon swims, and splashes out rain with the other.

In contemporary China, Yu Shi, like Feng Bo, is a vibrant, vital presence in computer games. Only very occasionally is the god featured in his more recent forms, however. Because of the nature of computer games and their heavy reliance on fighting, myth, and fantasy for their plot and character development, the earlier, more aggressive, forms of deities often persist or enjoy revivals in this medium. Two forms in particular have captured designers' imaginations: the snake form, often combined with gladiatorial and beast-like male bodies, and the female form, with an emphasis on erotic appeal, often wearing very little or, at times, nothing at all. You can make offerings at Xian Nong Tan (Ancestral Altar of Agriculture), which is dedicated to Yu Shi and Feng Bo and other relevant deities. This is one of the Nine Altars and Eight Temples of Beijing.

In Western pop culture, one of the most widely recognized depictions of Yu Shi is as part of the Three Storms in the 1986 Hollywood movie *Big Trouble in Little China*. The character design in this film harks back to a god born in ancient China thousands of years ago. Rain, one of the Storms, appears with flowing hair reminiscent of the wild hair of the god's original form. The Chinese harness armor he wears is a nice nod to Chi Song Zi's original leather kilt. He displays his immense powers, not only by generating localized rain during his first appearance in the alley fight scene, but also in the huge storm that follows. Later in the film, the Three Storms perform a kind of martial dance to hypnotize the brides of Lopan into submitting to his will, an emulation of ancient shamanic dances that were performed to summon rain. The character's flowing hand movements, which look softer than those of Lighting and Thunder, the swooping movements of his cape, and his flying attacks are all reminiscent of Chi Song Zi in dragon form, flying, gliding, and swooping through the air.

Chang'E with the Jade Rabbit, Yu Tu

Chapter 5

Chang'E, Lady of the Moon, and Other Lunar Spirits

The moon is a reflective entity, both astronomically and culturally. Just as it reflects the sun's light, the moon is also a celestial entity that reflects the desires and hopes of people in many cultures. As clouds move in the earth's atmosphere, they obscure our views of the moon and are transformed into various celestial beings by the human imagination.

Texts of the Warring States tell of a toad who lived on the moon to explain the mysterious lunar "shadows" we see when we look into the night sky. Later texts and Han iconography have this toad standing on its hind legs and pounding medicine with a mortar and pestle. In other legends, the "shadow" is a rabbit the color of white jade, hence its name Yu Tu, or Jade Rabbit. The two stories seem to have co-existed for some time before the toad was phased out and only the rabbit remained, sometimes pictured running, sometimes pounding the elixir of immortality for Xi Wang Mu, who was famous for her elixirs (see chapter 2).

One of the celestial beings associated with the moon is a female personification called variously Yue Gu (月姑, Aunty Moon), Yue Liang

Niang Niang (月亮娘娘, Lady Moon), and Yue Po (月婆, Grandmother Moon). In early times, people venerated Yue Gu during the Moon Festival with offerings of harvest produce so that she would grant their wishes. Also known as Mid-Autumn[8], this festival takes place on the fifteenth day of the eighth lunar month. It is the second most important Chinese traditional festival after Spring Festival. In certain rural regions, it was believed that Yue Gu were seven immortal maidens from heaven (the daughters of Xi Wang Mu). On the appropriate night, people gathered around an outdoor altar, on which were placed a piece of lucky red cloth, lucky red eggs, and embroidered shoes for Yue Gu to consume and use when she descended from the skies. To complete the summoning ritual, a bowl of water is placed on the altar, with a mirror in it to reflect the moon. These offerings were often accompanied by fortune-telling rituals. Some southern Chinese women in their fifties and sixties to whom I recently spoke told me that, in their youth, they prayed to Yue Liang Niang Niang and believed that the goddess would come to their aid. Today, however, the most popular moon deities, known not only throughout China but around the world, are the immortal Chang'E and her companion Yu Tu, the jade rabbit.

Little is known about the origins of Chang'E (嫦娥), except that she was a goddess whose name may originally have been Heng'E, but was changed to Chang'E to avoid the taboo of sharing a Han imperial name. She may have been the daughter of a god, or she may originally have been called Chang Xi, who is mentioned very briefly in *Shan Hai Jing* as having given birth to twelve moons that she regularly bathed.

The Chang'E myth can be traced back to the Warring States text *The Storehouse of All Things* (*Gui Zang*), which tells a very simple tale of Chang'E stealing the elixir from Xi Wang Mu. By the Han Dynasty, a fuller story had developed and been documented in *Huai Nan Zi*[9], the elixir a gift from the supreme goddess to Chang'E's husband, Yi, the legendary archer.

Yi, also known as Hou Yi, was the Immortal archer recruited by Di Jun, an ancient supreme god, to shoot down the multiple suns in the sky. According to *Shan Hai Jing*, there were once ten suns, the sons of Di Jun and the goddess Xi He, that lived on a giant mulberry tree called the Fusang Tree in the Great Wilderness. From there, they rose and set in rotation every day. One day, the brothers thought it would be fun to rise into the sky all at once. When they did, the earth and all its rivers dried up, plants and crops shriveled, and even rocks began to melt. People died of thirst, starvation, and heat exhaustion. Strange beasts appeared and roamed the land. But the suns were so dazzled by the light they made and enjoyed their frolic so much that, despite the entreaties of their parents, they refused to return to the Fusang Tree.

Di Jun granted Yi magic arrows and ordered him to shoot down his ten wayward sons. Yi dutifully shot down nine, leaving one in the sky to do its job. While he was on earth, Yi also rid it of the strange beasts that threatened men's lives, slaying a giant bird of prey called the Great Wind in close combat. When he returned to heaven, he faced the wrath of Di Jun, who, despite having ordered it, could not face the

Hou Yi Shooting Down the Suns. An illustration from "Inquiry of the Heavens" by Xiao Yuncong, Qing dynasty, c. 1645.

loss of his children. So Yi and his wife, the goddess Chang'E, were banished to live as mortals on earth.

The goddess resented her earthly existence as a hunter's wife and could not forget the life of luxury she had enjoyed in heaven. She suggested to Yi that he request the elixir of immortality from Xi Wang Mu, the Great Mother of the West who lived on Mount Kun Lun. After listening to his tale, Xi Wang Mu was moved and granted Yi a small box of elixir she had made from Pan Tao, peaches from her celestial tree. Xi Wang Mu solemnly told him that there was only enough in the box to make one person immortal as a god, but that the contents were sufficient to grant two people immortality on earth. After he returned home, Yi entrusted the elixir to his wife for safekeeping.

While Yi went out hunting, Chang'E brooded over her fate discontentedly. She not only wanted to avoid death; she wanted to be the goddess she once had been. So she took the elixir from its hiding place and swallowed it all. As she floated toward heaven, Chang'E realized that she would still face the displeasure of the gods for her husband's deeds, as well for her own selfish actions. So she looked around for another place to settle, and ended up on the moon.

At some point in history, the Chang'E myth merged with other moon-spirit myths. Earlier versions have Xi Wang Mu transforming Chang'E into a toad as punishment, dooming her to remain on the moon pounding out the elixir she had stolen for all eternity. Tang scholars in particular emphasized the punishment aspects of the story, and portrayed the idea of living on the moon as punitive. Chang'E is presented thus by Tang poet Li Shang Yin (813–858 CE). His contemporary, Duan Cheng Shi, wrote about another inhabitant of the moon, Wu Gang, who chops at a cassia tree whose wounds immediately heal as eternal repentence for an error he made in his own search for immortality.

More modern versions of the myth have tended to minimize the Immortal origins of Yi and Chang'E, and present Chang'E in a good light. One tale describes Yi as a brilliant archer who was awarded the elixir by an Immortal for his services to the people. He didn't want to leave his mortal life and his wife behind, so, instead of drinking the elixir, he kept it in what he thought was a safe place. His apprentice, Feng Meng, who coveted immortality, learned of this. One day when Yi was away, Feng Meng broke into his house and tried to force Chang'E to give him the elixir. Chang'E refused and swallowed it all to prevent the apprentice from getting it. Greatly saddened to have lost his wife to the moon, Yi gathered her favorite fruit each year and presented it to her as an offering. Sympathetic people began to participate in these rituals—and thus began the Mid-Autumn festivities.

In another modern version, Yi is made king by the people after shooting the suns, but becomes a conceited tyrant. He acquires the elixir so he can live forever. Chang'E did not want people to be subject to the rule of a cruel king, so she swallowed the elixir herself. Yi found out and shot an arrow at his wife, who was already floating up toward the sky as she fled to the moon. People offer sacrifices to Chang'E on this day every year to give thanks for her sacrifice.

In other eras, the views expressed on Chang'E's lonely life on the moon in the poetry of the time became more sympathetic. She is once more depicted as a beautiful goddess. Here two strands of moon mythology merged, and Chang E' was given the companionship of Yu Tu (玉兔), the Jade Rabbit. Yu Tu became the more prominent moon spirit, eclipsing the toad, and acquired a new mistress. Thereafter, Chang'E is often seen with a rabbit by her side, and it is Jade Rabbit who pounds the elixir.

Whether you decide that your moon deity is Yue Gu, Chang'E, or Yu Tu, the best time to make offerings is, of course, on Mid-Autumn Festival. The most common types of offerings are fruit—pomegranates, dates, pomelo, watermelons, peaches, and apples, whose seeds are a symbol of fertility and whose name inspires lucky puns in Chinese. Seafood like crabs, which produce roe in this season, are also suitable and carry the same kind of symbolism. If you feel more enthusiastic about Yu Tu, make sure you have some Mao Dou (edamame) among your offerings, as this is believed to be Yu Tu's favorite food. Whatever specialities your region boasts will be the most appropriate.

Today, a favorite part of Mid-Autumn offerings is moon cakes (月饼), which you can purchase in many varieties at your nearest Chinese shop or supermarket in the period before the festival. Sometimes called Yue Bing, moon cakes have existed since the Song Dynasty.[10] They only became a Zhong Qiu custom during the Ming Dynasty. Moon cakes—usually very large and round to symbolize the moon and union—were made of dough and sometimes dyed red with fruit juice, then topped with sugar and osmanthus and inlaid with dates. They were then steamed or baked, with Yu Tu, Chang'E, or Fu Lu Shou printed on them (see chapter 11). A family usually made only one, and shared the pieces after the ceremony. One well-known Cantonese variety, with egg yolks to symbolize the moon, was introduced later.

Today's commercialized moon cakes come in much smaller sizes and much prettier packaging.

If it's a clear night, make your offerings in the open air on a table before the moon, with gifts of incense and wine from harvest fruits. Wishes and prayers that relate to matrimony and childbearing are appropriate on this occasion. Be sure to consume any food offerings with your family after the rituals are complete, then enjoy viewing the moon together.

As a child living in China in the 1980s, I first learned these myths through textbooks in literature class, which had the earlier version of Chang'E in which she coveted immortality and stole the elixir from her husband to attain it. Because of this, I have often wondered how Chang'E and her Jade Rabbit could have become so inseparable from the moon in the Chinese consciousness, given that part of their myth contains some rather unpalatable actions of greed and pride. Chang'E's beauty seems to transcend these actions, however. She has her own eponymous TV series (released in 2010) and her image has continued to grace colorful children's books and inspire beautiful contemporary iconography in online graphics, greeting cards, and moon-cake packaging designs, where she has largely kept her traditional appearance.

Computer games like Xuan Yuan Sword or League of Genesis, however, have re-invented her variously as a cute maiden with bunny ears, a tribal moon warrior, a voluptuous armored warrior with aerials that resemble rabbit ears, and a dark magician who derives her powers from gems and elixirs and dispenses phantom bunnies. There are plenty of Chang'E dolls in traditional dress made in fine detail to choose from on the domestic toy market, including China's version of the Barbie doll. Recently, the Yang Zhou Arts Theatre in Jiang Su performed *Chang'E Ben Yue* (*Chang'E Ascending the Moon*) in traditional Zhang Mu (wooden pole) puppetry on the stage of China's National Theatre for the first time.

Perhaps the popularity of Chang'E and Yu Tu is another manifestation of the Chinese admiration for fallible Immortals. Or perhaps it serves as a reminder of the dangers of hubris, of humanity's tendency to overreach itself. Only occasionally is Chang'E depicted looking wistfully down at the earth. More often, she is seen dancing, playing music, holding Yu Tu or a basket of flowers, or in the act of flying toward the moon with her lovely robes and hair streaming. In these depictions, one arm stretches upward and her feet are in a climbing posture, as if all her mind and spirit are bent on reaching some higher goal for which she yearns. It is this image of Chang'E that has propelled her into the modern Chinese consciousness and made her a symbol of great endeavors and aspirations. After the occupation and civil war, when the People's Republic was formed, her image was borrowed by artists to capture the mood of hope and optimism for a glorious future.

In 2007, China finally launched CLEP, its lunar exploration program, after a nearly thirty-year delay. It has since sent a series of robotic space probes into the moon's orbit that have successfully carried out missions on the lunar surface. What better mascot for these space crafts than Chang'E, who reached for the moon herself all those thousands of years ago. In 2013, a space probe named Chang'E 3 completed the first soft lunar landing since 1976. The rover it launched broke records for the longest operational time on the moon. So it is perhaps not surprising that it was named after Yu Tu, one of the oldest moon spirits in Chinese culture.

Wu Chang, Soul Hunters (provenance unknown)

Chapter 6

Guardians of the Netherworld

T he ancient Chinese believed that, when someone dies, his or her soul leaves the body and travels to another world. The Chinese Underworld is based on the Buddhist concept of *Naraka*, a place of torment, or hell. According to Buddhism, the netherworld has ten regions—the four holy realms, where the souls of the enlightened go, and six realms where the rest of the souls end up. One of these is composed of the Eight Scorching Hells, another of the Eight Freezing Hells. A third is the Hell of Loneliness, while yet another consists of eighteen tiers, among which are the Hell of Knife Mountains, the Hell of Flaying, and the Hell of Boiling Faeces. These tiers descend into increasing pain and suffering and progressively more rigid sentences, effectively rendering them infinite.

The Chinese love the gruesomeness of their hell. As a child living in south China, I loved to visit a simulation of the Underworld that formed part of the attractions of the local park. In Si Chuan, there is a full-scale model of the Underworld known as Feng Du that is one of the seventy-two sacred Daoist sites. Daoist wizards, who often act as intermediaries between the human world and other worlds, flock there. They are referred to as "ghost emissaries," and Feng Du has come to be known as the Ghost City.

Feng Du is considered the gateway to the netherworld. To enter, you must have a Lu Yin, a passport for the ghost guards to check. This is a document made of yellow paper with three required stamps—one from Cheng Huang (see chapter 10), one from heaven, and one from the governor of the city. Lu Yin can be purchased all over the country, and even in parts of Southeast Asia. You must cross over the Nai He Qiao bridge, which crosses the River of Blood Pond, to get to the otherworld. Bad souls guilty of evil deeds are thrown over the bridge when they attempt to cross.

As you pass through the Ghost Gates of Feng Du, you come to the Cave of Five Clouds, where the elixirs of immortality are made. This is also the entrance to the Underworld. The rustlings often heard in this windy place are believed to be the souls of the dead receiving the monetary offerings customarily made here. Inside Ghost City are renowned statues of the ten kings of the Underworld and representations of the eighteen tiers of hell, as well as the Wang Xiang Terrace, from which ghosts can see their home, and the Nie Jing Terrace, on which there is a mirror showing all the bad deeds committed by guilty souls.

Dong Yue Temple in Pu Xian, Shan Xi, which is famous for its cave architecture, contains an even more spectacular representation of the eighteen tiers of hell. The vast temple consists of around sixty structures in total. The fifteen underground caves, of which three have two tiers, make up the eighteen tiers of hell, housing 120 statues of kings, judges, and ghosts, as well as depictions of torture scenes. This Ming sculpture cluster is one of the largest and rarest among existing temples in China today.

YAN WANG,
LORD OF THE UNDERWORLD

阎王

As the Jade Emperor is to heaven, Yan Wang is to the Underworld, ruling over the vast realms described above. This deity, whose name means literally "king of the gates," originated from the legend of Yamaraja, or Twin Sovereigns, in Indian mythology, referring to the king who oversees male souls and his sister who oversees female souls. The name, which can also mean "just sovereign," implies a ruler who is completely impartial. The Thirteen Kings of Hell who ruled under Yamaraja evolved into the ten kings of the Underworld in Chinese mythology.

As a Chinese god, Yan Wang is said to be the distant great-grandson of Pan Gu, the giant who fashioned the world out of chaos (see chapter 1). His mother, the primeval female Mi Lun, swallowed two suns before bearing Yan Wang and his brother. Yan Wang rules under the jurisdiction of Tai Shan Wang, or the King of Tai Shan (Tai Mountains), located in east China—the foremost of its five mystical mountains. The ancient Chinese viewed the east as the source of change and development of all things. From the Xia Dynasty all the way through to the Yuan, emperors have paid their respects to Tai Shan when they ascended the throne. And entering the realm of Yan Wang—dying—is certainly the ultimate change in life!

As with many Chinese deities, the identity of the earthly Yan Wang varies. A long line of dramatizations and historical texts have attributed the title to various warriors, ministers of punishment, and upright scholars over the Song and Sui Dynasties (690–1279 CE and 581–618 CE respectively). The most famous Chinese Yan Wang is the great judge Bao Qing Tian, affectionately known by the people as Bao Gong. The commonality between all these different identities is the justice they represent—a distinct characteristic retained from the origins of this god. This is why Yan Wang is usually depicted with a black "iron" face that is impassive and impartial. His impartiality, however, is only matched by his severity. Crimes deemed to merit torture include not only murders, violence, and theft, but also swearing and the disrespecting of elders.

Yan Wang is often venerated today in video games and online artwork. His fierce, formidable, and horrific appearance also lends itself to tattoos and modern gothic art. He is sometimes pictured clutching *memento mori*, and sometimes as a traditional-style emperor at work with his writing brush on the administration of souls. Regardless of how he is portrayed, however, he is always larger than life, with a lugubrious and impassive face.

Throughout history, the involvement of Yan Wang has spiced up classics like *Journey to the West*, *Tales of Zhong Kui*, and *Tales from the Hearth* (*Liao Zhai*) a famous collection of ghost stories by Pu Song Ling (1640–1715 CE). Many of these have been successfully transferred to film and TV. The deity continues to appear in contemporary comics and online novels as well. *Here Comes Yan Wang*, by Li Qing, re-imagines the god as the head of the department of the affairs of life and death, while *Yan Wang Bu Gao Xing* (*Bu Gao Xing* means literally "unhappy") is a popular manhua by Shi Tu Zi about a new holder of this post who has a phobia about ghosts. *Yan Wang's Wife* looks at the life of the god's spouse, while *Yan Wang's Love*, by Tai Yang Yu, describes the love life of this famously impassive character. It is clear that a contemporary pattern is emerging that tends to subvert Yan Wang's traditional roles.

HEI BAI WU CHANG, SOUL HUNTERS
黑白无常

The Wu Chang, who conduct souls to the Underworld, are common to both the Buddhist and Daoist scriptures. They appear in two guises— Hei (black) and Bai (white). With the time of death being one of such mixed and extreme feelings, it's no wonder that a binary pair has evolved. Through the ages, these two spirits have cemented themselves, not only in China's spirituality, but in its pop culture as well, even today.

In almost all depictions of this pair, from classical paintings to modern artwork, the Wu Chang are presented shoulder-to-shoulder, gaunt and ghoulish, in robes that match except for their contrasting colors. Hei Wu Chang dresses in black, occasionally sporting white detailing, while Bai Wu Chang dresses predominantly in white. The two are sometimes portrayed with extraordinarily long tongues lolling out of their mouths. Their singular appearance and the nature of their role make them a fearful sight. Anyone who sees them knows instinctively that their time in the living world is ended. They both wield batons and wear tall hats with spell tags at the front. These tags, called Fu in Chinese, are made of long thin strips of paper or cloth with spells written on them by Daoist priests. Fu are routinely used in Chinese vampire films, in which they are hurled at the undead to subdue them.

While the Wu Chang are minor gods in the Daoist and Buddhist pantheons with the fairly neutral task of leading souls from the living world to the next, folklore has elevated their profile and given their image a highly emotional color. During the Qing Dynasty, when tales of the strange and supernatural were a prominent literary genre, urban legends of the Wu Chang abounded. In *Strange Tales of Drunken Reverie* (*Zui Cha Guai Shi*) by Li Qing Chen (1838–1897), a doctor who responds to a call in the night finds that he must take a coach past the Cheng Huang temple. The driver stops suddenly and some of the passengers catch a glimpse of two tall ghastly beings sauntering toward the temple. They disappear through the locked doors. The next day, the driver and all the passengers who witnessed the apparitions drop dead. The Wu Chang are also featured in *Tales from the Hearth* (*Liao Zhai*).

According to popular legend, the two Wu Chang were once very close friends, Xie Bi An and Fan Wu Jiu. Xie was tall, pale, and slim; Fan was short, dark, and stocky. One day, when the friends were walking near the river, it started to rain. Fan urged Xie to stay under the bridge and keep out of the rain while he went to fetch an umbrella. On his way back, the rain grew heavier and heavier, turning into a great thunderstorm. But Fan pressed on, determined to keep his word. The river burst its banks, sweeping over the small figure of Fan and drowning him. After the storm, Xie discovered the corpse of his friend and was heartbroken, wishing that he had died instead. Unable to contain his grief, Xie hanged himself from a beam of the bridge.

When the souls of Fan and Xie traveled to the Underworld, the lord of this realm, Yan Wang, heard their story and was moved. He gave Fan the new name of Hei Wu Chang, and Xie the new name of Bai Wu Chang and assigned them to work under Cheng Huang, the city god tasked with escorting wandering or wicked souls to face judgment in the Underworld (see chapter 10). In popular belief, these Daoist civil servants of the Underworld were seen as fearsome protectors and a scourge of evil-doers.

This is why Hei sometimes appears carrying a chain and handcuffs, and Bai is often shown holding an umbrella. The spell tag on Hei's hat reads "Peace Under Heaven" (天下太平) and is a testimony to his prowess as a hunter of fallen souls. His terrifying appearance is supposed to scare any wrongdoers into submission. Bai, by contrast, is often seen smiling and carrying the umbrella that Hei went to fetch for him. His spell tag reads "Instant Fortune Upon Sight" (一见生财) and reflects the good luck the Wu Chang bring by ridding places of mischief-makers.

The task of leading wayward souls to the Underworld, or capturing corrupt ones, is an eternal one. Today, the Wu Chang still retain their hold on the popular imagination. Where once they were portrayed in ink-and-brush paintings, today they appear in comic books. Their myth, which was once related in teahouses and by street storytellers, now appears on the Internet on forums and in blogs. People still love to share their versions of the legend of the Wu Chang on the Internet during Ghost Month (the second of three annual Chinese festivals of the dead), often accompanied by fresh artwork that depicts them as anything from Wuxia swordsmen, to wizard warriors, to cute little demon hunters in anime style. These "creepy pasta" (Internet urban legends) posts and fan art are well grounded in a long tradition of storytelling and art inspired by the pair. Their "employer," Cheng Huang, is the deity who governs both the Underworld and human cities, so wherever you see Cheng Huang's temples, you'll find a corner dedicated to the Wu Chang.

As ghoulish escorts of the dead, Hei Bai Wu Chang are also a favorite of those with a taste for the macabre. Tattoos of these deities are becoming increasingly popular among the growing crowds of punks, goths, and metalheads in China. On TV, the CGI series *The Delinquents of Jiang Hu* (*Bu Liang Ren*) presents the Wu Chang as a couple of ruthless assassins who wound their opponents with deadly poison before absorbing their essence, taking far more story cues from their horrific appearance than from traditional folklore.

If you like dressing up, the Wu Chang have become a popular "couple costume" in China, to be worn with either your partner or your best friend. Homemade or tailored costumes are a favorite for young people at conventions and have become increasingly popular at Halloween parties. Major Internet shopping sites offer inexpensive ready-made costumes, along with those of the more familiar vampires, zombies, and grim reapers.

MENG PO, GUARDIAN OF THE LAST GATE

孟婆

As with many Western religions, in Chinese religions, death is not the end. Daoism, Buddhism, and many folk religions believe in the concept of reincarnation. This concept implies belief in a deity who can keep the world from falling into chaos as souls take on new bodies to live fresh lives, undisturbed by their previous cycles. This very important deity—who is often, but appropriately, forgotten—is Meng Po, or Lady Meng.

According to literature and documented popular beliefs from the Song and Qing Dynasties, the Underworld is ruled by ten kings under Yan Wang, each with his own palace and each administering different punishments to those guilty of different crimes. Souls arriving in the Underworld go through ten stages of correction at these ten palaces before arriving at the residence of the Lord of Reincarnation, who assigns them their new lives. These souls are then ordered to the residence of Meng Po, Guardian of the Last Gate, in order to be cleansed of the memories of their past. Each soul is conducted into her arena of forgetfulness by her demon guards, where they are given the Mi Hun Tang (literally "soul beguiling soup"), which she makes from herbs of the otherworld. The soup, which is simultaneously sweet, briny, bitter, acerbic, and hot, makes them forget their past lives so they can be reborn into the world of the living. Any souls who refuse to drink the soup are immediately manacled and a sharp copper tube is inserted into their necks through which the liquid is forced.

Meng Po has been around as a deity since the Han Dynasty. Her earthly life feels rather one-dimensional. Legend says she was once a devout, virginal hermit who lived to a ripe old age in the mountains, where she spent her days studying the scriptures, never thinking about the past or the future. Once she became a goddess, however, her only memory of her previous life as a human was her surname. However, when the canonical rendition feels rather dry, Chinese folklore often finds a way to provide some color.

A far more popular version of Meng Po's life tells us that she was once an Immortal who was unable to forget her earthly life. She set up a cauldron at the foot of the bridge over the River of Forgetfulness. Gathering herbs from the banks and water from the river, she brewed an eternal supply of Mi Hun Tang—her secret soup—to help souls in torment and encourage them to avoid her own fate. The irony, of course, was that, if Meng Po were to drink her own soup, she would forget how to make it and therefore damn all other souls to the burden of their past.

Meng Po's harsh and unforgiving "service" seems a perfect setup for tales of horror and defiance. Among the best known is the love story of Ge Sheng and Lan Rui, which tells of the scholar Ge, who is too poor to marry the songstress he loves. When Lan, his beloved, dies of illness, he pines away. His soul travels past the teahouse at which Meng Po is serving her soup and sees people of all ages clambering to drink from the urn. Just as he is about to join the crowd, Lan Rui's spirit emerges. She tells him that she has pleaded with the goddess to allow him not to drink the soup of forgetfulness. With Meng Po's help, they manage to return to the world of the living with their memories intact in order to try their love anew. Like many things in China, the rules can sometimes be bent by negotiation.

The Qing Dynasty writer Wan You Guang tells a rather gruesome tale of a visit to Meng Po's home. The guest is ushered into a house of tasteful luxury by an old woman. Here, he meets the Meng sisters, three beautiful, elegantly dressed young ladies who urge him to sit down and serve him tea. Mesmerized, he drinks the whole cup in one swallow. Suddenly, the house disintegrates into desolate ruins and he finds himself in the company of three skeletons, just before he realizes that he has lost his memories. In another tale of the same era, a baby girl is born and immediately claims to be a recently deceased concubine of an official who lives nearby. It turns out that, as she lifted Meng Po's soup to her lips, a dog ran past and tripped her, so she ended up missing out on the chance to erase her past.

Traditionally, Meng Po is presented as a radiant and wise old woman, though pop culture tends to portray her as either a wizened old crone or a young gothic sorceress with silver hair and blue or green skin who is sometimes accompanied by demons and beasts. Contemporary devotion, like that of many of the gods relating to the Underworld and death, seems strongest in Internet art and fiction. A fascination with the omission or inefficacy of her soup still exists today, with urban legends spreading on forums about groups of people suddenly having phantom memories that seem to belong to another life.

A generic image used in festival to "usher in" the Cai Shen

Chapter 7

Gods of Prosperity and Good Fortune

A s civilization advanced and people learned to shelter themselves against the elements and grow, gather, and hunt for food and staples to sustain themselves, the natural aim for a good life became prosperity and plenty. For ancient societies, this often translated into wealth. In China, the attainment of wealth fell under the auspices of the Cai Shen, the gods of wealth. These gods have been as integral and natural a part of the Chinese annual calendar as welcoming in the new year.

The identity of the Cai Shen is very fluid and, throughout Chinese history, the title has been held by hundreds of heroes, warriors, and notables. In ancient China, the path to wealth fell into two broad categories. And accordingly, there are two main types of Cai Shen—Wen Cai Shen and Wu Cai Shen. Scholarly professions like the imperial council, the civil service, and the judiciary looked to Wen Cai Shen as patron; warrior professions and the military looked to Wu Cai Shen for success and fortune. A third god, Wu Lu Shen, looked after the fortunes of rural folk and that of their households.

WEN CAI SHEN,
PATRON OF SCHOLARS' WEALTH

文财神

Wen Cai Shen is the deity who looks after the wealth of devotees who hold scholarly posts. Typically dressed as a civil servant, he wears the official's gauze hat and has a long moustache and beard. He is often attired in a python-patterned robe and wears shoes in the shape of Yuan Bao (taels, a form of Chinese currency).[11] Two renowned historical statesmen have carried the title of Wen Cai Shen—Bi Gan and Fan Li.

Bi Gan was the uncle and advisor to the Shang king Zhou Wang. He offered sensible advice that the debauched and violent ruler loathed to hear. Nonetheless, Bi Gan remained loyal and fearless, never tempering his admonitions. One day at court, he became so abhorrent to Zhou Wang that the enraged king threatened to gouge out his heart. And he did.

Folklore always hates seeing the bad guys triumph, so an alternative ending to the story of Bi Gan evolved. In this version, Bi Gan gouged out his own heart in frustration, threw it on the floor, and stormed out of the palace. Having already taken an elixir granted to him by the mystic Jiang Zi Ya, he survived and roamed the country giving money to the needy. In Bi Gan, we can see the desire to associate prosperity with justice and righteousness, although he met a rather sticky end.

Fan Li, the other god of scholarly wealth, managed to remain true and avoid Bi Gan's fate. As minister under the Gou Jian, the king of Yue during the Spring and Autumn period, Fan's brilliant statesmanship contributed to the king's successful campaign, in which he defeated the kingdom of Wu and placed himself in the seat of power. In the triumphal celebrations, however, Fan Li was nowhere to be found. Knowing the king's ruthless temperament, he wisely foresaw his own demise if he stepped any closer to the seat of power. So he left his post, changed his name, and fled to the kingdom of Qi, where he made a fortune in agriculture and commerce. He always shared his wealth with the poor.

In a country subject to drastic political changes and tyranny, wisdom is valued as highly as loyalty. Both Bi Gan and Fan Li were wealthy, but

FROM KUAN YIN TO CHAIRMAN MAO

were generous with their money, especially when it came to helping the disadvantaged. In traditional Chinese culture, pursuit of wealth ideally comes hand-in-hand with charity. This is evident in traditional Spring Festival customs, in which peddlers and paupers go from door to door selling cheaply printed images of the Cai Shen, a custom called "ushering in the Cai Shen." These can be bought for a couple of cents. And even if nothing is purchased, the peddlers never leave empty-handed, but are sent away with at least a few buns to see them through to the new year.

In southern China, where faith in the Cai Shen is the strongest, performers are often employed to dress up as Wen Cai Shen. They wander the streets of the neighborhood, bringing blessings of prosperity to all its inhabitants. In Hong Kong and Guang Dong, shops and restaurants resound with the pop song "Here Comes Cai Shen" (Cai Shen Dao), much as "Santa Claus Is Coming to Town" or "Do They Know It's Christmas?" is constantly played in shops in the West in the weeks leading up to Christmas.

WU CAI SHEN, PATRON OF MILITARY FORTUNES
武财神

Wu Cai Shen, the warrior god of wealth, is the protector of the fortunes of devotees who work in the military. This mantle has been most famously born by Zhao Gong Ming. Clad head to foot in armor with a great beard on his black face, Zhao Gong Ming wields an iron whip and rides a black tiger he tamed. He is the epitome of the fierce warrior. According to Sui legend, he was one of the Wu Wen Shen, or Five Gods of the Plagues, who descended upon the Eight Demon Kings, erasing them from the living world. It is in Ming Dynasty texts—most famously in the *Investiture of the Gods*—that Zhao Gong Ming became Wu Cai Shen. It is here also that he assumed the power to call and control storms, subdue plagues, cure disease, and mitigate disasters, always setting the balance right. As people began to have faith in Zhao Gong Ming as a deity

Zhao Gong Ming carried the mantle of Wu Cai Shen

who could right wrongs, his role as a demon-slayer faded and he emerged as a bringer of fortune.

In an alternative version, Zhao Gong Ming manifests as a Muslim whose offerings had to be free of pork. This portrayal was related to Admiral Zheng He (1371–1433)[12], who took on the role of Cai Shen during the Ming Dynasty when he brought back rare treasures and rarer tales of distant lands from his voyages.

WU LU SHEN,
GODS OF HOUSEHOLD PROSPERITY

五路神

Another significant god of wealth is Wu Lu Shen, the God of Five Paths. The great Zhao Gong Ming has been given this title, and even He He, the gods of harmony, have lent their name to Wu Lu.

Wu Lu Shen is one of the Wu Si (五祀), or Five Offerings, deities intimately connected to the daily lives of people in ancient China. These are gods of the household, kitchen, earth, door, and paths. "Paths," in this context, refers to the four points of the compass and the center—in other words, the routes that people take everyday, physically and metaphorically. Wu Lu Shen's duties are to see that these paths lead to wealth.

The Wu Lu Shen continue to appear in popular religion today as a group of five gods led by Zhao Gong Ming. This portrayal was established in *Investiture of the Gods*, which dramatized Zhao's inauguration as a powerful Immortal who had mastered the secret ways of the Dao. He wandered the mountains carefree, until he met the Shang imperial tutor Wen Zhong, who implored him to fight an enemy of the state. Zhao agreed and fought along with his four trusted friends and fellow Immortals. After winning the battle, they were executed by the gods for breaking the heavenly taboo on meddling in earthly matters.

Jiang Zi Ya, impressed by Zhao Gong Ming's loyalty and bravery, made him the leading god in charge of wealth in the human world, a task in which he was aided by his four friends. Each of these warrior gods looks after the flow of fortune in one direction—east, west, north, and south—with Zhao presiding over the center. They also have ties to the principles of the Five Elements.

Research shows that the Wu Lu Shen may also have been derived from the Shan Xiao, who were malevolent mountain spirits. Books of myths like *Shan Ha Jing* describe the Shan Xiao as giants that live in the south who are depicted covered in black fur with long arms. They have strength beyond compare, are faster than leopards, and can easily rend tigers apart. They lie in wait for lone travelers in the mountains, ambush them, and lead them astray. Sometimes, they even devour them. The only common factor between depictions of the Shan Xiao and the story given in *Investiture*, however, is the violence, for Zhao Gong Ming and his friends fought violently and died before they became gods. As with other Chinese gods of fortune, they demonstrate the Chinese belief that it takes qualities other than avarice to bring good fortune—qualities like honor and bravery.

The Wu Lu Shen are worshipped in different parts of the house, and their shrine is usually on the wall to the left of the entrance. Here, the word "protection" is usually written on the wall with the words of the Dui Lian couplet on each side (see chapter 8):

> As the Jade Emperor is to the Heavens,
> So the God of Fortune is to earth.

In the old days, people visited temples and brought back paper Yuan Bao as a way of "inviting prosperity." Dumplings, made to resemble the shapes of Yuan Bao were also considered to be gifts worthy of the gods. They are a staple dish in north China, especially during the family meals at Spring Festival. In fact, the making of dumplings is an important part of reuniting the family and they have become an easy and accessible way of venerating the Cai Shen. You can find dumpling recipes with different fillings in cookbooks or on cooking websites. Don't forget to hide some nuts inside, as it is considered very lucky to find them during your meal.

The different guises given to the Cai Shen illustrate Chinese ideas surrounding the achievement of wealth and prosperity, and therefore their idea of the ideal life. It is not only important to possess intellectual abilities; you must also be wise, charitable, just, and physically powerful. This well-rounded picture is hard to achieve, however, so it is little wonder that a little help from the gods is needed. As civilization has become better at molding the environment to human needs, eliminating disease, and preventing natural disasters, the Wen Cai Shen have come to the forefront, superceding the Wu Cai Shen.

Throughout Chinese history, other deities of wealth have also been at work to ensure that every aspect of prosperity is covered. These include Li Shi, a minor god who looks after everyday fortunes and loose change. The money given to young people by married couples in small red packets decorated with lucky gold designs on New Year's Day is named after Li Shi. This Spring Festival tradition is also known as Hong Bao.

Chapter 8

Gods of the Household

Household gods are among the best known gods in China and also among Chinese around the world. Just as in most cultures, the home is the most important of places, and the Chinese like to feel at home, wherever their geographical location may be. It is not surprising to find a wealth of gods and goddesses tasked with overseeing and protecting every element of the home, from doors to beds, and even the kitchen stove. Those discussed here are some of the most signifiant in the wide range of spirits who inhabit Chinese households and watch over their members. Just remember that everyone's collection of household divinities can vary. Common additions to the set are Kuan Yin, Zhong Kui, Gods of Health and Happiness, even Chairman Mao.

MEN SHEN, DOOR GUARDIANS

门神

Even before people learned to build houses and huts, when they still lived in trees or caves, the threshold to a place that offered shelter, comfort, and security was considered sacred. The cult of Men Shen, or gods of the door, began as early as the Zhou Dynasty as part of the ancient ritual of the five offerings of the household—threshold, household, well, kitchen, and earth. These offerings, made by the Imperial as well as civilian households, took place on the ninth day of the ninth lunar month, the time for golden harvests and storing the year's work behind the door.

The earliest Men Shen were demon-slayers. These demons were not necessarily malignant spirits, however. They were often phenomena that threatened people's livelihood that couldn't be explained at the time—like wind, rain, and lightning. The first Men Shen were Shen Shu and Yu Lü, known together as Warriors of the Peach. Peaches, as one of the first wild fruits the early Chinese people relied on for sustenance, have traditionally been instilled with spiritual powers to bring good luck, along with the trees on which they grow.

Legend has it that, during the reign of Huang Di (see chapter 9), who ruled over the realms of humans and demons, Shen Shu and Yu Lü were assigned to guard the gate by a giant peach tree near the eastern sea and monitor demon activities between the realms. When they discovered any disruptive demon behavior in the human world, the gods were charged with catching the offending demons and throwing them to a devouring tiger. These demons could only roam freely at night. The crowing of the golden cockrel on the giant tree was the signal that dawn was near and their time was up.

People used to make sculptures of Shen Shu and Yu Lü to hang on either side of the doors to their homes. Later, these became simplified as drawings of the gods on wooden boards. Eventually, their names were simply written on tablets along with spells—the so-called Tao Fu (peach charms) that evolved into the Dui Lian, those iconic Chinese couplets usually written on red paper and pasted on either side of doorways.

The Men Shen can be any protective spirit that makes devotees feel safe. Because of this, their identities have been very fluid. Depending on the region, the doorway images made to venerate them may be of the golden cockerel or the tiger, the two beings the Chinese believe demons fear most. The tiger, king of beasts, is traditionally believed to be able to swallow ghosts and demons, although lions can sometimes serve this purpose as well. In many parts of China, you can hardly find any substantial building without its leonine door gods sculpted in stone.

It is important for Men Shen to look fearsome, so they can be a match for the hideous demons that may lurk in the doorway. So another fearsome-looking demon-slayer, Zhong Kui, arose to fill this role. He is usually depicted in armor, scowling and wielding weapons like metal whips or truncheons. He is sometimes on foot, and other times on horseback.

Other Men Shen include generals Qin Qiong and Wei Chi Gong, who served under Emperor Tai Zong, founder of the Tang Dynasty. Having taken many lives, the emperor was constantly haunted by a multitude of ghosts and could not rest until he summoned the generals to guard his door. During the Ming and Qing eras, regional Men Shen emerged and the role branched out into other professions to include not only warriors from the Three Kingdoms period like Zhao Yun, Han Xin, or General Yue Fei of the Song Dynasty, but also statesmen like Sun Bin of the Warring States and Wei Zheng of the Tang. The title has even been carried by a female warrior deity, Mu Gui Ying of Yang Clan, who proposed to her husband after famously fighting and capturing him. She ended up also capturing her father-in-law, much to his annoyance. No demon would dare disturb a household guarded by this goddess.

Although it is the iconic fierce warriors who have been most recognized as Chinese door guardians, the Men Shen also appear in scholarly guise—sometimes as the Fu Lu Shou, the gods of happiness (see chapter 11), and at other times as national scholars from the past. In paintings and prints, the scholarly Men Shen are surrounded by images associated with lucky homonyms—bats for Fu (happiness), vases for Ping (safety), deer for Lu (reward). Their role is to attract wealth and good fortune rather than to protect it.

Today, we still see the Men Shen everywhere, either painted or pasted on doors or as statues guarding temples—for instance, the Heng Ha generals at Buddhist sites. Even in the 21st century, larger-than-life images of Qin Qiong and Wei Chi Gong, the generals who guarded the Tang emperor, still watch over the ancient city gates of their home in Shaan Xi. Thousands of miles away, on the other side of the country, giant pottery sculptures of the Men Shen were recently unveiled in Fo Shan, Guang Dong. To keep the tradition alive for the next generation, Chinese companies now offer children's stories of these deities adapted for electronic devices. To appeal to contemporary players, games of Men Shen feature versions of them that resemble comic heroes like Marvel's Dr. Strange and Abe Sapien from the Dark Horse comic series, *Hellboy*.

The fluidity and adaptability of the Men Shen persist, with devotees creating and posting pictures on social media of their ideal contemporary door gods—Superman, Batman, Father Christmas, and Chairman Mao—surrounded by gadgets like mobile phones and laptops. Occasionally, the warrior gods are drawn brandishing their horns, their ferocity lending itself to a metal-inspired interpretation. The 2014 China Worldcon bid booth was flanked by Zhang Wang's artwork, featuring the Transformers Optimus Prime and Megatron as door gods.

You can purchase traditional Men Shen images for your doorway, or draw your own ideal guardians. Alternatively, you can place action figures at suitable positions on the lintel. For an easy way to be creative, purchase some red sheets or Hong Bao with white silhouettes on them, or draw your own Men Shen designs with colorful crayons.

For all their ferocity, stories about the Men Shen tend to be lighthearted. A very early example is the Ming play by Mao Wei (late 16th to early 17th century CE), about two door gods having a dispute. The other deities resident in the household, like Zi Gu and He He, had to make peace between them. A similar lightheartedness pervades more recent portrayals. In Light Chaser's 2016 animation *The Guardian Brothers*, two modern-day Men Shen finding themselves facing the prospect of unemployment, take action to save their jobs. The English language adaptation is now on Netflix, with the voices of Meryl Streep, Nicole Kidman, and Mel Brooks.

ZAO SHEN, KITCHEN GOD

灶神

A deity of the kitchen has been worshipped in China as far back as the Shang Dynasty. And today, when people in the West talk about Chinese gods, among the first to spring to mind is Zao Shen—literally "god of the stove, or hearth." Zao Shen is the kitchen god made famous in novels like Amy Tan's best-selling book *The Kitchen God's Wife*. The ancient Chinese believed that the stove, or hearth, represented the unity of the family, so Zao Shen's power stretches far beyond food and drink to issues concerning the heavenly administration and matters of life and death, as well as fortune and misfortune. The deity is also closely associated with pecuniary matters, and is greedy and fickle.

Zao Shen began life as an old lady who presided over food and drink. In Si Chuan, she was referred to as Tou You Po (Oil Stealing Granny), which is now a colloquial term for cockroaches, those regular frequenters of kitchens in hot climates. Later, she became a young goddess dressed in red. By the time of the Han Dynasty (206 BCE–220 CE), Chinese society had developed into a patriarchy and Zao Shen became male.

In his *Book of Rites*, Confucius records how Zao Shen was honored by state ceremonial sacrifices. During the Han period, popular worship of the god grew thanks to widespread tales of people gaining fame and fortune by making sacrifices to him. The feudal state, keen to preserve order and keep its citizens under control, promoted these stories. The twenty-third day of the twelfth lunar month is said to be the day that Zao Shen returns to heaven to make his annual report to the Jade Emperor of the merits and misdeeds of those on earth. People adhered to prescribed ethical codes so that the ruler of heaven would not shorten their lifespans as punishment for bad conduct.

Zao Shen is essentially the heavenly bureaucrat, the keeper of moral values, and the arbiter of bad behavior. Besides being used as a tool for social control, however, he also provides ordinary people with a modicum of power over their own lives and some hope of directing their own fates. Good behavior isn't enough; offerings and tributes must be made

Zao Shen, the Kitchen God
(*from* Myths and Legends of China, *1922, by E. T. C. Werner*)

to ensure that Zao Shen puts in a good word for you on the first and fifteenth day of each month when he travels to heaven to consult with the Jade Emperor. The more offerings you give, the more good luck you will have. You'd better watch out, however, because this not-so-benign but ever-present Father Christmas figure is watching you throughout the year—from your own kitchen. And he always knows.

Powerful though he may be, Zao Shen is allegedly afraid of women. This trait has several roots in tradition. One myth tells how, during the twelfth lunar month, a beggar pretended to be the kitchen god to obtain food and money, for which he received a severe beating, probably from womenfolk. Another speaks of the Kitchen King who coveted all the good food in the world. When he ran into a beautiful weaver, an Immortal who married a cowherd (see chapter 2), he saw the basket of jujube cakes she carried. He tried one, found them delicious, and wanted to marry her. She refused his proposal and used her Immortal powers to get through all the traps he set out for her. A nosy old woman colluded with the king to coerce the weaver into marriage, but she struck them both a resounding blow, sending them to the back of the kitchen range where they have remained ever since. And this is where effigies and posters are customarily placed for worship.

Clearly, the kitchen was a place where women's authority traditionally superceded that of Zao Shen. The story of the kitchen god being beaten is a tribute to women who may prove every bit as formidable as their male counterparts. This is why, in many regions, women are absent during offerings to Zao Shen, who would otherwise be too timid to accept the tributes.

In modern China, Zao Shen's role as bureaucratic reporter has been adopted by the elderly men and women of the local residential committees. Although residents in many modern high-rise buildings have consigned them to the past, in areas of older housing, they still patrol the neighborhood in their red armbands with extreme vigilance, often turning up unexpectedly in corridors and behind stairwells. No gossip escapes them; nothing goes on without their knowledge. They have the power to make your life hell if they choose to, but can be appeased with frequent gifts of food and drink, or whatever treats are available.

Today, Zao Shen is still venerated for luck and fortune. Over the centuries, he has acquired many different living and mythical guises. Many households in China still have a paper image of him or a porcelain statue behind the kitchen range. On traditional polychrome paintings, Zao Shen and his wife gaze out at you with composure and contentment, flanked by servants holding jars that contain rewards and punishments for the year's deeds. They are often surrounded by tributes and, behind their halos, the Jie Qi, or lunar twenty-four seasons, are often listed.[13] Contemporary art and children's books, however, tend to emphasize the rotundity and comical side of this deity and depict him in a rather undignified manner—as a fat god shoving food into his mouth. A few traditional paintings of Zao Shen can even be found in museums of world folk customs in the West.

The kitchen is Zao Shen's temple. To mark his shrine, use a paper image or place a tablet saying "Official Order of Zao Shen" behind your kitchen range. You can purchase porcelain effigies that often come with a free packet of incense and an incense pot. The day of worship varies between regions in China. In the north, Zao Shen is worshipped on the twenty-third or twenty-fourth day of the twelfth lunar month. In the east, devotees bring him offerings on the fifth day of the first lunar month. In other parts of the country, he is venerated on the day of the Lantern Festival, on the Winter Solstice, or on the twenty-third day of the last month of the year, when people give thanks for the past year and make wishes for the next. The Han Chinese refer to the last occasion as Xiao Nian, or Little New Year, as it occurs a week or so before New Year. During this time, you should clean your house to rid it of bad luck as well as dirt.

There are several things you can do to ensure that Zao Shen puts in a good word for you. Prepare a sumptuous meal to thank the god on the day of your offering. Or you can smear honey on the lips of his paper image so that his words will be sweet—or so that the sticky liquid prevents him from opening his mouth and reporting any bad behavior. Make an offering of Nuo Mi Ci (glutinous rice balls) cooked in sweet soup to stuff Zao Shen's mouth so full that he can't talk. Or even glue his teeth together.

This god likes meat, wine, fruit, and melon seeds; his favorite treats are brown sugar bars, so you may want to bribe him with these. After you lay your food offering before his image, burn it, along with paper chariots, horses, and money. And be sure to put a fresh image in place for the god's return from heaven.

CHUANG SHEN, PROTECTORS OF SLEEP
床神

Sleep is an integral part of life and so, of course, the Chinese have a deity to watch over the bedside and ensure restful sleep. His name is Chuang Shen, but he is sometimes known as Chuang Gong (床公). Like the gods of the doors and kitchen, this god's powers are territorial. He is one of the pantheon of household gods required to keep your home comfortable and secure. And he comes complete with a spouse—Chuang Mu (床母), also known as Chuang Po (床婆).

Veneration of Chuang Shen began in the Song Dynasty, during which the poet Yang Xun Ji (1456–1544 CE) wrote: "Sweets for Zao Shen (kitchen god), a drink for Chuang Shen." Like offerings to Zao Shen, those to Chuang Shen are made in the month before the new year—during Xiao Nian, Little New Year—when the house is cleaned and preparations are made for Spring Festival. Chuang Shen was worshipped not only by the people, but also by the emperor, since rest was a vital aid to his governance of the country.

In the old days, when children contracted chicken pox or other illnesses, parents prayed to Chuang Shen. In some areas, a mother and child prayed together, until the child reached the age of fifteen. During the Ming and Qing eras, respects were paid to Chuang Po at weddings, along with those offered to parents and in-laws. Offerings were also made at the An Chuang or "bed settling" ceremony, which took place a few days before the wedding to install the couple's new bed in the bridal chamber. Beds were placed carefully, according to the strict Feng Shui of the couple's astrological signs, as was the bedroom shrine.

The Chuang Shen were very popular deities along China's southern and eastern coasts and are still worshipped regionally. The people of Chao Zhou (Teochew) and Guang Zhou in Guang Dong make offerings to Chuang Po rather than Zhi Nü, the weaving goddess, on the Festival of Skills, which is celebrated on the seventh day of the seventh lunar month. There, local legend tells of a woman who loved to care for children and was well loved by her people. She came to be venerated as a goddess associated with caring nannies and is referred to as Chuang Jiao Po, or "granny at the foot of the bed." Her name was then shortened to Ah Po. According to Song folklore, shortly after the emperor Ren Zong was born, he would not stop crying. The doctor could do nothing, so he recruited a nanny, who proved effective. One day when she was breastfeeding the baby prince, his father suddenly appeared. The nanny ducked under the bed to maintain her modesty and suffocated. Later, the emperor made her a protector goddess of children.

In Zhou Shan, Zhe Jiang, life used to revolve around a set of rituals dedicated to Chuang Shen, starting with Xi Chuang, or "bed washing," on the third day after a baby was born. For this ceremony, glutinous rice was steamed in two wine cups, each with a date (homonym for "early" or "quick") on top. These were then held reverentially over the bed during prayers for the child's rapid growth. The rice was then gifted to neighbors' children in order to share the good luck. When a baby was a month old, it was brought to the shore to bond with the sea, after which incense offerings were made at the head and foot of the bed. This was done so that the baby would grow up treating the sea as his bed and the sky as his curtains. It was also said to prevent sea sickness.

In Zhou Shan, drums were played around the bed when someone fell sick to drive away the bad energy. After a death, the bed sheets of the deceased were burned by the sea to help the soul become one with it. These rituals are still performed in some of the surrounding islands today.

Today, effigies, icons, and rituals for Zao Shen tend to be far better documented and curated than those for Chuang Shen. The decline in the awareness and following of these gods of the bedside may have something to do with the hectic pace of modern life and our tendency to underrate the importance of sleep. With the postmodern revival of mindfulness and meditation practices, however, veneration of Chuang Shen is seeing a revival. Customs vary between regions. You can make offerings either on New Year's Eve after offerings to Zao Shen, or on the day after the Lantern Festival, the official start of the new year. Pray for restful sleep to be with you always. If you're in Beijing, you can visit the Daoist version of Chuang Shen at Dong Yue Temple.

Traditional images of Chuang Shen and Chuang Po resemble a well-fed, well-groomed middle-aged couple. You don't need an altar to worship them, just an earthenware pot for incense. Place fruit, cake, wine, and tea in your bedroom, and the gods will find them. Chuang Po likes alcohol, while her husband prefers tea.

If you're an antique collector, look for wood carvings of Chuang Shen in the Jiang Nan style. These come from a geographical region in China immediately south of the lower reaches of the Yangtze River and have recently become popular in the domestic market. Many images of Chuang Shen are also carved on the region's famously intricate traditional Qian Gong Chuang wooden beds (bed of 1,000 chisels). You can find these in Wu Zhen, a stunning old water city that now hosts an international theater festival.

In 2016, a Chuang Shen-centered film that is part of the comedy trilogy *The Visitation of the Gods* was being filmed in Tian Jin when an actor was injured. He returned after two days in the hospital in order to keep the filming schedule on track. I hope he made proper offerings to Chuang Shen to ensure a speedy recovery.

LIU HAI CHAN, THE GOLDEN TOAD
刘海蟾

Liu Hai Chan is an exceptionally popular small god, beloved for his associations with the distribution of wealth. He often appears alongside the gods of wealth, harmony, and happiness in Nian Hua, traditional new year household decorations common in regions like Shan Dong, Shaan Xi, Si Chuan, and He Nan until the mid-20th century.[14]

Liu Hai Chan is derived from Liu Cao, a Daoist monk who lived during the Five Dynasties in Yan Shan (Beijing). He had passed the Jin Shi examinations—the highest level of the Ke Ju, the notoriously difficult imperial examinations introduced in the Han Dynasty that were essential for any office in government administration. He was serving under prime minister Liu Shou Guang when he was visited by a mysterious Daoist master who balanced ten coins and ten eggs on top of one another. Liu remarked how precarious the construction was and the master pointed out that it was an illustration of Liu's circumstances, being so close to the seat of power. Later, Liu realized that he had been enlightened by none other than Han Zhong Li, leader of the Eight Immortals (see chapter 14).

In 909 CE, the prime minister under whom Liu Cao served became the king of Yan, eventually proclaiming himself Emperor. Liu rejected the call to office, and traveled far and wide in search of the Dao. After receiving training in inner alchemy from Lü Dong Bin, another of the Eight Immortals, he settled in the Hua Shan and Zhong Nan mountains, acquiring the Daoist name Hai Chan Zi (Hai meaning "sea" and Chan meaning "toad"). Thereafter known as Liu Han Chan, he came to be regarded as one of the founders of the Quan Zhen school of Daoism, well known thanks to its depiction in Wu Xia novels, a genre of Chinese fantasy and historical fiction that centers on the lives of martial artists and swordsmen.

From the amphibious connotations of his name, folk stories evolved that became the subject of many regional musical forms, like the Hua Gu ("flower drum") operas of Hu Nan. Phrases that describe his miraculous deeds—like "Liu Hai Xi Jin Zhan" ("Liu Hai's Antics with the Golden Toad")—even entered the *Tong Su Bian*, a Qing collection of popular words, phrases, colloquialisms, idioms, and proverbs by Di Hao, who died in 1788.

According to Qing legend, a mysterious man known as Ah Bao once called on Bei Hong Wei, a wealthy merchant in Su Zhou, asking for work as a servant. Exceptionally hardworking, Ah Bao never accepted any

Liu Hai Chan and the Golden Toad, by Zhang Lu (1464–1538, Ming Dynasty)

payment, or even ate or drank. It was said that he could turn chamber pots inside out for cleaning, and mold clay into pottery with his bare hands. One year, he took his baby master out during Lantern Festival and, having been rebuked for his late return, disclosed that he had taken the child to Fu Jian (at least a train ride away), where the lanterns were much prettier. Needless to say, the family did not believe him, but were astonished when they saw a fruit clutched in the baby's hand—a lychee, a specialty of Fu Jian.

Ah Bao found a large three-legged toad in the well, tied a ribbon around its leg, and told the family never to lose it. Sure enough, they lived in comfort and wealth for the rest of their lives. Thereafter, Liu Han Chan became known as a god for the flow and distribution of wealth, and the three-legged toad, a rare find in itself, became an auspicious sign. The real Liu Cao was around fifty years old before he supposedly became an Immortal, but popular woodblock paintings depict him as a small, fat, and grinning youth holding a string of gold coins in each hand and surrounded by lucky objects like lotus and plum blossoms—and, of course, a golden three-legged toad.

Images of toads are still considered very lucky, and remain among favorite household charms today. You can buy golden toads to place above your front door to facilitate the flow of wealth into your household. There are copper and bronze sculptures of toads holding coins in their mouths that you can place on shelves, desks, and worktops. Stone toads are also a popular decoration as a Cha Chong—a tea pet, usually placed in the corner of tea trays in traditional tea ceremonies as an ornament and as a connection to nature that can bring good luck to your guests. The toad gets to enjoy the tea alongside your guests, and any spare tea can be poured over it as a tribute.

Chapter 9

Gods of Invention

The Chinese are an immensely creative people, whose inventiveness has brought us everything from fireworks to the printing press. It's little wonder that some of these inventors have been raised to the status of gods. Chinese inventions range from many practical devices—like the compass, timepieces, geared locks, and the stone mill— to breakthroughs in weaponry like gunpowder and the recurve bow. Even in leisure, they created Cu Jü, an ancient precursor to soccer. Perhaps the most important Chinese invention, however—and certainly the one that has informed what we know about China's growth and development —is the invention of Zi, the characters that form the basis of the Chinese written language.

CANG JIE, FATHER OF CHINESE WRITING

仓颉

China's history and ancient culture are so well documented because its written language has existed for so long. The man who invented Chinese writing, who was also an imperial historiographer, was named Cang Jie, the man born with four eyes. The myth of Cang Jie's four eyes probably

Cang Jie, Father of Chinese Writing (1685)

derived from his remarkable abilities and unique vision. His notable deeds were, in turn, recorded during the Warring States and Han eras.

Cang Jie's job was to keep count of the livestock and food supplies for the ruler Huang Di. During wartime, Cang Jie found it hard to keep track of the cattle, sheep, and grain, even though he had a brilliant memory. But the emperor needed the figures so he could use them in diplomatic negotiations. After wracking his brain, Cang Jie created a system for counting high numbers by tying different-sized knots in ropes and painting them various colors. But sometimes he found himself forgetting what some of the colors represented!

As Cang Jie watched hunters track their prey by animal footprints, a bright idea popped into his head. He would make drawings like those footprints to represent and differentiate all kinds of things. He closely observed the appearance of everything around him—the shapes of all birds and beasts, even fine patterns like those that appear on tortoise shells. He took in the contours of mountains, trees, and rivers. Then he chiseled these symbols, or pictographic signs, on the inside of a cave and called them Zi (or characters). An animal footprint became 爪, or claw; a round shape came to represent the sun; a curved shape denoted the moon's distinct crescent form. Cang Jie soon ran out of space on the cave wall, however, and had to dig bigger caves to house all the Zi he had invented.

It was said that millet rained from the sky and ghosts cried at the momentous appearance of the pictographic signs called the Zi. This is why, ever since its birth, the Chinese have held writing as sacred and endowed it with magical powers. Chinese Fu—spell tags used to subdue Jiang Shi (僵尸, literally "stiff corpse") in horror films—are a good demonstration of these properties.[15]

Cang Jie traveled far and wide, teaching whoever wanted to learn to recognize and draw the Zi. Communication between people improved, misunderstandings were avoided, and records became available. Legend says that the characters carved in stone by Cang Jie weighed the equivalent of ten liters of seeds, and even the great scholar Confucius was only able to learn 70 percent of the entire store of Cang Jie's characters.

Cang Jie became widely venerated during the Song Dynasty. The Xu Li, imperial officials who processed documents and paperwork, referred to him as King Cang and held an annual festival to commemorate him. At this celebration, devotees drank all day and, by the end of the festivites, were highly likely to see the deity with four eyes.

Today you can still go to He Bei, He Nan, Shan Dong, and Shaan Xi to visit sites sacred to Cang Jie—his tomb, his temples, and the place where he is said to have had his great revelation. Cang Jie Temple in Bai Shui County, Shaan Xi, where he was born, holds an elaborate festival in April on the season of Gu Yu (literally "grain rain," inspired by the legend of the raining millet). Here, paper with writing on it is regarded as sacred and not to be thrown away. Young children make offerings to Cang Jie instead of Confucius before beginning primary school, and older students go to the temple and touch the sacred stone tablet so that the god will grant them good handwriting.

A practical way to venerate Cang Jie is to learn Chinese calligraphy. You can find a good set of brushes, ink stones, and calligraphy books on the Internet, in your local Chinese bookshop, or in shops in Chinatown. Chinese is rapidly becoming one of the world's most widely spoken languages. Although writing Chinese is considered to be a lot more difficult than speaking or reading it, it is very rewarding to access these miniature distillations of thousands of years of culture. Chinese characters provide interesting insights into anthropology, and a lot of etymology can be extracted from how the character for an object is written. Once you have cultivated your calligraphy to a certain level, it can also be beneficial to your health by aiding the flow of your Qi (inner energy). Like Chao Dao, the art of Chinese tea, Chinese writing cultivates the mind and spirit. To commemorate the millet myth, it is customary to bake bread featuring a calligraphic pattern. Why not design your own!

HUANG DI, THE YELLOW EMPEROR

黄帝

Unlike Western civilizations, in which monarchs and gods are typically separate entities, China has a long tradition of venerating great emperors and leaders as deities. The first great Chinese emperor to become a god was Huang Di, the Yellow Emperor, who was perhaps the greatest in history. According to *Huai Nan Zi*, five divine emperors ruled over the east, west, north, south, and central parts of the land. Each belonged to one of the five elements, and each was represented by a color. Huang Di ruled over central China and belonged to the earth element. He was represented by the color yellow ("huang"). Huang Di was by far the greatest leader of his age. He was worshipped as the ideal sage emperor, and was the founder of Chinese culture and civilization. He is venerated as the great ancestor of the Chinese race who, himself, fathered many gods and humans.

姓嬴名政始目始皇乙卯即王位庚辰併天下稱皇帝
在位三十七年居王位二十五年即帝位十二年壽五十

Huang Di, the Yellow Emperor, the first great Chinese emperor to become a god
(World History Archive / Alamy Stock Photo)

The ancient Chinese believe that astronomical signs mark momentous events and the birth or passing of great people. This is why the births of so many Chinese deities are surrounded by strange weather. In Huang Di's case, a great flash of light as strong as the sun illuminated the night sky and the land where his mother lived and, in this light, she saw a halo in the Great Bear constellation. When this faded, she conceived Huang Di and carried him for over two years before giving birth. He was born with the face of a dragon, and with the ability to talk.

Huang Di lived in a time when fantastical monsters and creatures that were half man and half beast were said to roam the land. The legends of his epic battles are still told today and have never lost their appeal. Huang Di fought his brother, Yan Di, the Flame Emperor, over who would rule the world. Yan Di drew on the force of fire in the battle; Huang Di invoked the power of water in rain and floods. He summoned the birds and beasts to his aid. Wolves bounded, panthers descended, tigers emerged, and eagles and falcons soared—all to fight alongside the Yellow Emperor. The brothers battled long and hard before Huang Di claimed his victory.

To govern the united land, Huang Di appointed the ox-headed Chi You as his minister—a creature with killer horns, four eyes, six hands, and ears and temples as sharp as swords and spears. As time went by, Chi You grew proud and coveted Huang Di's power. He challenged the emperor to battle, leading forth an army of followers with iron heads and copper faces who subsisted on stones and could make any weapons out of iron. Ying Long, the winged dragon, came to Huang Di's defense, while Chi You summoned Feng Bo and Yu Shi (see chapter 4) to support him in the fight. Rain poured down on Huang Di's army; storms obstructed his path and dank mists hid his enemies from view. But Huang Di used his new invention of the compass to guide his army, while Ying Long gathered and stored flood water. Just as their armies drew close enough to engage, Chi You ordered the gods of wind and rain to do even more damage. So Huang Di summoned his daughter, Pa, the drought fury. Pa swallowed all the excess water, leaving just enough for the rivers and streams of the world.

Pa refused her father's entreaties to return to the mountains, however, and wandered the land, periodically wreaking destruction. Ying Long could not return to heaven after failing to defeat Chi You, so he roamed the south of China and made the region very wet. After Huang Di's triumph, Chi You was executed and his manacles, stained with blood from his struggle, were thrown into the wilderness. When maple leaves turn red every year, people believe it is the anger of Chi You.

Huang Di governed the world from his palace at Kun Lun, the residence of the gods where Xi Wang Mu, the Great Mother of the West, lives (see chapter 2).[16] As emperor, Huang Di fought not only monsters on the battlefield, but also social injustice, savagery, and barbarism among his subjects. His was a time when gods and spirits mixed with humans, some even inflicting violence on them and behaving dishonestly. It took a just and impartial ruler like Huang Di to maintain order and justice.

When the other four divine emperors plotted against Huang Di, he fought them and won. The deities Chin Pi and Ku bullied the small god, Pao Chiang. They were arrested and executed by Huang Di. But after their execution, they managed to transform into terrifying giant birds who destroyed crops and foretold battles. The god Er Hu was driven by a servant's words to kill another god, Ya Yu. Huang Di arrested them both, put the servant to death, and sentenced Er Hu to thousands of years of torture. Then he summoned shamans to bring Ya Yu back to life. But Ya Yu went mad.

Some say that this emperor lived for 300 years. Slowly, after many years of effort, Huang Di brought order to the world. But not without a price, for the world still bears the mark of violence and bloodshed. Some beings and phenomena that lurk in the dark peripheries of more civilized times still remind us of these primitive struggles.

Apart from administering his domain with love and benevolence, Huang Di was also considered the source from which all ancient Chinese civilization originated. He was always keen to understand everything around him and invented a great number of things. He taught people how to drill wood to make fire so they could keep warm, eat cooked food, and avoid disease. He taught them how to build boats from hollowed tree trunks so they could travel to distant places, and how to build houses from trees. He tamed cattle and horses to draw carts, which gained him the nickname of Xuan Yuan—Xuan being the name of the ancient high-fronted, curtained Chinese carriage and Yuan referring to the shafts of a cart. The invention of coins, weights and measures, time-telling devices called clepsydra, and cauldrons are all attributed to Huang Di, who apparently also invented hats, crowns, mirrors, clothes, coffins, and even Cu Jü, an ancient sport resembling soccer.

According to folklore of the 1980s, Huang Di invented the compass after losing several battles against Yan Di during a particularly foggy autumn. Driven by his defeats, Huang Di worked hard to find a way of determining directions without visual references. He discovered that a type of magnetite was attracted to the south. So he made a wooden figure with a magnetite hand and fixed it on a cart. No matter where the cart went, the figure's hand always pointed south. This became the earliest form of the Chinese compass, which could be wheeled onto the battlefield.

The Yellow Emperor was clearly exceptionally intelligent, observant, and perceptive, but it is hard to believe that even he could have created most of Chinese civilization single-handedly. The secret lay in using all his resources to the full, one of which was his cadre of talented officials. According to the *Shi Ben*, the encyclopedic Qin book of origins and China's earliest genealogical text, systems for observing the stars, the calendar, arithmetic, and the Heavenly Stems and Earthly Branches that designate years, months, days, and hours in the lunar calendar were all created during Huang Di's reign from projects he assigned to different officials. Cang Jie, father of the written Chinese language, was among these talented men. Huang Di was the model for the wise emperor who promoted capable officials all around him and made good use of their skills for the nation, a model that many conscientious emperors subsequently emulated to earn the respect of their people.

Legend has it that, upon Huang Di's death, a dragon descended to earth and the Yellow Emperor rode it to the heavens. According to the *Shi Ji*, he knew the dragon would come, so he had a giant cauldron made so he could bring some of his officials and concubines with him to heaven.

Others say that, after his funeral, the mountain in which he was buried collapsed and his coffin was found empty.

Texts from the Warring States describe Huang Di as having four faces. Most traditional portraits depict him as authoritative, middle-aged, and scholarly. Twenty-first-century Chinese favor a younger Xuan Yuan dressed in primitive garb who looks fit for battling beasts as well as ruling his clans. In this guise, he is currently featured in major TV series and big-budget historical epic films.

Huang Di was a popular subject for writers during the Warring States, and interest in and adoration of him only grew after this period. Some research indicates that he and his brother were the actual historical leaders of primitive clans, including most of the Hua Xia people, who later became the Han. The Chinese still refer to themselves as Yan Huang Zi Sun, "descendants of Huang Di and Yan Di." It is interesting that, during the Qing period with its Manchu rulers, Huang Di began to be worshipped as the ancestral sage, not just of the Han people, but of "the Chinese nation." At the time, this evolution was supported by the Qing state in order to legitimize its power and authority.

Later, in the early 20th century, with aggression from European nations and later invasion from Japan, China's first president, Sun Zhong Shan (also known as Sun Yat-sen), called on the god again. Faced with a nation in crisis, the Yellow Emperor came to the rescue as Sun's government and their successors united the nation by invoking the god in sixteen public addresses given between 1911 and 1949, even sending officials to Huang Di's tomb in Shaan Xi to pay their respects. This truly demonstrates the power of Huang Di as a deity and paved the way for what Huang Di has become today—not only a symbol of the magnificence of Chinese civilization, but also of unity and solidarity between China's fifty-six ethnic groups. Today, during the Qing Ming Festival, it's not uncommon for Chinese leaders to come together with Chinese from around the world to worship this god, who is the common ancestor of the Chinese people.

SHEN NONG, THE DIVINE FARMER

神农

One of the wisest, most creative, and most resourceful of China's ancient gods is Shen Nong, who is venerated for the invention of agriculture, Chinese medicine, and a dozen other trades. China has a long and rich history in agriculture, and she has more than one god to thank for this. But Shen Nong is by far the most esteemed and popular of them. Every time we call his name, we evoke the Divine Farmer.

Early tales of this god can be found in a number of Spring and Autumn texts, and later, in *In Search of the Supernatural*, by Gan Bao (286–336 CE). In these stories, Shen Nong's mother is said to have copulated with a dragon in Chang Yang, so her child was born with a dragon's head on his human body. Three days after he was born, the child could talk. In five days, he could walk. And at the age of three, he knew everything about sowing and reaping crops. At the time, people ate and drank whatever they could find, including poisonous fruits, animal blood, and worms. Consequently, they suffered from sickness and pain. Shen Nong taught them to sow the five grains (rice, two kinds of millet, wheat, and beans), and showed them how to examine the quality of the land and cultivate it accordingly. Thanks to the Divine Farmer, people learned to distinguish different tastes and use their palettes.

Shen Nong invented many tools for farming—including the axe, the hoe, and the Chinese plow. He trained people to open and weed wastelands, excavate wells, and irrigate the land. The old way of preserving seeds, by dipping them into horse urine to protect them from worms, is attributed to this god. Shen Nong created the Jie Qi, twenty-four seasons around the lunar year that indicate changes in climate and the timing for agriculture procedures. These are still in use today, not only for farming, but also for traditional festivals.

Children in China learn about Shen Nong at school as the creator of Chinese medicine. Versions of the myth in which he tastes all the herbs he finds in the wild are generally more popular than those that tell of him thrashing the herbs with a whip to extract their characteristics.

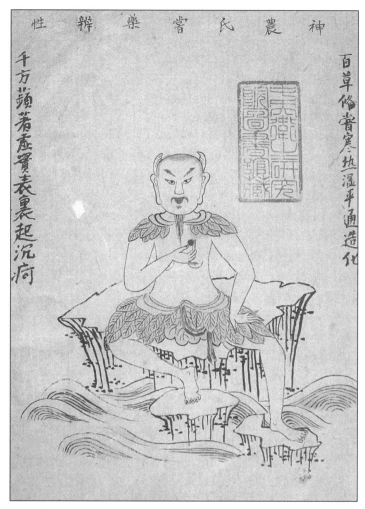

性 辨 藥 嘗 氏 農 神

千方蘋著虛實表裏起沉疴

百草修嘗寒熱溫平通造化

Portrait of Sheng Nong, the Divine Farmer, from Gudai yijia huaxiang,
created by Lin Zhong (Qing period, 1644-1911)

He distinguished the herbs' flavors and classified them according to the
principles of Traditional Chinese Medicine—coldness, warmness, mildness, and toxicity. Shen Nong was the first to study the human pulse
and to explore the use of acupuncture and moxibustion, a therapy in
which dried mugwort (moxa) is burned on particular points on the body.
He recorded all his findings in *Shen Nong Ben Cao Jing* (*Shen Nong's Materia
Medica*).

As a child living in China during the 1980s, I remember learning the version of the myth that had been collected around Zhe Jiang a decade before. In it, Shen Nong tasted all the plants he found so he could distinguish between food and medicine. He put the food in one bag, and medicinal herbs in another. Because he had a crystalline stomach, he could see exactly how his organs reacted to each new experiment. His two bags must have been pretty big, for he collected 47,000 flowers, roots, herbs, and leaves in the food bag, and 398,000 curative plants in the medicine bag. But one day, Shen Nong tried a small yellow flower. Soon after he swallowed it, he watched his intestines break into pieces and died. This plant became known as Duan Chang Cao—gut-shattering weed.

The very first plant Shen Nong tasted was a small green leaf that he found very refreshing—it made his entire system feel cleared. He called it Cha (查), meaning "inspected." Shen Nong tasted many other plants of all shapes and sizes, but whenever he felt unwell, he took a few of the little green leaves and felt restored and refreshed. That small green leaf became known as Cha (茶), a name homonymous with the name Shen Nong had given it. An entire culture was founded on this herb by the tea sage Lu Yu (see chapter 13). This tea culture flourished during the Tang and Song periods, eventually spreading to Europe via trade and the Opium Wars. It became known as tea, from the term for the beverage in the dialect spoken at the ports of Fu Jian, Hokkien. Today, even though English blends are well established and the English tea ceremony has become closely linked with the British identity, Shen Nong is still remembered as the discoverer of tea on packets of popular blends like Yorkshire. He also occasionally appears on mugs and tea towels.

Shen Nong's contributions to Chinese civilization are not limited to farming and medicine, however. The invention of the pestle and mortar, bowls, pans, pots, rice steamers, and the kitchen range are also attributed to him. If he hadn't taught people to plant mulberry trees, Lei Zu, the Mother of Silk (see chapter 12), would never have been able to learn silkworm breeding. The bow and arrow, the sixty-four diagrams for divination, the Qin and Se (respectively seven- and twenty-five-stringed instruments), and trading markets have all been credited to this god, who believed that music had the ability to calm and purify the spirit. The

Shen Nong era is seen very much as a golden age and an ideal dynasty—a time when people lived content, happy, peaceful, and self-sufficient lives.

The brilliance of Shen Nong has fueled the Chinese imagination for centuries. In fact, many outgrowths of his folklore were still retold as late as the 1980s in places like Chong Qing. His intimacy with plants seems to make them come alive. The popular tale of the once highly toxic ginger circulated in Cheng Du in the 1980s. Everywhere it grew, ginger was hunted and dragged out of the soil to be scorched in the sun. The ginger ran and ran until, one day, it came across a farmer who grew the most luscious flowers. A white gourd nearby told it that the farmer was Shen Nong. The ginger went to Shen Nong and asked for his help. And this is how the ginger lost its toxicity and became known as both a hot-tasting spice and a warming herb.

Historically, emperors themselves have made offerings to Shen Nong, who is considered the founder of many trades, including cultivating grain, pastry-making, salt-mining, and even storytelling. There are temples, mausoleums, and relics across the country that you can visit, as well as over 100 temples in Taiwan. In the Chinese epic tradition, there is a long narrative poem, the *Hei An Zhuan* (*Epic of Darkness*), that tells the tale of Shen Nong and his exploration of plants, combining with it many interpretations of myths and lives of other gods. The poem is often sung at funerals.

Two locations claim to be Shen Nong's home—Hu Bei and Shaan Xi. Shen Nong's tripod cauldron is featured in Tai Yuan and on the Shen Nong Plain, where he investigated the herbs. In Shaan Xi, there is a Five Grains Temple and even a Shen Nong town. Hu Bei offers a beautiful mountainous area called Shen Nong Jia, or Shen Nong's Ladder. Legend says that the god built a rattan ladder so he could climb high and reach the rare plants at the top of the mountains. The ladder eventually turned into a forest. In the same province, you'll find Shen Nong's cave and his nine wells. Festivities are held at these locations on the twenty-sixth day of the fourth lunar month, believed to be Shen Nong's birthday.

Today, China's younger generation still have enormous admiration and reverence for Shen Nong. Artwork posted online re-imagines him— sometimes as a female forest sprite clad in leaves, sometimes as a powerful eco-warrior in beast form, and sometimes even as a plant-loving giant robot with a see-through belly. Even more than Pan Gu and Nü Wa (see chapter I), domestic Chinese companies invoke his spirit across all trades and industries, from hot-spring resorts, to herbal health plasters, to rice brands. Food markets borrow his name, as do manufacturers of glass, honey, and wild-mushroom food products. A company in Hao Zhou, An Hui (the home of Chinese herbs), pays tribute to the god by commissioning giant golden statues of him surrounded by flowers. Jiao Zuo in He Nan holds a cultural festival of traditional rituals on their Shen Nong Mountain, while the Lovely Taiwan Foundation offers a day-long educational program for children as part of their Project Shen Nong to encourage them to understand how their lives are connected to the land, and to help them discover their heritage.

The forty-episode *Legends of the Ancient Times* (*Chuan Shuo*) TV series, one of modern China's many ventures to reconnect with its heritage, features Shen Nong as a fierce warrior who, after witnessing the strife caused by war and plagues, turns his attention to plants and relieves people's suffering. On the other end of the spectrum, online novels have carved out many contemporary Shen Nong reincarnations as poor farmers and agriculture students being granted the powers of Shen Nong after rescuing people or finding mystical Nü Wa stones. There is even a Shen Nong channel on YouTube.

Chapter 10

Protectors and Guardian Spirits

Throughout its millenia of turbulent history, which has been passed largely under imperial and totalitarian rule, the Chinese people have always been at the mercy of emperors and others in office who have not always been wise and benevolent. A country so vast, diverse, and complex that it has been virtually impossible to govern as a whole has seen more than its fair share of social unrest, internal political struggles, and foreign occupation. With so little certainty over their fate, the Chinese need guardians and protectors, and these figures have become a key part of Chinese spirituality. Some of them, the spirits of places and objects, arose from the Chinese imagination. Others were once just officials or folk heroes that sprang from the populace and were embraced, adored, and elevated to the status of gods.

CHENG HUANG, GUARDIAN OF THE CITY

城隍

The Chinese believe that all objects, especially those connected with everyday lives, possess spiritual powers, whether they are big or small. Just as

Cheng Huang, Guardian of the City

there are gods that protect doorways, wells, and kitchens, there is a spirit that protects cities—Cheng Huang. Cheng means "city," while the Huang refers to the dry moat around a city fortress. The earliest temple built for Cheng Huang dates back to the 3rd century in the Kingdom of Wu.

Cheng Huang's popularity rose during the Northern and Southern Dynasties because of a legendary battle. When the Qi army was blockaded by the enemy with no means to access supplies, General Mu Rong ordered his men to pray to Cheng Huang at the city's temple. Suddenly, a storm descended on the Liang army and their entire offensive force was washed away by floods. By the time of the Tang Dynasty, with the rise of trade and commerce that came hand-in-hand with the growth of cities, belief in Cheng Huang became widespread as cities around the country built their own temples. It was only a matter of time before Daoism incorporated him into its official pantheon, as a vanquisher of evil and a protector god who tempers the climate.

Water is associated with Yin energy and the Underworld. With his watery realm (rivers) on the borders of cities serving as a metaphor for the borders of the realm of the living, Cheng Huang also became the administrator of souls of the dead. Before priests conducted souls from the living world to the Underworld, they "gave notice" so Cheng Huang could update his records. In *Tai Ping Guang Ji*, the imperial collection of Song stories, a legend appears that illustrates Cheng Huang's ability to foretell the amount of time someone has left in the living world.

During the Ming Dynasty, Emperor Zhu Yuan Zhang brought Cheng Huang to the peak of his power, raising his status to that of the highest official in the realm, equivalent to a prime minister. Under imperial orders, every prefecture, county, and state refurbished their Cheng Huang temples. The temples in the capital cities introduced wooden statues of the god painted in crimson and flanked by his attendants, Yin and Yang. Although the emperor later revealed that he did this to instill fear of the god into his subjects to deter them from wrongdoing, his edicts also ensured the preservation of temples across the country.

Because of Cheng Huang's evolution into a god of the Underworld, generations of Chinese have designated their city's dead heroes as local Cheng Huang—including loyal courtiers, fierce generals, and just officials, many of whom sacrificed themselves for the good of the people. The tradition of electing heroes by popular consensus to bear the title of the god continued for hundreds of years, until at least the 19th century. A more recent Cheng Huang of Shanghai is navy commander Chen Hua Cheng (Tiger Chen), who fought valiantly against invaders in 1842. Sinking eight of the enemy's ships in two hours, the seventy-year-old Chen eventually gave up his life in this battle.

In the old days, invalids moved into Cheng Huang temples, believing that this would cast out the demons that possessed their bodies. Exorcisms were performed in the temples at night, with one spiritualist acting as a medium for channeling the deity and another chanting the spell and persuading the demon to exit the patient's body. If the demon "agreed," it was rewarded with paper money and boats to help it on its way. If it refused, various methods of extortion were employed to persuade it. Those who died away from home had to obtain their "ticket" from Cheng Huang at the temple before their hearses could be brought back to their hometowns. People who received unfair trials at court presented their cases on paper so they could be burned before the god's statue. And in times of natural disasters and plagues, Cheng Huang's statue was paraded around the affected areas so he could cure these evils.

You can make offerings to Cheng Huang during the three annual Chinese festivals of the dead. During the first—Qing Ming, in the spring—Cheng Huang is believed to emerge to restrain ghosts that are bothering people who are busy tilling their fields. During the last—in winter—ghosts are released from the Underworld to roam for a short time after the year's farming has been completed. The most popular festival for worshipping Cheng Huang is Zhong Yuan, commonly known as the Hungry Ghost Festival, which is celebrated on the fifteenth day of the seventh lunar month. Here, the wrongful deaths of lost souls are presented before Cheng Huang and dealt with so they can be released to their next incarnation. During this time, banquets are left outside for wandering ghosts, and lotus lanterns are floated on rivers to guide their way to the Underworld. Giant effigies of Cheng Huang are also paraded in procession and burned to ensure success.

Today, you can still find many Cheng Huang temples in older parts of towns. Unlike other temples, which tend to stand out as places of worship, these structures are often unobtrusive, natural, and part of the street scene. Going to see Cheng Huang is a bit like running other errands—visiting the optician or dropping something off at the tailor's. His temples vary in format, often featuring altars for other popular gods like Yan Wang, Lord of the Underworld, the local earth god, and even the Monkey King (see chapter 10). This gives local devotees the convenience of making multiple offerings and worshipping multiple gods in one location. The presence of Cheng Huang's subordinates—the Wu Chang, Niu Tou, and Ma Mian, the ox-headed and horse-headed attendants—make these temples exciting ones for children to visit. You can see these subordinates in the corridors of Lopan's lair in the movie *Big Trouble in Little China*.

GUAN YU, LORD OF LOYALTY AND JUSTICE
关羽

If you like computer games more than mythology, the one Chinese character you will have heard about, apart from the Monkey King, is Guan Yu. Guan Yu was a real person—a great warrior who is also a god to Chinese all over the world. They pray to him before battles, before going riding or traveling, when swearing brotherhood, and before seeking their fortunes. He is endowed with the power to exorcize evil.

Guan Chang Sheng, or Guan Yun Chang, was born in Yun Cheng County, Shaan Xi, in the Han Dynasty during the reign of emperor Han Yuan, a time when government was dominated by eunuchs who overtaxed the people. He was either an ironsmith or a bean-curd merchant by trade, and was a man of extraordinary strength who was always ready to defend the underdog.

Legend tells us that a man named Yun Chang flew into a rage at an injustice he witnessed, committed murder, and then was forced to flee. The stories vary. Some say he was furious with a local landowner who

Guan Yu, Lord of Loyalty and Justice,
depicted with the Green Dragon Crescent Blade

filled the communal drinking well with stones in order to force people to buy water from him. Others say he was passing by a house in which he heard weeping. When he inquired within, an old man told Yun Chang that his daughter, already promised to someone else, was being forced to become the concubine of a local official. Whatever the cause, Yun Chang eventually fled to the Tong Guan Pass in Shaan Xi, and was surprised that the gatekeepers did not recognize him. He checked his reflection in the river and saw that his face had turned bright red. He changed his name to Guan Yu (Yu meaning feathers). This is why Guan Yu is usually depicted with a crimson face, indicative of his rage against injustice.

In 184 CE, Guan Yu answered a call to arms put out by the governors of prefectures against the powerful Yellow Turban rebellion. This is when he met Zhang Fei—son of a butcher and wine-seller, and an impetuous defender of justice—and Liu Bei, an impoverished gentleman of noble descent. Guan Yu swore brotherhood with these two in a peach orchard, just one of the many famous episodes of his life dramatized by Luo Guan Zhong (circa 1330–1400 CE) in his timeless classic *Romance of the Three Kingdoms*.

In 189 CE, a new emperor ascended the throne who was controlled by the tyrant Dong Zhuo. General Yuan Shao led an army to destroy Dong Zhuo. Guan Yu and his sworn brothers were permitted to participate in a contest of champions in this campaign, despite these contests being a privilege of the aristocracy. Guan Yu shone and impressed a warlord named Cao Cao, thus assuring his future. Guan Yu had been so sure of victory that he requested that the victory wine be poured before he started. It was still warm when he returned with his opponent's head.

Thirty years of unrest and factional disputes form the backdrop for Guan Yu's story. This continued until the three kingdoms were established—Wei in the north, Wu in the south, and Shu in the west. Guan Yu's companion, Liu Bei, moved from patron to patron, and eventually became the ruler of Shu, while Cao Cao became the ruler of Wei. Guan Yu stayed loyally by Liu's side, not once deserting his sworn older brother, despite a multitude of temptations Cao Cao laid in his way. Once, Guan Yu was captured by Cao Cao in a battle. During his captivity, Cao Cao tried to win him over with seductive servant girls and attempted to break his loyalty to Liu Bei by putting him in a room with his wives. He even tried to make him fight Liu's army. All to no avail. Guan agreed to work for Cao Cao during his captivity only on the condition that he be allowed to rejoin Liu Bei if the occasion arose. He performed his duties admirably and embarked on a long trek to rejoin Liu as soon as he got news that he was still alive, bringing his wives back to him.

Fearless in battle, Guan Yu is said to have killed thousands on the battlefield. Indeed, he is famous for saying: "Death is only a return home." Stories of his valor still fill the pages of Chinese children's books and Western comics today. Once, when Guan Yu was wounded by a poisoned arrow, the doctor had to operate without anesthesia in order to scrape the toxin from his bone. During the operation, Guan Yu played a game of chess and showed no signs of distress. Despite all his bravery, fighting skill, and strength, however, Guan Yu neglected his own strategy and so was eventually captured and beheaded.

As a god, Guan Yu is shared by all China's established faiths, as well as by folk religion. According to Buddhist records, he was venerated as early as the Sui Dynasty, when the monk Zhi Ji dreamed that Guan came to him seeking to be converted to the Buddhist faith. The state officially conferred the title of Luo Han (*arhat*, meaning "guardian god") on Guan Yu. In Hang Zhou's Ling Yin temple, his statue is erected alongside those of the eighteen Luo Han.

Most gods are commemorated by temples at their birthplace or the place of their deeds. In the case of Guan Yu, his greatness in life made him immortal in people's minds. This contradicts his actual mortality and indicates that, when his mortal form perished, he transformed into a deity, in which guise he became an immortal. The first temple dedicated to Guan Yu was built in Dang Yang County, Hu Bei, where he met his death, during the Northern and Southern Dynasties.

From the Song Dynasty on, emperor after emperor granted Guan Yu posthumous titles, the longest composed of twenty-six words. These include Heroic Lord, Lord of Loyalty and Justice, Great Emperor Who Seconds Heaven, and Marquis of Shouting of the Han Dynasty. He is now popularly known as Guan Di (Emperor Guan), or affectionately as Guan Gong (Uncle or Grandfather Guan).

Today, Guan Yu represents many things. He is commonly known as the god of war, which is not entirely an accurate description, for he is not a symbol of the brutality and destruction that war brings. During his lifetime, he was a fierce warrior, but not unequaled—he was bested by a few. However, his righteousness, integrity, and loyalty have never been excelled. These are the qualities for which he has become a symbol, and these are the qualities for which he is most respected and adored. Guan is the epitome of Zhong (loyalty) and Yi (the closest English term being honor), which, in all that it encompasses, is a unique Chinese quality often found in wandering swordsmen of Wu Xia stories. He was also said to be a learned man, capable of remembering whole books after only one reading. For the nobility, he was a defender of the state; for intellectuals, he was an upholder of civilization; for common folk, he was the pillar of ethical behavior. For the Chinese, might and strength must go hand in hand with morality.

There are very few facets of society that Guan Di cannot protect. He is venerated by the military, by law keepers, by those in positions of power, by civil servants, by the literati, and by ordinary people making their way in the world or seeking protection. He is also venerated by businessmen, particularly owners of restaurants and pawnshops, as well as by curio dealers. There was once a shrine to Guan Yu in virtually every household in China. Today, you can still find his image in many homes, and in shops and restaurants in China as well as abroad. A large shrine still graces every office of the CID of the Hong Kong Police. For his famous loyalty to his sworn brothers, Guan Yu has also been assigned the role of patron god of brotherhoods and secret societies, and is even a favorite of the Triads. Everyone needs a supernatural being to turn to.

Legend has it that Guan Yu once went to a banquet where he knew he would be ambushed, but he terrified the host so much with his daring that the host never gave the signal to have him struck down. Stories like this have endowed Guan Yu with yet another power—the power to exorcize evil, whether in the form of an evil ghost, a demon, or just a wicked intent. This is why he has been named Miraculous Demon Subduing Sage Emperor Guan. He supposedly stole a horse when he escaped from his hometown and rode it through the Tong Guan Mountain Pass. For this reason, he became the patron god of journeys and horse-riding. His surname has the meaning "to be concerned" and "to observe," as well as "gate" or "post." This is why his devotees make offerings to him before embarking on journeys. In sea temples, where merchants pray for safe journeys or the safety of their cargo, there is often a statue of this crimson-faced god in a side temple.

Guan Yu is usually depicted with a long moustache and beard on his crimson face, and dressed in green from head to foot, in contrast to his golden armor. He rides a horse called the Crimson Hare and is armed with the Green Dragon Crescent Blade. His image from the 1989 TV series *Three Kingdoms* remains iconic, although there have been many others since. In ancient China, playing Guan Yu in a dramatization is no laughing matter, however. Being costumed and made up in the image of one of the pantheon's most powerful gods is believed to involve actually absorbing his essence. An actor portraying Guan Yu must undergo abstinence to purify his body and soul, pay respects to the god before and after going on stage, and abstain from profanities while in the role or even just while in costume. Though not all these rituals are strictly observed in modern times, only actors possessing a certain on-screen persona, gravitas, and integrity are considered fit for the role. Only one international star has qualified so far—Donnie Yen, who has a long history of playing righteous cops and who won acclaim for his portrayal of Ip Man, another Chinese national hero.

Contemporary artists have envisioned Guan Yu as a biker with a bandana instead of his headscarf, sitting astride his mechanical Chi Tu, a bright red motorcycle. He has also been portrayed as a ghost, which tends to be his favorite way of appearing in people's dreams. Guan Yu is also sometimes depicted in female form. He has been represented in anime as a voluptuous battle maiden, but Chinese versions of his female form tend toward androgynous warrior types. Today, Guan Yu's image is found not only in homes or as giant statues in holy places, but also in squares and courtyards. He has even been adapted into a Gundam robot and a Transformer. In some computer games, he has fully mechanized armor and weapons that include an oversized metal left arm, the one that was shot by the poisonous arrow. In contemporary English literature, he is often re-imagined in alternative histories by renowned writers like Ken Liu.

JI GONG, THE MAD MONK

济公

There are approximately 500 high-ranking Buddhist saints (*arhats*), most of whom are portrayed in typical saintly fashion, and are therefore not particularly memorable. This makes the occasional colorful character among them stand out even more and explains why these few are capable of really capturing the popular imagination. Ji Gong is such a deity, known and loved by all.

Ji Gong began his incarnation as a historical person who lived in Tai Zhou, Zhe Jiang, during the Song Dynasty. Born Li Xin Yuan, he took the name Dao Ji when he became a monk. He practiced at Ling Yin Temple, where he disregarded the rules of abstinence and freely consumed meat and alcohol. Because of this, he came to be known as Crazy Monk Ji.

Crazy Monk Ji traveled far and wide, preceded by his reputation for jester-like behavior. Many stories about him were circulated throughout the country, one of the most popular telling of how he outwitted the corrupt minister Qin Gui. These stories reflect a brave and honorable monk who stood up to injustices wherever and whenever he found them. His attire was unkempt and his manners ludicrous, but he was, nevertheless, a learned man and an accomplished poet who often used his skills as an herbalist to heal the poor. This is why he came to be known as a guardian of the common people, who, out of respect, began to refer to him as Ji Gong (Lord Ji), or Huo Fo (Living Buddha). Buddhism astutely canonized this hero, giving him the title of Jiang Long Luo Han, the Dragon Descended Arhat.

Ji Gong has a big following in Taiwan, where he is worshipped at temples and by certain charitable organizations. Some devotees commission carved sandalwood effigies of the god, which they bring all the way to Lin Yin Temple in Hang Zhou—the temple where Ji Gong once served as a monk—to have the statues blessed.

Ji Gong's deeds have been well dramatized ever since his earliest appearance in Ming novels. Both early and late Qing periods produced large-scale collections of legends about him. He features in many Qing plays, as well as in Peking opera. More recently, Shanghai Animation Studio told the story of *Ji Gong and the Cricket Fight* (1959) in traditional paper-cut animation. Here, the god saves a carpenter by defeating a bully, a minister's son, in a cricket match. From the 1980s on, there has been at least one TV series about Ji Gong made on the Mainland, Hong Kong, or Taiwan every other year. Actors and directors who pride themselves on comedy—like Johnnie To and Stephen Chow—have presented their versions of the god's story.

Ji Gong's temple at Hang Zhou's picturesque West Lake and his ancestral pagoda, where his holy relics are kept, are both popular places for venerating this deity. You can bring the poems composed by him on West Lake and read them in the very surroundings that inspired him. Across from Lin Yin Temple is Fei Lai Peak, so named because the summit is so formed that it looks as if a rock flew out of nowhere and landed on it. There are many grottoes and caves there, among them one where Ji Gong once lived. Of course, while he was practicing at Ling Yin, he also hid there to drink, eat roast meat, and sleep when he was supposed to be chanting sutras.

When you visit the hall of arhats at Beijing's Bi Yun Temple, you won't find Ji Gong among the neat rows of images of holy persons. But if you look up, you'll see him on the rooftop, hiding there because he was late for his inauguration. In big temples around Jiang Nan (regions to the south of the lower Yangtze River), the deity, who is never where he is supposed to be, will frequently surprise you in the corridors.

Ji Gong's iconic image has remained unchanged for hundreds of years, and his disheveled appearance doesn't seem at all out of place in our times. The lanky deity sports an old, patched-up cone-shaped monk's hat that he usually wears askance on a head of messy hair. He has long Buddhist beads strung around his neck over a monk's robe with countless patches that is never properly secured over his body. He carries a broken calamus fan and, of course, his inseparable gourd of wine.

Those who grew up in post-Open Policy China all know and love the 1986 classic *Ji Gong* produced by Shanghai TV and starring You Ben Chang. The series derives its plots from the most colorful and unfettered source—folklore. In fact, You Ben Chang became so inseparable from the role that he filmed a sequel ten years later. Now eighty-four years old, the actor is currently filming a third series that portrays Ji Gong at the same age. It's clear that the public has never tired of this mischievous deity, who has a heart of gold and who has performed enough good deeds and generated enough stories to support a lifetime of retellings. The 2016 film *Ji Gong*, directed by Liu Jia Jing, has moved away from the deity's traditional image to present a cleaner, tidier, saner, and more handsome hero. Although this film does re-invent the god for a new generation, I can't help but feel that it somewhat detracts from the qualities that make Ji Gong so unique and lovable.

TIAN HOU, CELESTIAL QUEEN OF THE SEA

天后

The Chinese, inventors of the compass, were once great explorers. Even before Admiral Zheng He's famous 15th-century sea voyages, regions within China relied heavily on coastal trade, the Southern Song capital of the trade being Lin An (Hang Zhou). All types of materials and food were shipped along the coast to supply coastal towns and inland areas. The unpredictable sea, with its potential to devour lives, was, however, both a blessing and a bane. Thus a powerful goddess arose in the coastal towns to offer seamen protection and assure safe journeys. She is Tian Hou, or Ma Zu, goddess of the sea.

According to legend, Tian Hou was once a woman named Lin Mo (960–987). She was born on the island of Mei Zhou in the district of Pu Tian, Fu Jian, and was the daughter of an inspector. According to the Ming collection *Gods of the Three Faiths* (*San Jiao Sou Shen Da Quan*), Lin Mo's mother dreamed of the Bodhisattva Kuan Yin (see chapter 3), who granted her an elixir in her dream. When she woke up, she found herself holding it in her hand, and she drank it. Fourteen months later, she gave birth to Lin Mo. When the child was born, the floor of the bed chamber flooded with purple clouds and the whole room was permeated with a celestial glow and a heavenly scent. The child was said to have an uncanny connection to the sacred and mystic. She could recite sutras at the age of five and had the power to forecast future events. Moreover, she had an intuitive bond with the sea and seemed to know its "moods." Needless to say, she was also a good swimmer.

One day, Lin Mo's father and four elder brothers each went out on a business trip on separate boats. That night, her mother saw Lin Mo thrashing around in her sleep and woke her, concerned that she was having a bad dream. Distressed, Lin Mo revealed that her eldest brother was in danger. There had been a storm at sea. In the dream, she had been trying to save her father and brothers, tethering one boat in each arm, one in each hand, and one between her teeth. Distracted by her mother awakening her, she had to let go of the rope tethering the boat between her teeth. The next day, Lin Mo's father and brothers returned safely with accounts of their hazardous journeys. On the verge of capsizing, they were rescued by a woman who walked on the waves as if they were a flat floor and pulled all five boats to safety.

Lin Mo became a legend across Pu Tian. When she grew up, she rejected marriage, instead taking frequent trips out to sea, where she rescued many fishermen and merchants in distress. People began to refer to her as a goddess even during her lifetime. One day, during a particularly heavy storm, Lin Mo was overcome with exhaustion during a rescue effort and fell into the arms of the sea. The locals refused to accept that she had died, preferring to believe that she had ascended to the sky to become an immortal. They built an ancestral hall in Pu Tian by which to remember her.

Accounts and legends of her appearing to mariners grew more and more fantastic. The Song emperor Hui Zong's fleet was embroiled in a violent storm on its way to Korea. The leader of the expedition closed his eyes and prayed to Lin Mo for help. When he opened them, he saw the goddess dressed in red standing on the deck—and the sea grew calm. Fishermen reported seeing her set overturned boats upright, one by one, with a fish fork. An antique dealer from Guang Dong sought her help during a windstorm. She appeared before him, waved her arm, and the storm subsided. Even the great Zheng He, upon his return from his sea voyages, reported to the emperor Yong Le that he had repeatedly been aided by the goddess.

The goddess of the sea began life as a local protector and gradually earned the veneration of emperors. Her powers expanded from safeguarding those at sea, to protecting the land against drought and pestilence. She also became known as a protector of women's fertility and a healer of sick children. Like Xi Wang Mu (see chapter 2), she became an all-encompassing super-goddess, but, unlike her peer, she did it without the benefit of mythical origins.

As China made great advances in sea trade and seafaring in the Yuan period, the people gave thanks to the goddess after every shipload of food arrived safely in port. During the eight centuries between the Song and Qing Dynasties, Lin Mo was honored by royalty forty times and granted sixty titles, the highest-ranking among them being Tian Hou Niang Niang (literally, "celestial queen"). Belief in Tian Hou's powers spread along the Fu Jian coast, south down to Guang Dong, and as far north as Tian Jin.

There is a large population in Taiwan who moved there from Fu Jian and took their love of Tian Hou with them. This is why in Taiwan, where there are now an astonishing 500 temples dedicated to her, Tian Hou is primarily referred to as Ma Zu, the Hokkien variation of her name. There, at the Ma Zu temple in Zhu Nan, you'll find the world's largest statue of the goddess, which stands twelve stories high.

Many legends surround the origin of the name of Hong Kong ("fragrant harbor"). According to one, when a mysterious red incense pot floated in from the sea, people believed it was a manifestation of Tian Hou. They built a temple to honor her and named the region Hong Xiang Lu Gang (Fragrant Harbor of the Red Incense Pot). Eventually, this was shortened to Xiang Gang, Fragrant Harbor—in Cantonese, Hong Kong.

Offerings to Tian Hou are traditionally made during the first, third, fifth, eighth, and ninth lunar months of each year. These times grew out of the Niang Niang Hui (Queen's Temple Fairs or Lady Temple Fairs—referring to Tian Hou) and featured offerings of thanks to the deity after successful voyages. There are temples all over the southern and eastern coasts, with sixteen in Tian Jin alone, including some considered to be particularly efficacious for those wishing for fertility and healthy children. If you visit these, be sure to touch Tian Hou's "dragon bed."

Tian Hou's birthday, which falls on the twenty-third day of the third lunar month, is an extra-special occasion in Tian Jin that became more elaborate during the Qing era. Apart from the usual incense offerings and parading of effigies, this festival is also seen as an occasion for local art performances featuring drums, stilt-walkers, and martial arts. Tian Hou's effigy is brought to the Fu Jian-Guang Dong Guildhall in the city so that the goddess can pay a visit home. It remains there for three days before returning to the temple. At the National Museum in Beijing, there is a 100-meter painting that documents the festive traditions and customs of this celebration.

Another great place to venerate Tian Hou is Macao. The earliest temple for her there is 500 years old, erected during the Ming period (1368–1644), when Macao was still a desolate island. Later, when Portuguese colonists arrived, they did not know the name of the place where they had landed, but immediately noticed the Tian Hou temple. They began referring to the island as Ma Ge (the local name for the Tian Hou temple) or Ma Gang (Tian Hou Temple Harbor). This is how the English name of Macao was born.

Tian Hou traditionally appears as a regal queen with full headdress. She has captured the imagination of Western writers like the renowned Anthony Horowitz in his *Power of Five* novel series for young adults, which reincarnates Tian Hou as a teenage Southeast Asian adoptee who comes to realize that she possesses the powers of Lin Mo. As China became a manufacturing powerhouse during the 1990s, companies that set up factories in Guang Dong or headquarters in Hong Kong and export their goods by sea across the world have contributed to a revival of veneration of Tian Hou, which remains strong today.

At temple fairs that celebrate the anniversary of Hong Kong's return to China, celebrities dress up as Chinese deities, Tian Hou among them. At Nan Hai Shen Temple on the outskirts of Guang Zhou, incense burns bright and the wishing trees are tied full of red ribbons from which are suspended small golden figurines of boats, wishing for safe journeys at sea. So if you're an importer of Chinese goods or work with Far East manufacturers, the next time you travel to China on business, pay your respects at a Tian Hou temple and offer prayers for the safe transport of your goods.

If you like to go off the beaten track, Tian Hou Temple in Nan Shan, Guang Zhou, is well worth a visit. Built during the Ming Dynasty, it was damaged during the occupation and later renovated with funds from Huo Ying Dong, a renowned tycoon and politician born in the province. Many Chinese temples are built on mountains, but this temple *is* a mountain. As you gaze up at the glorious fourteen-and-a-half-meter statue of the goddess that stands before the temple benevolently looking out to sea, you can really feel her might, her grandeur, and—almost—her presence. As you climb the steep stone steps to the top of the mountain, you find effigies of her associates—the dragon kings and renowned devotees like Admiral Zheng He—housed in different temple halls. At the back of the temple, you can even see her private quarters. Plan to spend a day at this fascinating place so you will have time to enjoy the seaside resorts and visit the museum.

Ensuring the safety of merchants, sailors, and passengers at sea is a hefty job, even for a powerful goddess like Tian Hou. She is aided by another deity, Chuan Shen (船神), the god of water vessels. Until the beginning of the 20th century, sacrificial boats offered to this god were still made in Fu Jian. Rituals and offerings to Chuan Shen, together with a permanent shrine for Tian Hou on fishing boats, shipping liners, and tourist cruise ships, are believed to be able to keep the passengers, crew, and cargo safe from storms, sharks, and pirates.

WONG TAI SIN, IMMORTAL OF CRIMSON PINE
黃大仙

Apart from Guan Yu and Kuan Yin, probably the most popular Chinese deity outside of mainland China is Wong Tai Sin. I use the romanization of the Cantonese pronunciation of his name here (rather than the Mandarin of Huang Da Xian) because this god's legacy has primarily been sustained in the region of Guang Dong and Hong Kong, where it later spread. He is now known around the world by his Cantonese name, Wong Tai Sin.

There are numerous legends surrounding the origins of this immortal. One is that he was born in Zhe Jiang as Huang Chu Ping (Wong, in Cantonese). Regional records of the time note the miracle of Wong turning stones to goats. The story goes that Wong was a goatherd who one day disappeared into the mountains. After searching for him for forty years, his brother finally found him on Crimson Pine Hill and flippantly asked him: "Where are the goats?" Wong led him to an opening, pointed to a group of white stones, chanted a spell, and transformed the stones into goats. This is why Wong Tai Sin is also known as Chi Song Zi, Immortal of Crimson Pine.

Wong Tai Sin, by Sesshu (c 1450), after Liang Kai (c 1200) (Kyoto National Museum)

Wong explained to his brother that he had spent the past forty years living as a hermit in a cave, learning the ways of the Dao[17] from an immortal he had met in the moutains (he is said to have taught military strategy to the great Han statesmen, helping them achieve many victories). The temple in Jin Hua County in Zhe Jiang, where the miracle of the stones and the goats is said to have occurred is the most magnificent Daoist construction in the entire region.

The cult of Wong Tai Sin was first brought to Hong Kong in 1915 by a man from Guang Dong, where Wong was, and still is, a local deity. At first, the man erected a small altar in Wan Chai and graced it with a painting he had brought with him from his hometown. Its power to grant devotees' wishes became so well known that enough funds were soon raised to build a temple in Kowloon. The growing popularity of Wong Tai Sin ensured that more than enough donations were received to rebuild the temple in 1973. In addition, millions were raised in Wong's name for educational charities. It is likely that faith in the deity increased with the influx of migrants from Zhe Jiang to Hong Kong in the 20th century. Today, Wong has his own district in Kowloon, in the heart of the city, and his temple is just a ten-minute walk from Wong Tai Sin station.

As I write, Wong's temple receives about 10,000 visitors each day, supporting a temple industry that thrives on a whole range of provisions for worship and the merchandizing of talismans and charms. In the 21st century, worship is going digital, however. In 2011, an underground palace opened within the temple, Tai Sui Yuan Chen Hall, that was dedicated to the sixty Tai Sui and the Yuan Chen, protectors of each year and gods of the calender cycle. The hall's ceiling features a digital representation of the twenty-eight Chinese constellations. It features environmentally friendly LED lights and motion detectors. Air-polluting incense is prohibited. Different electronic devices acknowledge the prayer slips visitors offer with an electronic puff of smoke on their screens.

Outside the temple, many contemporary devotees now opt for an electronic online casting of Qian, or divination sticks (yarrow stalks). Indeed, this has become one of the most popular activities of worship. Smart-phone apps provide a number system for casting, and a beaming cartoon Wong Tai Sin is there to explain the meaning of the divined message.

It seems that almost everyone in Hong Kong has his or her own story of Wong Tai Sin. His specialities are healing the sick, saving the wounded, and punishing evil, although his assistance is also requested on matters of fortune, happiness, health, love, professional advancement, and offspring. This deity is even asked to provide racing tips! Many fortune-tellers have set up stalls by the temple to channel the powers of Wong.

Chinese states and Chinese speaking regions outside the Mainland have proved interesting places for the development of these deities. Faiths in native Chinese goddesses and gods like Tian Hou and Wong Tai Sin have been transplanted into new lands, brought there by migrants. Faiths in these deities have transmuted, sometimes by elaboration and sometimes through the growth of a new branch. For example, in Taiwan, Tian Hou evolved into Ma Zu.

Sometimes these migrated faiths have kept the incense burning for certain gods, even after the embers were extinguished in their native land. You can still find statues of Chi Song Zi or Huang Chu Ping in old temples of Zhe Jiang, although there is lukewarm enthusiasm for the deity there. But a great number of people in Guang Dong, and certainly on Hong Kong and around the world, know and revere Wong Tai Sin.

There is a theory that Wong may be a reincarnation of Huang Di, the legendary ancient ruler and symbol of Chinese civilization (see chapter 9). This is indicated by the Luo Shu Square calculations (an ancient tool used for divination in Feng Shui) derived from the legend of Huang Chu Ping transforming the stones into goats. Now this sacred stalwart of ancient China has evolved into the immortal guardian of Hong Kong.

ZHONG KUI, THE DEMON SLAYER

钟馗

The Chinese traditionally believe that death is not the end—that ghosts and spirits co-exist with human beings at all times but are only noticed when they are restless and need to be appeased. It is no surprise, then, that they have many demon-slaying deities. For instance, the legendary archer Hou Yi (see chapter 5) not only shot down nine suns, but also slew numerous monsters and saved people from their clutches. Likewise Chi Guo, a seventy-foot-tall giant with an immense stomach who sports a waistband of giant snakes and lives on a diet of thousands of ghosts and demons per meal. The highest-ranking of these demon slayers is Zhang Ling, a founder of Daoism and chief minister of the Heavenly Ministry of Exorcism. But none of these gods have enjoyed nearly as much popularity or been as enduring as Zhong Kui.

Zhong Kui's first appearance, immortalized by Song Dynasty writer Shen Kuo, sheds light on his deification. The Tang emperor Ming Huang was plagued by a mysterious illness. Imperial doctors, shamans, and herbalists all labored to no avail to cure him. One night, Ming Huang dreamed of catching a small crimson demon in the act of stealing his valuables. Furious, the emperor began to reprimand the demon, when

Zhong Kui, the Demon Slayer. This painting has been traditionally attributed to Wu Wei (1459–1508), but was most likely painted by an anonymous painter from the Ming dynasty.

a bigger demon appeared and swallowed up the smaller one. The bigger demon identified himself as Zhong Kui, scholar of Zhong Nan, who, in life, had passed the Jin Shi examinations but failed to attain the title. In sorrow and frustration, he ended his own life.

The emperor awoke and found himself cured of his illness. He arranged for Zhong Kui's body to be exhumed and dressed in imperial clan robes. He was then reburied with full rites, laying the malign spirits to rest. Ming Huang commissioned the renowned painter Wu Dao Zi to draw Zhong Kui's likeness and declared that it should be used as a talisman. In addition, he granted the dead scholar the title of Great Spiritual Chaser of Demons for the Whole Empire, propelling him to national fame.

There are numerous versions of how and why Zhong Kui took his life. Tang novels set his story during the reign of De Zong, an emperor prone to superficiality and the influence of slanderous rumors at court. He refused to grant the talented scholar the title of Jin Shi on the grounds of his hideous appearance. In a fit of fury, Zhong Kui immediately took his own life. Some works say he dashed his head against the wall; others say he threw himself into a river. According to early Qing legends written by Zhang Da Fu, Zhong Kui's repulsive appearance was the result of a disfigurement suffered in an attack by ghosts. The ghosts were ordered to descend on Zhong Kui by Kuan Yin as punishment for having once interrupted a ceremony of Buddhist rites while drunk.

Little is known of the origins of this god, but he seems to have embodied the wishes of generations to keep evil and bad luck at bay. His name may have originated from several objects regarded as powerful talismans. In China, a person's name is seen as a powerful talisman to protect against harm. One theory is that Zhong Kui's name may have derived from the name of a type of mallow used in poultices and the treatment of fevers (终葵). Notables through the ages have been named after this herb, including generals, kings, and eunuchs. Another theory, popular in the Ming Dynasty, is that Zhong Kui is the personification of the Zhui, a large cudgel made of peach wood traditionally used to beat and chase away ghosts and demons. According to definitions in the *Rites of Zhou* (*Zhou Li*), 终葵 was another name for the Zhui. Somewhere along the line of development toward human-centric deities, 终 became 钟, an actual surname, and 葵 became 馗, meaning "crossroads"—an apt name for a being who dwelt at the threshold between the living and the dead.

Zhong Kui's popularity was reinforced by the Da Tan ceremony, a state ritual performed in masks, animal skins, and bright beaded gowns during the last month of the year to ward off evil. Ceremonial props include the Zhui and a jade axe. In the Han Dynasty, these ritual dances were performed by courtiers and military leaders who re-enacted the slaying of monsters by the gods. Later, these rituals were replaced by Zhong Kui talismans and dances retelling his story. These practices spread from imperial grounds to desolate graveyards, from the landscape gardens of the wealthy to the most obscure of back alleys. During the Song period, troops of beggars performed Zhong Kui dances at night to beg for money. Thus the legend of Zhong Kui became known to all under heaven.

The occasions to make offerings to Zhong Kui are Spring Festival and Duan Wu (Dragon Boat Festival) in May, considered a crucial time of transition and the point at which the forces of Yang outbalance the Yin. Appealing to the vanquisher of the dark is part of these seasonal activities, along with outdoor sports and the making of five-poison talismans out of herbs that are worn or hung on the doors of dwellings. Zhong Kui was considered a household protector god by emperors and citizens alike, and he relates closely to everyday life.

It's fairly easy today to make your own Zhong Kui talisman. The god has been a favorite of famous painters from the Tang through the Qing eras, and has been depicted by modern artists like Xu Bei Hong (1895–1953) and Qi Bai Shi (1863–1957).[18] You can find photographs of a lot of these paintings on the Internet. Just print out one that you like in high resolution, mount it in a frame, and hang it somewhere near your door. These also make good gifts for friends and relatives. There are also plenty of sculptures made of choice wood, pottery, and copper, as well as Bu Dai Xi puppets. Bu Dai Xi is a form of glove puppetry theater that originated in 17th-century Fu Jian and Guang Dong and has now been revived in Taiwan. Charms featuring the god's head are also popular talismans that you can carry around with you.

Images of Zhong Kui have retained the ferocity that Wu Dao Zi gave him in his very first portrait, which set the tone for folk art like Nian Hua and Jian Zhi (paper cutting). Here he is shown with wild hair and one eye blinded while the other one glares. He clutches a demon in one hand and gouges out its eyes with the other. He boasts a massive beard and has bushy eyebrows and a moustache that shoot out from his face. Indeed, his imposing appearance is itself a powerful weapon that helps him frighten ghosts into submission. As a remnant of his scholar roots, he is sometimes depicted carrying a fan with a magical inscription on it, as well as a sword. He is often seen with one foot in mid-air and brandishing a sword as if ready to charge and strike. Sometimes peaches hang from his hat—his business may be gruesome, but he brings good fortune. Like the Wu Chang (see chapter 6), his grotesque appearance has appealed to tattoo enthusiasts, some of whom sport full-length images of the god on their backs, complete with a demon under his foot.

In images of Zhong Kui, he is almost always accompanied by a bat. According to some historical texts, this was a bat that Zhong Kui encounterd while crossing the Nai He Qiao, the bridge over the Chinese Lethe. It was originally a mole that drank the waters of this river and grew wings. Other texts say that one of the door gods, Shen Tu, had transformed into a bat. The bat is the demon slayer's constant companion and acts as a sort of guide and radar to evils and bad ghosts that need to be vanquished. The Chinese word for bat, Fu, is a homonym of the Chinese word for fortune, or happiness. You'll notice that the bat is often portrayed upside down, a representation of Fu Dao (*dao* meaning both "upside down" and "to arrive"), the arrival of good luck. The image of the bat descending from the sky is also a wordplay on "happiness descends from the sky," which sounds identical.

Since the earliest dramatization of Zhong Kui appeared during the Ming era in *Five Ghosts Frolic with Zhong Kui in the Year of Qing Feng*, stories based on him have become a staple of the Chinese stage, and have been adapted into many kinds of opera. He also appears in many novels. Needless to say, Zhong Kui has made modern appearances on stage and screen, not only in China but also in other Asian countries like Singapore.

Hong Kong cinema has presented an updated take on the god as a cop revived from the dead in *The Blue Jean Monster* and as *The Chinese Ghost Buster* (1994), while recent Chinese comic books depict him as a rough and handsome half-demon warrior. The 3-D fantasy film *Snow Girl in the Dark Crystal* (2015) tells the story of Zhong Kui's origins, his painful rise to his role as a demon slayer, and his forbidden love for a beautiful reformed snow demon. I recommend this as a suitable introduction to Zhong Kui. Plans are now afoot for a film series based on the manhua *King of Demons* (*Gui Wang*) by Xie Feng.

Buddhist and Daoist pantheons are structured according to an elaborate hierarchy. In fact, it seems that China's systems of deities have mirrored the structure of its bureaucracy. But this is only how things appear, or how they have been presented, both now and in the past. If we look at how popular religion has interacted with these pantheons, we can see that, in many cases, it is the bureaucracy that has come under the influence and sway of popular beliefs. Because of this, the bureaucracy is, to some extent, held accountable to the public. This is one reason why Chinese devotees have been drawn to a long line of transgressors and rebels. The tale of Zhong Kui is a great example of this—a warning to leaders against unwise and hasty decisions, and a reminder to the state to adhere to its system of meritocracy. Zhong Kui remains, through all time, a god who exorcizes the metaphorical demons of those who have been betrayed and wronged.

NE ZHA, CHILD HERO,
REBORN PROTECTOR

哪吒

The majority of Chinese deities take adult form, although occasionally younger ones appear—like Ne Zha, whose origins lie in Buddhism. Ne Zha was the son of Vessavana, one of the Four Heavenly Kings. He entered Chinese culture during the Tang Dynasty, the age of the Silk Road, when he appears on many Dun Huang murals along this route.

During the Song Dynasty, China really developed its native beliefs in this deity. In a work of Buddhist history, Pu Qi tells the story of Ne Zha as an Immortal sent to the living world to protect it against the increasing number of demons it faced. The Jade Emperor ordered him to be reborn as the son of Li Jing. As a young child playing at the seashore, Ne Zha became embroiled in a rage-filled fight with the dragon gods and ended up slaughtering the nine sons of the dragon king and the king himself. He also accidentally killed the son of the goddess Shi Ji, and then the goddess herself. Facing judgment before the Jade Emperor and the shame to his family, Ne Zha cut off his own flesh and bones to repent his sins. Impressed with his efforts, the Buddha granted him a celestial lotus, which became his new body—the stalks his bones, the roots his flesh, and the leaves his new clothes. With this new body came immense new powers. As the leader of the thirty-six heavenly generals, Ne Zha now guards the gates of Heaven.

We can see that Chinese Ne Zha gained a completely separate identity from his original foreign persona—one that was a mixture of Buddhist and Daoist influences. In most depictions of Ne Zha today, we see him in his final form, with lotus-themed attire, chakras, six arms, and sometimes three heads. He carries his signature weapons—the Yin Yang ring, Feng Huo ("Wind Fire") wheels, a fire-tipped spear, and the Hun Tian ("Heaven Confusing") stole. It is in this guise that he is famously portrayed in *Journey to the West* in an epic battle with Sun Wu Kong (see chapter 10). A later work of popular literature, the Ming Dynasty *Investiture of the Gods*, tells the story of his early life, describing in great detail his birth as a wondrous ball of flesh, his violent fight with the dragon princes, his own dismemberment, and the rare beauty of heaven.

The raw power, mischief, and unruliness of Ne Zha are very reminiscent of Sun Wu Kong. It is remarkable that a god whose story entails such violence and cruelty could be so popular, especially among children. Parents are happy, however, when their children watch cartoons or fight their way through computer games based on this god's exploits, because they know that, in the end, Ne Zha provides the perfect example of self-sacrificing filial piety. For others, Ne Zha, like Sun Wu Kong, symbolizes the eternal free spirit that refuses to be controlled by any force.

Apart from China's 1986 classic TV series *Journey to the West*, most Chinese see Ne Zha as depicted by Shanghai Animation Studio's 1979 *Ne Zha and the Dragon King*. Animated in the curved lines and bright colors of traditional Chinese art, the film makes Ne Zha into a folk hero who rids the land of dragons that brought chaos by manipulating water supplies. Ne Zha gains further respect by ultimately sacrificing himself.

Since then, Ne Zha has appeared in many TV, film, and animated adaptations of *Journey to the West*, *Investiture of the Gods*, and *Lotus Lantern*, not to mention computer games and stage performances including ballet. Contemporary adaptations sometimes portray the child god in street clothes, but still carrying weapons that are faithful to the originals.

Ne Zha is also venerated in other parts of Asia, like Thailand, where you can find temples dedicated to him. There used to be Ne Zha temples across China, but many have been ravaged by time. Since Ne Zha is said to have been born in Xi Xia, He Nan, his magnificent ancestral temple, which was sadly destroyed in the 1940s during the Sino-Japanese War, once stood there. At the start of this millennium, with a combination of local government effort and support from Chinese around the world, the temple was rebuilt. You can also visit his temples in Hong Kong, Taiwan, and Macao. If you are in Macao in May, be sure to join in the very active celebrations. Cantonese operas, re-enactments, and lion dances welcome the god, while his effigy is carried around streets, hills, and the waters of the city in processions that draw hundreds of followers. The chair on which the statue is carried is said to be over 100 years old.

Ne Zha Conquers the Dragon King,
25th anniversary DVD artwork © *1979*
Shanghai Animation Film Studio,
all rights reserved

Mainland China has certainly made up for the contemporary lack of Ne Zha temples with media entertainment. A major film directed by Ann Hui, *League of Gods*, features a dazzling array of deities and demons, including Lei Gong, Li Yuan, and Ne Zha. The film gives them a stylistic treatment that is heavily influenced by the fantasy world of on-screen Tolkien. In this work, Ne Zha's tale is continued, although he is still haunted by the consequences of his past actions. He has lost his fire wheels and is unable to control his form, alternating between a baby and a grown youth. Ne Zha continues to inspire writers as well, especially in new genres that explore alternative histories like the "magic and machine" genre.

ZI GU, GODDESS OF THE TOILET

紫姑

It's a good thing that there's no actual committee to decide who becomes god of what, or they might have to answer some pretty lively letters of complaint. Zi Gu—also known as Ce Gu, Mao Gu, or Keng San Gu—has the dubious honor of being Goddess of the Toilet, her various names relating to regional approaches to lavatory-building. Zi Gu is primarily a fortune-telling deity, but also one who provides protection for women. Her origins are very much based in the physical side of human nature.

Legend says that Zi Gu was once a scholarly woman named He Mei who lived in Shan Xi province. Although she was happily married to a musician, the local governor lusted after her and eventually arranged for the murder of her husband and took her as his concubine. The governor's first wife grew exceptionally jealous and arranged to have He Mei murdered while she made her nightly ablutions, after which the locals heard her spirit weeping nightly in the toilets. Word of this eventually spread to the imperial court and to Empress Wu, who dubbed the weeping spirit Goddess of the Toilet.

Another origin story holds that Zi Gu was once Qi Fu Ren, or Consort Qi, the much loved concubine of Emperor Liu Bang. She bore him a son, which made her a challenge and a threat to the already jealous empress. After the emperor's death, Qi Fu Ren suffered a most gruesome death at the hands of the Empress. Her limbs were cut off, her tongue cut out, her ear drums pierced, and her eyes rendered blind. She was then left for dead in the toilets.

While sympathy for this tragic figure was strong among the common people, many Song Dynasty scholars were also drawn to the deity. Shen Kuo wrote about meeting an exceptional young woman who was skilled in chess, calligraphy, music, and art—the four qualities of a traditional Chinese gentlemen. He declared her to be the living embodiment of Zi Gu. Su Shi, the famous exiled poet also known as Su Dong Po (1037–1101)[19], wrote two pieces on the goddess: *The Tale of the Goddess Zi Gu*, about her origins, and a fantastical account of the daughter of an imperial minister. The daughter became a receptacle of Zi Gu's spirit during a ceremony of ritual offerings and composed *The Collection of Female Immortals* while possessed.

Zi Gu's various origin stories, emerging both from within the royal courts and from the general populace, show how women were mistreated throughout the patriarchal system of ancient China. The system allowed polygamy, but had no place for talented and capable women, who suffered gross injustices with virtually no protection. In many cases, women found themselves banished to outbuildings during menstruation and were sent to the toilets to give birth, since these activities were considered unclean. Zi Gu became a symbolic protective spirit for women during these times, and her protection ultimately was extended to those generally in need.

Traditionally, offerings are made to Zi Gu on the day He Mei died, the fifteenth day of the first lunar month. Paper offerings are burned along with incense to honor her. Paper and wooden or rice-straw likenesses of the goddess are placed outside lavatories, while songs that tell her tale are sung to invite her presence, which is indicated by the movement of the effigies. The day of Zi Gu coincides with the Yuan Xiao Jie (Lantern Festival), which marks the end of Spring Festival and the official start of the new year. This is another reason why, by the Ming and Qing Dynasties, she was consulted on so many parts of life, from agriculture and commerce to marriage and death.

A key part of Zi Gu's fortune-telling is the scrying ritual of Fu Ji— Fu meaning "to hold" and Ji referring to the shallow bamboo basket used to clean solid waste from toilets. A long hairpin is skewered through the upturned basket, which is then placed on a bed of sand or rice flour. A medium then holds the basket, moving it while channeling the will of the goddess, leaving a trail of automatic writing to be deciphered in response to the inquirer's questions. For purposes of hygiene, the custom was moved out of the lavatories and away from night-soil baskets, and is now performed on T-shaped wooden frames that are held by two scryers who "draw" with the trailing tip.

Today, you can still pay your respects to the goddess's statues at temples on the Wu Dang Mountains, the home of Daoism. There, Zi Gu is depicted in her Daoist tri-form, as three comely celestial maidens struck down by the gods after trying to avenge the death of their brother, Zhao Gong Ming. The welcoming of Zi Gu remains part of Lantern Festival traditions in many rural regions, where fiberglass statues of the goddess join those of the Buddha and Kuan Yin. As period dress has recently become a fashion among Chinese cosplayers, many young women take part in the Zou Bai Bing (Hundred Diseases Walk) in traditional Song and Ming outfits to honor Zi Gu and ward off illnesses. The walk, which is performed at night strictly by women, occurs after lighting incense in the bathroom and consuming the very heavy and rich celebratory meals traditionally eaten around the new year.

Zi Gu's story has been retold for generations. At the turn of the 20th century, she was celebrated in plays and poetry, and has since been captured in *Lian Huan Hua* (early Chinese comics) and in several historical TV series and films that feature the tragic Qi Fu Ren and her gruesome end.

CHONG WANG, PATRON OF PEST CONTROL

虫王

Because their civilization grew out of agriculture, pest control was vital for the Chinese, and the deity who had responsibility for this was Chong Wang. From the Zhou Dynasty onward, Chong Wang had temples all over the country. Offerings were made during the twelfth lunar month at the end of a year's farming. Ceremonies addressed the eight aspects of agricultural life, called the Ba Zha (八蜡)—veneration of Shen Nong and Hou Ji, inventors of agriculture and farming, the safeguarding of fields, the protection of mills, the efficacy of cats (at catching mice), the support of irrigation, and the success of pest control.

By the Song Dynasty, Chong Wang's powers were attributed to five living persons—stalwarts all with the surname Liu. This is why the god is also known as Liu Meng ("fierce") Jiang Jun, or Fierce General Liu. These five stalwarts are Liu Ge, Liu Qi, Liu Rui, Liu Zai, and Liu Cheng Zhong, four of whom saved the crops from locust infestations in eastern and northern regions of the country. The most significant of the five was Liu Qi, the general famous for his Ba Zi soldiers, who had an eight-character patriotic slogan tattooed on their faces. Liu Qi's military strategy broke the ranks of the invading Jin army, but he was framed by minister Qin Hui and demoted to a regional post. Liu performed wonders for agriculture practices, and pest and disaster control there. Eventually, he was deified by the Song emperor Li Zong.

As we have seen, just about anything can become the object of veneration in China. In the mid-12th century, farmers in An Hui and Jiang Su were about to reap a golden harvest when a huge swarm of locusts fell on their crops. Their year's work and livelihood were about to vanish when a large flock of black drongo flew over and devoured the locusts. After this, the imperial court granted this bird the title of National Guardian General.

Today, the name Chong Wang refers to ferocious battling insects in Pokemon and other computer games. To some extent, the job of pest control has been taken over by pesticides, many of which carry the name of the god and even have the word "god" in their product names. However, in the villages across Shan Dong, An Hui, and Jiang Nan regions, traditional rituals of venerating Liu Meng Jiang Jun are still alive. On the fourteenth day of the eighth lunar month, villagers carry around a statue of Liu Meng, either on a sedan chair or a palanquin in the Dai Meng Jiang (Carrying the Fierce General), a ceremony to welcome the god. You can still visit some of the temples dedicated to him in these regions, where a lot of local sites are connected to the deeds of the five Liu personages.

Sun Wu Kong, The Monkey King
孙悟空

Sun Wu Kong is probably the best-known mythological figure in Chinese culture. Also known as Qi Tian Da Sheng (齐天大圣, the Great Sage, Equal of Heaven), this mythical being is characterized by his staff, his flying cloud, his unruly nature, and his immense powers.

The story of Sun Wu Kong comes from the Ming classic novel *Journey to the West* by Wu Cheng'En (the earliest surviving edition published in 1592), which collects a series of folk tales that tell of the historical pilgrimage of Xuan Zang, a monk who traveled from the Tang Dynasty capital of Chang'An to the heart of India, a journey that took more than seventeen years. The monk brought back over 600 sutras and recorded his travels for the imperial court in his *Records of Western Regions Visited During the Great Tang*. His disciples retold this story, embellishing it with encounters and examples of Buddhist teachings. As the stories grew, gathering local flavor and myth, they eventually became popular entertainment.

By the time these stories were told through the Buddhist oral tradition, they had evolved into Yuan dramas. The Monk gained three traveling companions, a group of disciples, a lecherous pig demon, a bloody-minded god of the deep sands, and a bestial monkey spirit whose tricks and prowess elevated him to the role of main protagonist. Wu Cheng'En collected these stories, scripts, and plays into a long novel of over 100 chapters, neatly dividing the epic into three or four chapters per demon or strange encounter. By the Qing era, two dynasties later, the work had swollen to almost twice its original size, but the Ming novel has remained the definitive version of the Monkey King's story.

The legend tells of a rock in the mountains that was thousands of years old. The rock exuded a mystical aura, for it was one of the rocks that the goddess Nü Wa had created to repair the sky (see chapter 1). One day, it burst open and, from it, leapt a full-grown monkey spirit. The monkey spirit was very clever and soon found his own kind, becoming a leader among them. They discovered a mountain forest that was full of trees that bore juicy plump peaches, and a cave behind a great waterfall

Sun Wu Kong and Xuan Zang in a scene from Journey to the West
(1592), republished in 1864

that made a safe and idyllic home for them. The monkey spirit named these the Mountains of Flowers and Fruit, and their new home within these mountains the Cave of the Water Veil. Then he declared himself its Beauteous Monkey King. For a while, the monkey troupe lived there carefree, but, although he was very clever, the Monkey King was new to the world. Eventually he learned about death from the expiration of all kinds of wondrous creatures around him, and this made him very sad.

The Monkey King wanted to improve himself to protect his subjects. He met an Immortal who was greatly impressed by the monkey spirit's potential and named him Sun Wu Kong. Wu Kong learned the technique of Jin Dou Yun, a magical cloud otherwise known as the Somersault Cloud, that allowed him to travel 10,000 miles in one somersault. He also learned the seventy-two transformations. It was only when he raided the treasury of the dragon king of the eastern sea, acquiring a suit of mystical armor and the great iron staff whose theft caused the collapse of the palace, that the Jade Emperor acted to subdue the rebellious Monkey King.

The Jade Emperor invited Wu Kong to join the court of Heaven, offering him minor posts like Keeper of Heavenly Horses and Guardian of the Celestial Peach Garden. When Wu Kong eventually tired of these lowly duties, he rebelled against the gods, defeating heroes like Ne Zha (see earlier in this chapter) and Li Yuan Shen (see chapter 12). Wu Kong was eventually bested by the Buddha himself. Unable to escape from the Buddha's palm, he was sentenced to 500 years of imprisonment, at the end of which his spell was lifted by the monk Xuan Zang.

Grateful for his rescue, Wu Kong agreed to become Xuan Zang's disciple, and even to wear the power-limiting headband that tightened whenever Xuan Zang deemed it necessary to chastise his new ward. Centuries and centuries of audiences and readers have loved living through the battles of Sun Wu Kong and the fantastic array of demons seeking to devour the holy flesh of Xuan Zang, including the Ox King and Princess Iron Fan, the alluring spider demons, and the deadly White Bone Spirit.

The story of Sun Wu Kong grew out of China's oral tradition, which relied heavily on interaction. Thus he is truly a deity created by the people—and therefore, he is a reflection of society. In the 20th century, this action-packed fantasy story was bound to make itself present in every form of media, from early short films and ground-breaking animated movies like *Princess Iron Fan* and *Uproar in Heaven*, to computer games like Pokemon and League of Legends.

Throughout history, Sun Wu Kong has been a tool for accomplishing different purposes. The original novel used entertainment as a means to glorify the teachings of Buddha. Subsequent versions have shown Wu Kong as cruelly treated by orthodox religion, or even manipulated by bad gods in league with demons. He has been many different things to different devotees. To children, he is the mischievous Monkey capable of all sorts of trickery. To some, he is a riotous demon reformed to do good. To others, he is a rebel misfit whose spirit is irrepressible despite his confinement and enslavement.

If Sun Wu Kong were to be associated with any specific area of life, he would probably be the god of freedom and of unrestrained power. It may seem odd that a mythical being who is so chaotic in nature should be created and revered by one of the most prescriptive traditional cultures in the world. But through the ages, the Chinese have been drawn to a range of outcasts, rebels, and misfits, and faith in these deities has sometimes had the power to check tyrannical and corrupt leadership in society. Wu Kong, as the Monkey King, is among the most unruly of all gods—a mythical ape who represents the primate in us all.

Doubtless this monkey spirit will be around for a long time to come. If you are in the process of accomplishing something arduous or challenging or difficult, and feel that all the odds are against you, you may find solace in the story of the Monkey King's journey, which is now available in English thanks to Arthur Waley's 1942 abridged translation. Or try losing yourself in any of the films or cartoons that commemorate Wu Kong's indomitable nature.

The Fu Lu Shou, Gods of Happiness, Success, and Longevity (from Myths and Legends of China, *1922, by E. T. C. Werner)*

Chapter 11

Gods of Health and Happiness

Fu (福), best translated as "happiness" in English, has been an age-old concept for the Chinese. According to texts on the philosophy of governance written during the early dynasties, this concept traditionally involved five aspects of life: longevity, wealth, health and security, morality, and a natural death.

If you walk into any Chinese household, you will mostly like see statues or pictures of three rotund and ruddy-faced elderly gods who are usually surrounded by peaches and laughing children and beaming at you through a glowing haze of auspicious clouds on which cranes are perched. These are some of the best known of all Chinese gods, both at home and around the world—the Fu Lu Shou, gods of happiness, success, and longevity. They are worshipped as separate entities, and each began life very differently. But just having your physical well-being, prosperity, and material comforts cared for is not sufficient to be happy. There are also deities who look after your mental and matrimonial well-being as well.

FU SHEN, GOD OF GOOD FORTUNE

福神

At the very beginning, people entrusted their hopes to the stars, and the planet that represented the idea of Fu was Saturn. Later, during the Eastern Han Dynasty, the Daoist concept of the three realms entered popular belief. This attributed the granting of happiness to the realm of the skies, the absolution of sins to the realm of the earth, and salvation from distress to the realm of water.

This explains the traditional depiction of Fu Shen, the god of happiness, as a celestial official dressed in a heavenly court robe of red, belted with a sash embroidered with dragons and decked with jade. He usually appears wearing court boots, sporting a long beard and eyebrows, and carrying a Ru Yi (如意), a ceremonial scepter or talisman symbolizing power and good fortune. Some iconic images, like the Nian Hua images produced to celebrate the new year, show him surrounded by or holding small children carrying auspicious objects like peaches, pomegranates, spring plum blossoms, koi carps, Buddha's Hand fruits, orchids, and rhododendrons.

Like many Chinese deities, Fu Shen's supernatural identity evolved out of a living person whose qualities and characteristics were felt to embody those he eventually assumed as a god. In Fu Shen's case, this was Yang Cheng, governor of Dao Zhou (now in Hu Nan) during the Tang Dynasty, who stood up for the little people—literally. The region was known for people of very short stature. Because their peculiar physique amused the emperor, they were ordered to enter the court as tribute when they reached a certain age to become performing slaves. Yang protested their treatment before the emperor, making him realize that, despite their diminutive stature, the people of Dao Zhou were also his subjects, not performing monkeys. The emperor saw the error of his ways and stopped mistreating the locals, who began to venerate Yang Cheng as a god who brought them happiness.

Today, Fu Shen has evolved beyond representations in porcelain statues, wall posters, and shrines, and has entered everyday life. His veneration now pervades all aspects of Chinese life. Artwork of the god appears in every style, from his traditional image, to super-cute forms, to limited editions of trademark characters like Hello Kitty and Mickey Mouse. Dolls and figurines of him abound—even as plush toys. His name is borrowed by all areas of commerce, from makers of rice crackers, pineapple pastries, and popcorn, to restaurants and even clothes designers. His image is also featured on mobile card games and lottery artwork. He is a character in the Sina game Voyage of the Millionaire, which tests players' knowledge of economics, math, and physics.

Like the hammer of Thor and the power of Iron Fist, the powers of Fu Shen can transcend individual identities and have the ability to migrate between those who are worthy. The Han emperor Wu Di and the demon-slayer Zhong Kui (see chapter 10) have both taken on these powers at different times. You can, therefore, name your own personal Fu Shen, whoever he or she may be.

Fu Shen is a deity you will want to keep a constant watch on your household, so regular tributes—weekly or even daily—are more important than offerings made only on special occasions. Incense and auspicious fruits like oranges, apples, peaches, and pomegranates are good offerings to make at your personalized shrine, on which you can also place different tributes you may have found during the week—for example, a packet of Oreos or a cup of tea. Whatever makes you happy is a fitting thanks to the god of happiness.

LU SHEN, GOD OF SUCCESS
司禄神

The 18th-century novel *The Scholars* (*Ru Lin Wai Shi*) by Wu Jing Zi (1701–1754 CE) mentions a performance of Jia Guan (加官) before the start of a play. The Jia Guan, which means literally "raise one's office," is an act that signifies the conferring of advancement or good fortune that usually takes place before the main performance. The being represented in this ceremonial act is Si Lu Shen (popularly known as Lu Shen), the god of rank and success. Nian Hua, fortune paintings, and other folk art tend to represent Si Lu Shen through a play on words—as an old man riding a deer with an attendant who carries a peach, a symbol of longevity. The Chinese word for deer is a homonym for Lu, meaning "good fortune" or "official salary." Above them flies a bat, the Chinese word for which is a homonym of Fu, which means "happiness."

Lu Shen usually appears with Fu Shen and Shou Xing, the god of longevity. He rarely appears on his own. Like Fu Shen, Lu Shen too was first born out of a star, the Wen Chang star (see below), after which his most famous incarnations are named. He evolved from a mythical regional deity, became a deified hero, and eventually developed into a national god.

SHOU XING, GOD OF LONGEVITY

寿星

The third member of the happiness trio is the god of longevity, Shou Xing (literally, "star of longevity"). He appears as the oldest of them all, often portrayed propping himself up on a dragon-headed staff and holding a giant peach in his other hand. With his large round head, flowing white beard, long wispy eyebrows, and benign smile, he is the picture of a benevolent old man.

Shou Xing was traditionally represented by two groups of stars in the Virgo constellation. The brightest of them, Spica, is particularly associated with longevity. Spica is the brightest evening star in the southern Chinese skies from deep winter to late spring. The great historian Si Ma Qian wrote that, when this star appeared, it brought peace; when it did not, chaos reigned. Shou Xing is also known as Nan Ji Xian Weng, the Immortal of the Southern Pole.

Shou Xing has been around since the Zhou and Qin Dynasties (1100–256 BCE and 221–207 BCE respectively), and has been venerated by the imperial state throughout history. He also enjoys great popularity among civilians. He first appeared as a deity who watched over all living creatures. In multiple literary versions of the famous legend of White Snake, he appears in this capacity as Nan Ji Xian Weng. In the story, White Snake is forced to reveal her true form, which frightens her lover, Xu Xian, to death. She travels to Mount Kun Lun in search of Ling Zhi, an elixir that can bring Xu back to life, but she is defeated by the spirits who guard it. Nan Ji Xian Weng comes to her aid, presenting her with the elixir she needs to save her lover.

Since the Han Dynasty (206 BCE–220 CE), veneration of Shou Xing, which takes place during the eighth lunar month, has been combined with veneration of the elderly, during which gifts are given to those over seventy. The intertwining of the two had a major impact on the way Shou Xing has been venerated ever since. The custom has continued to this day and, on birthdays of the elderly, gifts are still given to Shou Xing.

In Yuan plays, Shou Xing appears with a lotus crown and an overcoat of crane feathers to supplement his white hair and beard. It was during the late Ming period that he gained his present form, with his big round bald head and staff. In *Journey to the West* by Wu Cheng'En (西游记, 1368–1644), when Sun Wu Kong (see chapter 10) tracks down the trio of Immortals Fu, Lu, and Shou to restore the tree he accidentally destroyed at Wu Zheng Temple, Ba Jie, the pig demon, makes fun of Shou Xing's big bald head and mockingly offers him his hat to cover it up. And the crane-feather overcoat of the Yuan plays eventually evolved into actual cranes that surround Shou Xing and complete his present form. Cranes are considered auspicious birds and represent immortality.

A piece of artwork appeared in the China Digital Times as a response to the early deaths of 10,000 people as a result of China's air pollution. In it, a shrunken and unhappy Shou Xing is depicted with a gas mask, the withered peach in his hand also covered by a mask and the lucky gourd on his staff a radioactive green. In the background, the character for Fu (happiness) is replaced by the character for Du (poison) and surrounded by bats. This cautionary image has proved an extremely potent warning, precisely because the concept of Shou Xing is built into the Chinese consciousness. China has heeded warnings of this kind and introduced active measures to reduce pollution, as well as to clean up its air.

Shou Xing's godly domain is not as wide and varied as Fu Shen's. He is specifically the patron god of old age and birthdays and, like his peer, he pervades all levels of Chinese society. His image graces birthday cakes that can be ordered from bakeries in major cities or made at home. He is also venerated in other Southeast Asian countries like Vietnam, where he appears in kitsch artwork on tins of evaporated milk. And there are countless icons in all formats—traditional Nian Hua, sculptures of different materials, or cute figurines featuring the god and his wife. Shou Xing also appears with Fu Shen and Lu Shen in missions and challenges in computer games, and on lottery artwork. On the thirty-fifth anniversary of Hong Kong's ocean park, Shou Xing was called upon (with the aid of a costumed performer) to join the celebrations.

The Wang Zhang, or "staff of kings," is an imitation of the deity's nine-foot-long staff—nine symbolizing the highest or ultimate in Chinese culture. This staff is given to the elderly on their birthdays during the Shou Xing venerations. This is a good example of how old age is honored and venerated by the Chinese. Today, Shou Xing has become almost exclusively the star of old age and the patron god of the elderly. Western society and culture, which tends to dismiss the elderly as decrepit or useless, could benefit from a little bit of Eastern reverence for the aged. The elderly deserve our care and respect.

So, during the eighth lunar month, spend some extra time with your elderly relatives; cook them a bowl of longevity noodles—long thin noodles that are cooked in pork or chicken stock. Meat, mushrooms, vegetables, and herbs like ginseng and angelica are also commonly added to the dish.

Help your elderly relatives or friends follow advice from the Shi Sou Chang Shou Ge, or Song of Longevity—a folk song supposedly made up of advice given by ten people who lived to 100: don't drink, take a walk after every meal, live on a diet of vegetables and grains, walk instead of taking transport, be self-sufficient, take up Tai Chi, maintain regular sleeping patterns, bask in the sun, don't worry, and always look on the bright side of life.

The spirit of Shou Xing can also be invoked on Chong Yang, or Nine Nines Festival. This festival of the elderly occurs on the ninth day of the ninth lunar month. Arrange an outdoor excursion with your grandfather or elderly aunt, and make sure you help them climb to a high place.

HE HE ER SHENG, THE SAGES OF HARMONY
和合二圣

The Chinese have gods that look after everything from the great out-doors to the provision of material comforts. They also have deities who look after the mental realm. He He Er Sheng, the gods of harmony, also known as He Shen, are an example of this. He means "harmony," and the He Shen fittingly originated from the story of friendship between Han Shan and Shi De in the Tang Dynasty.

Han Shan (寒山), which means "cold mountain," was also known as Han Shan Zi. He was a famous poet monk who once practiced at Qing Guo Temple in the Tian Tai Mountains of Zhe Jiang. As a minor monk who performed chores, he often went out into the wilderness in the vicinity of the temple. He was indifferent to the mockery of the other monks, and preferred a hermetic existence among the mountain rocks. He was also a prolific poet who wrote about 300 poems that were gathered into a collection. His poems were imbued with Buddhist doc-trine, but also commented on current events. Their simplicity and clear language make them popular in modern literary studies.

Shi De (拾得), whose name means "picked up," was an orphan who was found in the same mountains by one of the head monks of the tem-ple. He was raised by the monks and put to work in the kitchens. Also a poet, he wrote verse that explored the principles of Buddhism. When he met Han Shan, they often sang together and went into the mountains, where they both found inspiration for their poems. Shi De always gath-ered all the extra food and leftovers from the kitchen and gave them to his soul mate, Han Shan. Posterity has portrayed the two as so inseparable that their poems were published in the same volume.

A secular version of this story says that Han Shan and Shi De were from the same village in the north, where they were as close as brothers. Then they fell in love with the same woman, who was betrothed to Han Shan. On the eve of his wedding, Han Shan found out about Shi De's love for his fiancée. He forfeited his marriage, shaved his head, and lived as a hermit in Su Zhou. Shi De eventually discovered the whereabouts of his friend and brought him a blossoming lotus flower. Han Shan, in turn, welcomed him with food placed in a type of bamboo box traditionally used for carrying food—not unlike a bento box. Shi De shaved his head, as Han had done, and together they founded the renowned Han Shan Temple on the spot where they were reunited. In time, the pair gained the title He He Er Xian (和合二仙), the United Immortal Duo, drawing on two meanings of the word He, which can mean "together" or "union."

He He Er Xian enjoyed religious as well as secular fame. Buddhism was keen to glorify these two earthly representatives for posterity, presenting them as the incarnations of two Bodhisattvas. In 1733, at their temple in Su Zhou, the Qing emperor Yong Zheng formally dubbed Han Shan and Shi De the He He Er Sheng, the Two Sages of Harmony.

This pair of gods became a symbol of happiness and matrimonial harmony. For celebrations of the new year, they are often depicted as two ruddy-faced frolicking children. In other paintings, statues, and sculptures, they are presented as two chubby, carefree, and disheveled laughing men, with Han Shan usually standing and gazing off into the distance with wonder while Shi De looks at him adoringly. It is a little odd to find their images adorning the walls at weddings, but understandable because sometimes matrimonial harmony was the best people could hope for in the arranged marriages that were the norm in traditional Chinese society.

In contemporary society, He Shen are considered patron gods of social harmony and friendship. A framed paper cut, a porcelain statue, or a shrine all make appropriate and jolly decorations on the premises of any business. Offerings of fresh flowers made to your best and closest friend are popular for venerating these gods. If lotus is not easily available where you live, local flowers that symbolize friendship—like yellow roses—can be good alternatives, as are chrysanthemums, an oriental flower that represents loyalty and support.

It is best to abstain from eating meat and dairy for a day before making your offering, as a respectful nod to the vegan dishes that Shi De and Han Shan ate. These also serve as a sign of devotion for your friend. Offerings of food should also be vegan and contained in a lacquered wooden or bamboo box, which can be purchased at oriental supermarkets. For devotees more inclined to spirituality, Han Shan Temple in China is the place to visit. Of course, worship can also take the form of reading Han Shan's *Cold Mountain Poems*, which have been translated into English by Zen poet Gary Snyder, a friend and mentor to the beat-generation writer Jack Kerouac, who introduced him to Buddhism. Kerouac was so captivated by Zen Buddhism that he spent sixty-three days on Desolation Peak in Washington State replicating the hermetic experiences of Han Shan, after which he recounted his experiences in his 1965 book *The Desolation Angels*.

WEN CHANG,
GOD OF SCHOLARLY SUCCESS
文昌帝君

Since the Han Dynasty in ancient China, those wanting to enter the court or the civil service needed to sit the Kei Jü, a national exam that tested a candidate's knowledge of classical texts, military and agricultural strategy, statecraft, taxation, the law, and written composition. This exam was merciless, with only a few entrants of exceptional merit succeeding to make The Golden List, a select group of qualified people whose names were posted outside capital buildings and handed to the Emperor himself. It is not surprising that worried students seeking to qualify for this list looked for divine intervention.

In his more recent godly depictions, Lord Wen Chang is represented as a scholarly man holding a writing brush, a book, or a Ru Yi (literally, "as desired"), a curved, decorative scepter used for Buddhist ceremonies

Wen Chang, K'eui-Hsing (Kui Xing), and Chu I (from Myths and Legends of China, *1922, by E. T. C. Werner)*

and as a folk talisman. He is usually flanked by his two young apprentices, Tian Long (Deaf Sky) and Di Ya (Mute Earth), who symbolize the immutability of his character. His silence on the exam results meant that the fate of scholars is not to be tampered with. Earlier versions of Wen Chang, which are still prevalent around the province of Si Chuan, have him in battle armor on horseback, clutching a sword in one hand and an eagle's claw in the other. The interesting mix of warrior and scholar symbolism in this god is a result of how he evolved through the generations.

The name Wen Chang originally referred to a constellation of six stars adjacent to the North Star and parallel to the Big Dipper. It was the name given to the earth god and guardian of the Si Chuan region. Legend has it that the region was suffering from a host of diseases spread by the Five Gods of the Plagues. Wen Chang personally battled these gods and saved the people, who began to look on him as their protector from sickness. This powerful guardian was also given the duty of protecting the locals from thunder and snakes. A temple was built for him on Qi Qu Mountain in Zi Tong.

Celebrations honoring Wen Chang as the region's most important god continued unchallenged for around five centuries, until the age of Zhang Yu, a military leader born in Yue Xi during the Eastern Jin Dynasty (4th century). Zhang Yu led the people of Shu (Si Chuan) in uprisings that drove off invading barbarian tribes before eventually dying a heroic death in battle. After his death, a temple was erected to him on the same mountains that housed the temple of Wen Chang.

Locals, as well as the emperors of subsequent dynasties, flocked to the temple of Zhang Yu, who was posthumously knighted and showered with titles to reward his valor, his fortitude, and his familial loyalty. Pilgrims to his shrine in the heart of the Qi Qu Mountains also tended to visit and venerate Wen Chang while there. The worship of these two deities became so intertwined that, in the 14th century, 1,000 years after Zhang Yu's time, Wen Chang was granted the title of Lord Wen Chang by the Yuan Emperor Ren Zong, thus merging the mythical savior and the deified warrior into a single god.

It was customary for scholars, before they went to the Ke Ju exams, to appeal to their own local gods to bring them success. Of course, the scholars of Si Chuan prayed to Wen Chang. When the Sichuanese scholars began to do particularly well, market forces came into play and entrants from other regions who could afford it began to make the pilgrimage to Zi Tong or to create small local shrines to Wen Chang in order to offer him their prayers—although they still prayed to their regional deities as well. Thus Wen Chang became the patron god of scholars and exams, as we know him today.

China is massive and, more often than not, several gods are appointed to manage a given role between them—especially when that role concerns something as common as exams. Guan Yu is thus appealed to at times for success in scholarly pursuits and exams, as is Kui Xing (魁星), who also started off as a constellation in the sky that represented scholars' fortunes to the ancient Chinese. These stars were collectively named 奎星, meaning "Highest Stars." In Western astronomy, these are the sixteen stars of Andromeda, and Pisces. During the Han period, the character 魁, homonymous with 奎 (both meaning "highest"), came into use alongside 奎 to denote this star group and played a role in its eventual anthropomorphism.

Due to the ghost radical 鬼 in the character 魁, Kui Xing's representation (魁星) was transformed from a star into a blue demon with crimson hair who stood with one foot on a tortoise, a very auspicious creature in Chinese belief.[20] He held a pen in one hand and a dipper in the other. The symbol on the right of 魁 (斗) means "dipper," an instrument used for dubbing the highest achiever in any contest. This ceremonial dubbing was once part of the inauguration of the new Jin Shi, as was the possession of Kui Xing icons. Shrines to Kui Xing were built around the country, with major ones in Fu Jian and Kun Ming, where he appears alongside Wen Cheng and Guan Yu. Since Kui Xing had very little history, myth, or story to support his tradition and existed only as a literal representation of a written character, people eventually turned from his unapproachable demonic appearance toward the solemn, but dignified and authoritative, legendary Wen Chang.

About eighty literary works have been written on Wen Chang by authors from all over mainland China, Taiwan, and throughout Southeast Asia. Major temples have been devoted to him by all of China's various faiths, each of which is adorned with different elements from folklore.

Wen Chang is worshipped three times during the year—during the Welcoming of the Gods from the twelfth to the eighteenth day of the first lunar month, on the third day of the second lunar month (Zhang Yu's birthday), and on first day of the eighth lunar month, the day of Zhang Yu's official titling as Wen Chang. Works inspired by him are read on these occasions, including self-help books that instruct readers on the importance of unassuming good deeds, assuring them that Wen Chang is watching over them. These teachings are made accessible by social media sites that send out short extracts on a daily basis and offer animated online videos.

Of course, Wen Chang has been "kept alive," not just by these ceremonies, but by hundreds of thousands of private, solitary prayers offered up by anxious scholars and their families throughout the ages. Appealing to this god can help them open doors to a life of opportunity, honors, and rewards. The Kei Jü system was abolished during the Qing Dynasty and has today been replaced by the Gao Kao, the national exams for university entrance, in which millions of Chinese students compete to get into the very limited places at top institutions. Kindergarten-aged children are even required to take exams to qualify for attendance at certain daycare centers. The pressures on modern children in China are even greater than those faced by ancient scholars, and the "need to succeed" is very intense. Failure is seen not just as an obstacle to an individual's future, but also as a shameful circumstance for the family—the cardinal sin in Chinese society.

Many worried parents look to Wen Chang to intercede on their children's behalf out of fear that they aren't working hard enough. Indeed, sometimes teachers pray to him for their whole class. But this god's temple floors see more wear from the feet of the young than from those of the old. Devotees place offerings of celery (芹, "qin," a homonym for 勤, "diligence"). Cartoons circulated on the Internet suggest other suitable offerings to Wen Chang, including spring onion (葱, "cong," a homonym for 聪, "bright"), garlic (蒜, "Suan," a homonym for 算, "calculation"), Zong Zi or Bao Zi (for retaining good luck), and cooking oil, because a Chinese motivational term for cheering people on literally translates as "add oil." And it is very important to consume these foods after offering them to the god, because this helps you absorb the good luck created by the worship.

Apart from the usual gifts of incense, fruit, and tea—as a scholar god, Wen Chang shuns wine—these temples contain a lot of peculiar items that people have created to hold their prayers. In front of the main hall of some temples you can find ornate replicas of exam-result boards that are laden with lucky charms placed there by individuals. These are usually small thin gold tags just big enough to hold a short message. These are hung from red chords tied with elaborate lucky knots. Some also feature enamel bells and tassels. Some temples offer votive candle racks where students can leave notes along with their candles that give the details of their exams, so that Wen Chang will know exactly who to protect and when.

Wen Chang is a very busy god. With the hundreds of candles lit and prayer tags left at his temples, it is evident that the temple industry does very well by providing young people with a place to petition this god for aid. More distant temples pay for Internet advertising, selling pre-exam good-luck tours and cute paper cartoon versions of Wen Chang. And, of course, students are encouraged to boost their luck by equipping them-selves with a golden Wen Chang talisman that is packaged in a box that looks like a temple and is sold as a "must have" for exam entrants.

Japanese students offer Kit Kats to their equivalent god (whose name is a homonym for "100% marks"), while Chinese students offer the same sweet because its Chinese name, 奇巧, means "spectacular skills." Some prefer to offer more traditional cakes—like 糕点, a homonym for 高点, which means Gao Dian, or "a little higher"—if they feel they need only a bit of an edge, rather than response to a full-on cry for help. Moreover, Wen Chang's patronage does not stop at graduation. He is also the patron god of social climbers. For this role, he often appears as Lu Shen.

Many business leaders attribute their success and position to Wen Chang's aid, including the manufacturers of one brand of Chinese nougat that often makes its way onto pre-exam altars. During the Ming Dynasty, a Zhe Jiang scholar named Shang Lu, who was a devotee of Wen Chang, dreamed that he went to pray in one of his temples and, as he knelt, found a pile of sugar and peanuts under the altar. The god smiled down on Shang and the pile transformed into a cow that galloped toward him. These were fortuitous signs, the local soothsayer explained. Shortly after this dream, Shang achieved success in the civil-service exams, and created Chinese nougat by combining rice powder, malt sugar, and peanuts. To this day, the company still promotes their products using this story.

Since the 1400s, belief in Wen Chang has grown. He became a tow-ering, mammoth god and remained so, even after the Kei Jü system disap-peared. Indeed, as long as there are exams, and people aiming to "move up in the world," there will always be a need for him. As a god who grew organically out of local faith in an earth god and a flesh-and-blood hero, Wen Chang gained the favor of emperors and was accepted by all major belief systems in China. He is to the people of the south what Confucius was to the people of the north. The Daoists have assimilated him into their pantheon and, judging by the kinds of publications inspired by him, the Buddhists have also adopted him to further their teachings of karma. In modern times, Wen Chang has found favor with commercial enterprises. All these factors ensure his continued existence as a venerated god.

YUE LAO,
THE OLD ONE UNDER THE MOON
月下老人

The moon and moon symbolism are common in Chinese mythology, and many gods are said to dwell there, including the lady Chang'E and her companion, Jade Rabbit (see chapter 5). The moon is also home to an ancient deity whose role is to make sure that all loving couples come together as predetermined in a great book. This deity was known as Yue Xia Lao Ren, commonly shortened to Yue Lao.

The legend of Yue Xia Lao Ren (meaning "The Old One Under the Moon") began in the Tang Dynasty as the story of the Chinese god of love from Li Fu Yan's ninth-century *More Records of the Mysterious and Strange (Xu Xuan Guai Lu)*. In this story, a man named Wei Gu who lived in He Nan was wandering one night when he saw an old man sitting in the moonlight with a sack beside him, perusing a book. Wei asked the old man what he was reading. "The matrimonial pairings for all under heaven," he replied. Wei asked the old man what was in the sack. He answered: "Crimson threads, to be tied to the foot of husband and wife. No matter the gulf of rich and poor, no matter the remoteness of office, no matter the distance between hometowns, the thread can never broken."

When told that his future wife was to be the daughter of the blind local vegetable seller, Wei hired someone to kill the girl, who narrowly escaped death but was marked by a permanent wound to her brow. Years later, Wei became a soldier and impressed the provincial governor with his performance. The governor offered Wei his attractive daughter as a bride and Wei was shocked to find that she was the woman he had tried to kill all those years before. He recognized her by the wound on her forehead. The girl had been adopted into the governor's family and brought up as his own daughter.

This popular story, with its reliance on fate and fortune, was subsequently retold during the Ming Dynasty in the play *The Man Under the Moon Match Makes the World* (*Yue Lao Ding Shi Jian Pei Ou*). Living as they did through uncertainty and hardship under a totalitarian state, political turmoil, and natural disasters—all of which were beyond their control—the ancient Chinese tended to be drawn toward an unshakable sense of Fate—hence the imagery of crimson threads that led you inexorably to the love of your life had a strong appeal. Those who wished for love and matrimony prayed to Yue Xia Lao Ren to knot their crimson threads.

These threads are often referenced in literature, including in the 1754 classic *The Story of the Stone* by Cao Xue Qin (Cao Zhan, 1715–1763).[21] It was inevitable that the crimson threads of the Yue Lao legend would become a part of China's matrimonial traditions. The earliest recorded instance of this was found in Tang Dynasty official records when a marriage was performed by having both parties stand behind a curtain, each holding the ends of red threads. By the following dynasty, the Song, red sashes, and veils had begun to appear in weddings. The bride and groom proceeded into the bedchamber holding opposite ends of a length of red cloth as a symbol that their union was endorsed by Yue Lao.

At temples and on icons, Yue Lao is represented as a benign, smiling old man with a long beard, a common symbol of longevity. Dressed in colorful, auspicious-looking clothes, he holds the book of matrimony in one hand and red threads in the other. Sometimes he also has a staff decorated with lucky peaches. The kind of love represented by Yue Lao is not the hot, passionate, and frivolous kind associated with the Greek god Eros, but rather a contented and mature requited love of the kind represented by Eros's brother, Anteros. While some see Yue Lao as merely an auditor, ticking off names on a predetermined list, others believe that he is a very experienced matchmaker who himself makes the pairings by considering the subjects' personalities, nature, and interests.

To this day, China still calls its matchmakers Yue Lao, and the sage deity's image is commonly found on Internet dating sites, where the goal is a long-term relationship. For contemporary devotees, a mixture of ritual and custom from China and Chinese-speaking regions is still evident. Staff in many temples in Taiwan dress up as Yue Lao on festive occasions and, for a small donation, you can take a selfie with them. To ensure that your prayers are effective, you can buy embroidered pouches, or wooden tablets with a lucky message, or a cute figurine of Yue Lao himself to carry around with you as talismans. The full "Yue Lao gift kit" comprises a golden paper offering, incense, a coin talisman, a wishing letter stamped with your fingerprint that presents your personal details to the god, a pair of round longan (a tropical fruit that symbolizes union), and a pair of dates (homonym for 早, meaning "early"). Yue Lao has even inspired contemporary fantasy fiction writers like Crystal Gail Shang Kuan Koo.

Yue Lao is a powerful and very busy deity in modern China. With several generations of single children now achieving adulthood and the rise of the middle class, many feel family pressures to get married. Some families even take their sons or daughters to marriage markets that are held in public squares. At these markets, young people write their personal details on a card that they tie with thousands of others at a central point. Then they hope that the right person picks theirs. In the 21st century, the traditional red threads have been replaced by parental pressure and choosing a mate today is often influenced by annual income and other status symbols. So it seems that Yue Lao has his work cut out for him!

Women preparing silk, painting by Emperor Huizong of Song, early 12th century

Chapter 12

Patrons of Trades and Crafts

The gods of the old trades are a major feature in the pantheon of Chinese gods. Workers in each trade prayed to the appropriate gods for skill in their work, reward for their labors, and protection from occupational hazards. Craftsmen have Lu Ban, wine makers and cloth merchants have Du Kang and the Mei Ge Sages, and pottery makers have the Yao Shen. Even those plying the "oldest trade," sex workers, have deities to protect them (see below). Like household and happiness gods, these old gods are some of the most transferrable and applicable deities for today's society.

DU KANG, IMMORTAL OF WINE

杜康

While there are many differences between the world's civilizations, there are also many similarities. Common experiences and trades, like brewing and wine-making, are thus common to many cultures. Chinese archaeological studies of the Long Shan civilization indicate that alcohol has been a part of the Chinese diet since as early as the New Stone Age, although the legends of consumption of wine are a relatively recent development, harking back to the time of Huang Di in the third millennium BCE.

In one of the earliest legends of a wine god, Du Kang, quartermaster of the food stores, agonized over the problem of how to keep excess crops from rotting. He tried storing dried sorghum in a tree trunk in imitation of wintering animals, but when he returned to check on the grains, he found wild animals lying around the tree as if dead. Water had apparently dripped into the tree trunk and wet the stored crop, which had fermented and was emitting an unusual fragrance. The resulting liquid leaked onto the ground, where it pooled. And the local beasts had drunk themselves . . . well, drunk.

Other stories of Du Kang place him as one of the strongest political leaders of the Xia Dynasty. When his father was assassinated by the Han, he wrestled power back from the usurpers and began a reign that consolidated this 400-year-long dynasty, all while making excellent wine.

During the Zhou Dynasty, Du Kang was represented as the descendant of a minister who was executed by the king, Xuan Wang. Du went into hiding in the country as a shepherd. While out minding his herd, he often threw his lunches into a pit rather than eat them. As time went by, he discovered an alluring scent rising from his cast-off meals. This is how he learned the secret of fermenting great wines—a skill that earned him a welcome back to court as the royal wine-maker. He was eventually granted the title of Jiu Xian (酒仙), Immortal of Wine.

A more fantastical legend tells of an Immortal who came to Du Kang in a dream and granted him a spring, telling him that its water would turn into the world's most delicious wine if he could persuade three people to give him a drop of their blood within nine days. Du woke up to find the spring outside his door and set about searching for people who would give him their blood. On the third day, he encountered a scholar who gave him a drop of his blood after he composed poetry with him. On the sixth day, he met a warrior who, upon hearing Du's cause, gallantly volunteered a drop of his blood. On the ninth day, Du approached a lunatic he found asleep by a tree. After some meaningless talk and desperate pleading, Du managed to persuade him to give up a drop of his blood.

Du raced home to pour the three drops of blood into the spring. The spring bubbled and hot steam rose from it, along with the most delicious smell. The wine that came forth from the spring tasted like the elixir of the gods, but it carried the characteristics of Du's three blood donors. This is why, when you drink wine, you first become as eloquent as the scholar, then as bold as the warrior, and finally as incoherent as the lunatic.

All these tales may actually be based on a figure from historical records. These indicate that a wine-maker named Du Kang lived in Shaan Xi during the Han Dynasty. The spring in Kang Jia Wei village, from which he took water to make wine, was named Du Kang Spring. The villagers there have marked Du's grave with a temple, where they venerate him each year.

By the time of the Ming Dynasty, the myth of Du Kang and the evolution of fermentation had been gathered by Feng Shi Hua into his *History of Wine (Jiu Shi)*. Like other nations, China developed its own wines and spirits, like Huang Jiu and the famously strong Bai Jiu. Veneration of Du Kang pervades China's wine culture today, with trading companies and hotels adopting his name. Thousands of brands package their wine in the most stunning historical art styles, calling on China's ancient heritage and the aid of this mighty god to boost sales.

Researchers at Fu Dan University recently discovered the presence of an "alcohol-resistant" gene in ancient East Asians that is linked to the early development of agriculture in Asian civilizations. Their results were published in 2011 and the scientists dedicated this gene to China's legendary god of wine, calling it the Du Kang Gene.

Du Kang is usually portrayed in statues and paintings as simply clothed, bearded, and either reclining against a vat of wine or raising a Zhong (traditional Chinese goblet) to the skies. His feast day is the twenty-first day of the first lunar month. Festivities are held at the temple at Kang Jia Wei, and also at Du Kang Village in Ru Yang, Luo Yang. Not far from this village is Du Kang House, whose grounds include an ancient mulberry tree and a pit in which the deity allegedly created the first Bai Jiu from his rotten lunches.

The best way for contemporary devotees to venerate Du Kang is to drink Chinese wine. You can now find a range of Huang Jiu, Mi Jiu, and Bai Jiu even in the West. After a cup or two, when you're feeling scholarly, perhaps indulge in some poetic works of renowned Tang and Song poets who sang the praises of Du Kang, like Du Fu, Bai Ju Yi, and Su Dong Po. Hopefully, by the time you reach the second stage of boldness, you will have the courage to read them aloud. I don't recommend reaching the third stage.

LEI ZU, MOTHER OF SILK

嫘祖

Silk production is one of the oldest Chinese trades. Silk has been in use for over 5,000 years, ever since the New Stone Age. The silk trade was instrumental in building the ancient Chinese economy, and those engaged in the trade needed a powerful guardian deity to ensure large harvests and protect their crop from disease. The Chinese believe that every living thing has a spirit; even objects, if they're around long enough, can acquire spiritual powers. This belief can be seen in the tale of Ma Tou Niang (马头娘), the Horse-Headed Lady. Like the silkworm she protects, this goddess's legend is one of metamorphosis.

Ma Tou Niang, so legend tells us, was the daughter of an itinerant trader who often traveled on business, leaving her at home to look after the horses. While tending to a stallion, the girl revealed that she missed her father. She jested with the horse, offering to marry it if it could bring her father back to her. The stallion neighed, shook off its harness, and galloped all the way to its master and carried him home. In the following days, the stallion turned away the extra fodder he was granted as a reward and whinnied in excitement whenever the girl approached. When he found out the promise his daughter had made, the trader was furious and shot the horse dead with his bow and arrow. He then skinned the horse and put its pelt out to dry. The next time the trader went away, his daughter went to look at the horse pelt. The pelt suddenly rose up, wrapped up the girl, and whisked her away.

The father finally found his daughter hanging from a mulberry tree, having been transformed into a creature with a worm-like body and a horse's head, from which silk spun out and twined around her body in a cocoon. This is why mulberry trees are called Sang Shu (桑树), "Sang" being a homonym for mourning. A neighbor took the cocoon home, nurtured it, and eventually bred others to harvest silk. So the trader lost a daughter, but the world gained silkworms. During the Han Dynasty, the empress herself picked mulberry leaves to feed to silkworms as an offering to Ma Tou Niang, whom she addressed by the title of princess, as if she were her own daughter.

An alternative origin myth portrays Ma Tou Niang as an animal and human hybrid. In this story, the goddess of silkworms is recognized in a more sophisticated form as Lei Zu. The earliest records of Lei Zu date from the Zhou Dynasty, when she was venerated as Xian Can (Ancestor of Silkworms) or Can Mu (Mother of Silkworms). This figure is widely accepted to be Xi Ling Shi, wife of Huang Di, legendary first ruler of the Chinese people (see chapter 9). Research in the 1990s revealed that she may have been a woman from Yi Chang, Hu Bei, who married Huang Di and moved with him to nearby Xi Ling. By chance, she found a wild silkworm cocoon and, after painstaking experimentation, mastered the skills of breeding and extracting silk—skills that she passed on to her people.

In another version, Lei Zu was born in Yan Ting, Si Chuan, where she observed wild silkworms spinning their cocoons and brought one home to teach herself how to breed them and extract silk. She was made a leader by her tribe, the Xi Ling, before she received her proposal from Huang Di. While the origin myths of deities often involved the intervention of a *deus ex machina*, most research indicates that Lei Zu was an exceptionally intelligent and resourceful woman who was herself responsible for her important invention.

Fashions may change, but, through the ages, silk has never lost its enduring appeal. It has been sought after by the West since at least the Middle Ages and continues to be considered a material of immense beauty and value. Veneration of Lei Zu is still very much alive in contemporary China in all places connected to the deity—Si Chuan, Hu Bei, and He Nan. Ceremonies tend to take place twice a year—once in the spring on her birthday, when people pray for a good crop from the worms, and once in the autumn, when they give thanks to the goddess for a bountiful harvest.

At Yan Ting (Si Chuan), where fossils related to the silkworm industry were found, you can join in large-scale ceremonial venerations before an immense altar. Red-carpeted official ceremonies involve the lighting of giant incense, elaborate re-enactments of ancient rituals, ethnic weaving performances, and processions of banners bearing the names of all the festival patrons. In folk celebrations, people carry effigies of the goddess around town. They also make paper offerings and burn incense at every temple, shrine, or altar, and hold operatic performances that can last two to three days.

With state involvement, Lei Zu has become a major symbol of native Chinese culture. She has also come to be considered a forebear of Chinese civilization. Thus there are many festivities dedicated to her. Yuan'an in Hu Bei is now a site of cultural research and a new Lei Zu Cultural Festival is held there in March. As many as 80,000 people take part in this extravaganza of cultural exhibitions, folk performances, craft fairs, and conferences, watched over by a giant sculpture of the goddess. Xi Ling in Yi Chang is also a popular pilgrimage destination, boasting a Lei Zu Temple, a Lei Zu Memorial, and a Lei Zu Cultural Park. The goddess's ancestral cave in Yan Ting, her alternative birthplace, is in a neighboring province.

Like Pan Gu and Du Kang, Lei Zu has become a symbol of indigenous industry and commerce, and her name is frequently borrowed by different sectors of the economy. Yan Ting specialities include spring water and preserved eggs—and, of course, silk. Silk merchants there invoke the heritage of Lei Zu to promote their products.

The traditional image of Lei Zu is of a dignified, matronly woman in Han dress, either standing by a spinning loom tending to her silk worms with basket in hand, or holding a piece of spun silk. Her attire in more recent artwork has turned toward a more authentic depiction of her in tribal wear. If you like costume dramas, you may enjoy the forthcoming *Age of Heroes* (*Ying Xiong Shi Dai*), a major CCTV series directed by Zhang Jiz Hong. The production, which is based on the reign of Huang Di and his wife, portrays Lei Zu as a wise, enterprising, and selfless stateswoman.

Judging by Zhang's work on *Journey to the West*, this is likely to be a stylistically bold series packed with exciting moments. The 2016 3-D historical epic *The Great Emperor* (*Xuan Yuan Da Di*) was released just before Qing Ming, the time for ancestral worship. This is a story of ancient warfare, invention, and love between Huang Di and Lei Zu, who is depicted as strong, brave, and industrious. Experts were consulted on ancient weaponry, scenes of daily life, and even the use of language, which I hope doesn't get lost in translation. You can find this film with English subtitles.

LI YUAN SHEN,
PATRON OF PERFORMING ARTS
梨园神

It used to be that, when you went backstage at a Chinese theater, you were very likely to see a shrine that belonged to the theater troop—perhaps not big or elaborate, but most theater companies had one. These shrines were dedicated to Li Yuan Shen (literally "god of the pear garden"), god of the performing arts. This deity was named after a pear garden because of two different versions of his origin myth.

The first identifies him as Er Lang Shen (二郎神), who was best known for subduing the great floods. Both Tang Xian Zu (1550–1616), the great playwright of the Ming Dynasty, and Li Yu, renowned playwright of the Qing period, named him as the celestial patron of their trade. Er Lang Shen was the nephew of the Jade Emperor. He was said to have three eyes, fingers as sharp and strong as needles and knives, and a celestial hound to boot. He is best known in pop culture as the god who subdued the Monkey King (see chapter 10). A handful of heroes, both real and imaginary, have carried the mythical title of Er Lang—for example, Deng Xia, who supposedly slew flood dragons in Hu Nan, or Li Bing, the engineer and supervisor in the building of the Du Jiang Yan Dam, the greatest achievement in ancient Chinese irrigation.

But why should a god of the floods come to be associated with the performing arts? The answer lies in the way Chinese religion was disseminated among China's vast populace. The greatest achiever of all the incarnations of Er Lang was Li Bing, who had turned the basins of Si Chuan from "flood country" to "land of paradise." He lived during the Warring States, a time when wizards and shamans played a key role in the pastoral care of the community. These shamans exercised their powers by leading worship on the stage. These performances, which were referred to as the Yang Xi (literally, "sun theater"), consisted essentially of exorcisms. During these ceremonies, offerings were made to three key deities: Chuan Zhu, who watched over the rivers; Tu Zhu, guardian of the land; and Yao Zhu, patron of medicine. Li Bing, due to his role in controlling the floods, was granted the title of Er Lang and came to be seen as the guardian of the rivers. Thus he became part of the Yang Xi tradition.

Er Lang's deeds were brought to the stage in these shamanic rites, which were the primary medium through which Chinese religion—whether Buddhist, Daoist, or folk—was disseminated, propagated, and evolved through thousands of years. The majority of the populace were semi-literate or illiterate. But they could all happily enjoy a story told orally or performed on the stage by state theaters or traveling troops of amateurs who delivered China's vast array of traditional dramatic forms through regional opera and theater, puppetry, musical theater, and storytelling. These performances sometimes took place in teahouses, sometimes in tents, and sometimes on street corners. So it was only fitting that Er Lang, who had performed such powerful miracles in taming the floods, should eventually be linked to China's most powerful means of transmitting its religious traditions, and become guardian of it. As a deity, Er Lang Shen's role became twofold. He was charged with subduing the floods, and also with watching over the theaters of China.

A completely separate and much more popular legend that has become predominant today places the origins of the god of the theater in the royal pear garden. The Tang emperor Li Long Ji (685–762 CE), formal title Xuan Zong, was a talented, knowledgeable, and passionate musician. During his life, he amassed some several hundred male and female court musicians and dancers, and trained them in the pear garden of his inner palace grounds, which included rooms in which he played music himself and a pavilion for outdoor musical activities.

Xuan Zong loved the Fa Qu, a major court musical form of the time that combined the styles of the Han people with those of the more culturally diverse Xi Yu (western regions). The Fa Qu came to be a speciality of the pear garden. With his *de facto* royal academy of music, he gave large-scale performances of music and dance, for which he acted as composer, director, and coach, as well as performer. His imperial orchestra operated on a system of merit. Talented commoners who managed to pass the strict selection criteria were trained up by the emperor himself. His influence became so widespread that those in the performance trade referred to themselves as "disciples of the Li Yuan," or "disciples of the pear garden." Eventually, the emperor became the god of their performance venues—Li Yuan Shen, god of theaters.

Li Yuan Shen is sometimes affectionately referred to as Lao Lang (Lang meaning "boy" or "child"). In Chinese, Lao is an affectionate term for the youngest child in the family, and Xuan Zong was himself the youngest prince. It was also said that the emperor sometimes referred to himself as Lao Lang, especially while he was wearing theatrical masks, to put his subjects at ease and work with them in a more egalitarian way.

There are Li Yuan temples all over China, but the most famous is his ancestral temple in Guan Xian, Si Chuan. The mountains and waters surrounding the Hua Qing Palace in the old capital, Xi'an, where Xuan Zong first set up his studios in the pear garden, are so beautiful that they may make you to break into song. Even in present-day China, Li Yuan is still synonymous with theater and musical performances, and with all performing arts. Spring Festival performances of song and dance are commonly advertised as Li Yuan Chun (Spring in the Pear Garden). Online sellers of traditional theatrical costumes and face paints also borrow the name of the god when labeling their wares. Classically trained singers with successful pop careers are still referred to as gods or goddesses of the pear garden.

Processions on Li Yuan Shen's birthday, the eighteenth day of the third lunar month, take place in many locations across China and in other Chinese-speaking regions. In Beijing, "disciples of the Li Yuan" take part in large-scale folk music and dance performances that include drums, lion dances, and performers on stilts who progress through the city, passing as many markets, shops, and busy streets as possible to welcome the deity with an abundant display of the very arts he protects. To this day, in Wu Han, ritual ceremonies to Li Yuan that include a musical performance are still held. In Chao Zhou, offerings are made to Tian Yuan Shuai, the musician who was the supervisor of the emperor's pear garden academy.

A great way to remember Li Yuan Shen and invoke his powers is to catch a performance of traditional Chinese theater when one tours near you. Kun Qu and Peking operas, and even some more modern works, are being brought to the stage in the West, with some English adaptations produced by collaborative projects like the Royal Shakespeare Company's Chinese Classics Translation project.

LU BAN, MASTER MAKER AND GOD OF CRAFTS

鲁班

Lu Ban, god of craftsmen, was not only a highly skilled architect and craftsman; he was also an ingenious inventor. So it is no wonder that this historical personage was deified as the god of master craftsmen practicing carpentry, stonemasonry, and many other crafts as well.

Lu Ban first became known in the Spring and Autumn and Warring States period, a time when Chinese society underwent drastic changes from a slave-based to a feudal economy, with a huge increase in the use of iron and wood for weaponry. Carpentry and woodworking became highly refined master crafts, with wood being used for building chariots, carriages, and ships, as well as houses and coffins. Key texts from this period—like the encyclopedic *Lu Shi Chun Qiu* (*The Spring and Autumn Annals*) by Lü Bu Wei,[22] and the *Li Ji* (*The Book of Rites*)[23]—give varying origins for Lu Ban. Some identify him as a poor artisan, some as a member of a family of craftsmen. The general consensus is that he was born around the 5th century BC in the Kingdom of Lu, hence his surname.

It is highly probable that, thanks to social changes, Lu Ban was able to free himself from the life of a bonded servant and become an independent craftsman working for the Kingdom of Chu. According to his biography by the great philosopher and statesman Mo Zi, the eventual architect first created weapons that improved Chu's warfare capabilities—inventions like the Yun Ti (siege engine) and Gou Ju (boarding hooks).

Influenced by Mo Zi's philosophy, Lu turned his focus to improving the everyday life of people. Gathering wisdom from his own daily experiences of building and working wood, he invented the *chan* (shovel), the *zao* (chisel), the *pao* (wood plane), the *zuan* (auger), and the *qu chi* (set square), all tools that are indispensible to construction as we know it today. These tools greatly reduced the strenuousness of labor and increased its efficiency. A precurser to the stone mill and the lock with hidden gears have also been attributed to this master builder.

Lu Ban, Master Maker and God of Crafts

The exceptional level of Lu Ban's genius can be gauged by erudite and critically acclaimed Han Dynasty essays on society and the sciences, like *Huai Nan Zi* and *Lun Heng*. Even these level-headed works attribute super-human abilities and near mystical powers to the man. He was said to have chiseled out a wooden bird (crane or eagle) on which he flew for three days. He may also have been China's first proponent of automation, for he crafted a mechanical carriage that could drive itself to replace the horse-drawn cart. He put his mother in the carriage, which apparently went so fast that Lu is said never to have seen her again!

During the Tang Dynasty, Lu Ban's reputation became nationwide and the trades by which he was revered expanded from carpentry and woodworking to plastering, furniture design, architecture, and construction trades in general. It was only a matter of time before his deeds were dramatized and finally became myth.

The most famous Lu Ban legend is *Lord Lu Ban Repairs Zhaozhou Bridge*, which first appeared in written form in Yuan Hao Wen's fantasy novel during the Yuan Dynasty. The story tells of the river Jiao in Zhao Zhou, which was so incredibly wide and deep and with such whirling sands that no architect had ever attempted to build a bridge over it. That is, until Lu Ban successfully designed and built a stone bridge that allowed the inhabitants of the region to cross the river with ease. It was said that no other bridge was as solid and as sturdy as this one. One day, the Immortal Zhang Guo Lao was passing by and wanted to test the strength of the bridge. So he drove a cart containing Wu Yue, the five great mystical mountains of China, onto it. The bridge wobbled a bit, but then steadied itself. The mountains, the cart, the Immortal, and his donkey drove over safely. Legend claims that you can still see the hoofprints of Zhang's donkey imprinted on the bridge.

Legends of a similar nature circulated around the country telling of the building of temples, pagodas, and tombs. Though he was brilliant, Lu Ban never got above himself and was usually described as mild-mannered and shabbily dressed. Stories of the great inventor making small wooden gifts like cricket cages for workers and passing on useful hints and tips were popular among craftsmen and artisans. As the trade societies of the Tang and Song eras turned into the guilds of the Qing period, it became very common for tradesmen to venerate their craft's founder and Lu Ban became established as the father of carpentry, stone-masonry, bricklaying, and tiling. Considering that his devotees are mostly builders, it is easy to imagine the enthusiasm with which temples were built in his honor across the country. Lu Ban's wise counsels were collected in the three-volume Ming work *Classics of Lu Pan*, which became a sort of trade manual for craftsmen and builders.

The days on which to make offerings to this god vary between regions and trades, but they are usually made during the fifth, sixth, seventh, and twelfth lunar months. On these days, rates, contracts, and other matters are discussed within the trade. For example, the sixteenth day of the sixth lunar month is the Lu Ban Festival for construction workers in Hong Kong. During this holiday, they make offerings at the Lopan Temple.

Lu Ban epitomizes the skills and wisdom of the people. In China, he is especially revered, even making it into primary school literature texts and children's stories and cartoons. As a mark of respect and to show appreciation, contemporary architects or craftsmen of great skill are referred to as the "Living Lu Ban." This deity also inspired the idiom Ban Men Nong Fu (literally, "wielding your axe outside Lu Ban's door"), meaning displaying your skills to an expert.

Lu Ban, who is very much a workers' hero, survived the anti-superstition campaigns during the turbulent years of Chinese history. The now iconic black-and-white film classic *Legend of Lu Ban* was released in 1958. He has not been as popular in modern media as other deities have been, although he has reincarnated into a deadly wooden android in the computer game Wang Zhe Rong Yao and been revamped as a main character in the fantasy novel series *The Curse of Lu Ban* by Yuan Tai Ji. In this story, the King of Chu orders the master builder to construct nine deadly secret mechanisms in his palace to dispatch any enemies and assassins. When the courtier Mo Zi defeats them all, Lu Ban bows to his intelligence and his pacifist influence. One night, Mo Zi is visited in secret by Lu Ban, who reveals nine more deadly traps, then leads him to his hidden mentor. Together, they accomplish incredible feats. This story presents a much darker Lu Ban than we find in his original form.

These novels may have taken their inspiration from the villain in John Carpenter's *Big Trouble in Little China*, Lopan being a Cantonese corruption of Lu Ban. Lopan, once a great warrior defeated by Qin Shi Huang, has little to do with the master builder, but, like the character in the novel, he also suffers a curse.

Among specific trades, this god still enjoys immense veneration. Quality furniture makers, tool makers, and double-glazing manufacturers have all borrowed his name for their companies and for trademarks for their products—for instance, the "Luban Wall"—but respect for this god isn't just limited to crafts and construction. A wide range of highly skilled trades also invoke his spirit as the master of other skills—among them a programming language, a software company, and an interior-design firm.

You can find museums and temples to Lu Ban all over China, as well as in other Chinese-speaking regions. The temple in Macao features a giant

Lu Ban lock adjacent to the altar. For devotees who want to attempt to solve this puzzle, smaller ones are available. The Lu Ban lock is based on the principle of multiple beams of wood laid across each other into an interlocking system. The number of beams can vary from six to thirty-six. A variation of this is the Lu Ban circle, which is made up of semi-circular components. It was said that Lu Ban invented these wooden puzzles to educate and amuse his children. They are still very popular in China today, and puzzle-lovers around the world can purchase them on the Internet.

The Lu Ban lock has become something of a national obsession, with domestic news reports of retired carpentry workers collecting scrap materials and teaching themselves the master builder's craft, some even applying for it to be listed as an Olympic sport. This principle, when used in architecture, can produce whole buildings based on its interlocking system without using a single nail or bolt.

Lu Ban also continues to inspire the young. Undergraduates studying architecture and engineering employ his principles in their assignments with astonishing results. The gifting of a Lu Ban lock from premier Li Ke Qiang to German Chancellor Angela Merkel confirmed the status of this invention in the 21st century, and it has become a global symbol of traditional Chinese crafts and skills.

MEI GE SAGES, PATRONS OF CLOTH-DYING

梅葛二圣

The Mei Ge Er Sheng, Mei Ge Sages, are the patron gods of cloth-dying. One legend says that they were originally two Immortals, Mei Guo and Ge Niao, who were sent by the Jade Emperor to grant the earthly emperor his desired red robe. People then began to worship the likeness of these Immortals as the forefathers of cloth-dying. A more popular version bases their origins on two real people—an officer named Mei Fu, who was born in An Hui, and an imperial guard, Ge Hong, who was born in the neighboring region of Jiang Su. Before their military careers, the two may have been friends who grew up together.

Before the art of dying cloth became known, the Chinese wore linen and cotton in their natural colors of white and grey. One day, young Mei Fu fell into a muddy puddle and stained his white shirt. He washed out the mud, but some yellow tint remained in the cloth. The villagers admired the shade of the fabric and began to dye their own clothes with mud and earth. Mei Fu told his friend Ge Hong what had happened, and they began to look for more ways to dye cloth.

As they experimented, they discovered the green stains of grass, which seemed to resist washing. Excited, they cut a basketful of grass, ground it up, and added it, along with some white cloth, to a vat filled with water. The results were dissappointing. In despair, after repeated failures, they drank heavily to steel their nerves for one final attempt. In fact, they actually vomited into the vat before passing out. When they awoke, they were delighted to find that the cloth had turned a brilliant, steadfast blue. Luckily for them, and for the region's tailors, they managed to refine the fermentation process so that it included time and alcohol—but not the act of vomiting.

Indigo dyes were immensely popular in China during the early 20th century in both villages and cities. In fact, the indigo cotton cheongsams worn by teachers, students, and intellectuals in the 1920s and 1930s have become iconic of the era and a symbol of nationalism.

The Mei Ge Sages were revered throughout the country, particularly in places that either specialized in the dying trade or had a vibrant tradition of woodblock art, like Mian Zhu and Jia Jiang in Si Chuan and Kai Feng in He Nan, where many temples were dedicated to them. With the shift toward new technologies and away from traditional printing and dying methods, these temples have fallen into disrepair. But if you are visiting other folk temples around China, you are quite likely to find altars or grottoes dedicated to the Mei Ge Sages.

If you are in the garment or printing industries, the Mei Ge Sages are the perfect pair to pray to for the safety and success of your business, and it is traditional for printers and cloth merchants to have small shrines to them at their workplaces. Even without temples, it's quite easy for contemporary devotees to observe these traditional customs. Offerings for the two deities are a little different from those for other gods, however, with paper horses rather than incense being burned in their honor. This is a reminder that animal products are used in the dying and tanning process—a practice far more humane than the animal sacrifices that were originally offered up. Alcohol, which played a key role in the Mei Ge's discovery, is also important here, and the gods can be honored by sharing a stiff drink with the founding fathers of your trade. Ask them to grant prosperity to your business and safety to your premises and staff.

In Mi Yun (near Beijing), you can visit the old Yong Shun cloth mill, where you will find a museum of traditional Chinese dyes made out of indigenous plants, along with displays of techniques like Tang Dynasty multi-colored dyes and knotting methods that produced traditional patterns. Yong Shun is still a working mill, and is dedicated to the Mei Ge Sages, who appear at its entrance. On the second day of the second lunar month, the employees of Yong Shun still make offerings to the Mei Ge Sages, though the special dates for veneration of this pair vary from region to region.

Because of the nature of the dying trade, drawn or printed images of the Mei Ge Sages traditionally take priority over sculpted effigies. They are popularly depicted as two plump and bearded wise men, sometimes in line paintings on yellow paper, sometimes wearing the most vibrant colors in recognition of the dyes they invented. They are usually shown busy at work among pieces of cloth. In relatively recent depictions, Christian-style halos appear behind their heads. This is, perhaps, appropriate, given how important the Chinese printing and garment industries have become to the West.

YAO SHEN, SPIRITS OF THE KILN

窑神

China has been producing pottery ever since the New Stone Age, reaching an advanced stage in this field during the Yang Shao civilization (5000–3000 BCE). At first, pottery was made in the open air; then kilns were developed to house the craft. The earliest Chinese pottery was constructed of bricks and tiles, followed by porcelain, and specific kilns were dedicated to each type of product. As pottery became an important industry, it acquired its own guardian deities. The Chinese word for kiln is Yao (窑), so this art is appropriately watched over by the Yao Shen, spirits of the kiln. In fact, there are many Yao Shen, as pottery requires an amalgam of many elements. The identities of these deities also vary from region ro region.

The earliest personages regarded as Yao Shen include the mythical ruler Shun and Lao Zi, the Old Sage (see chapter 13). As the maker of elixirs and master of alchemy, Lao Zi was also revered as patron god of other crafts involving the powers of fire—like blacksmithing and metal foundry, and woks in particular. Since the earliest pottery was crafted outdoors, the process was highly dependent on the weather, as wind and rain affected the wood and coal fires and the quality of the clay. It is no wonder, therefore, that offerings were also made to Lei Gong, lord of thunder and the ruler of wind and rain (see chapter 4), so he would grant sunny and dry conditions to ensure a good batch of quality pottery.

Other Yao Shen are Shan Shen and Tu Di, gods of the mountains and earth that were the sources of clay, and Niu Shen and Ma Shen, gods of horses and oxen that pulled carts to transport this raw material. Yao Shen temples were built all over the country and dedicated to these four supporting gods of the industry. A theater was often built opposite the temple, where singing and dancing were performed in the second and third lunar months. Combined with days of feasting, this makes up the custom of "frolicking with Yao Shen." Some historical figures were also given the title—for example, Lei Xiang, the expert local potter of Bai Shui County in Shaan Xi.

The Yao Shen also double as the patron deities of the coal and mineral industries, and in particular, refineries. The Yao Shen of the coal industry can appear as an erudite scholar or a fearsome warrior, mirroring the hazardous nature of the mining trade. Major refineries used to have shrines to Yao Shen at their entrances, the owners making offerings for prosperity and the workers for protection and safety on duty. These offerings were made in the last lunar month of the year, when the owners paid their respects to the gods with incense and treated their workers to banquets, which were open to cart drivers and even beggars.

China is a vast country with many variations in soil and climate, producing vastly different clays in its different regions. In the 21st century, the Chinese pottery and porcelain industries have expanded and regional kilns that have been in use for centuries are responding to increased domestic demand and a growing export market. The Yao Shen that watched over workers in the trade and the inhabitants in areas that thrived on the trades through the ages are still with them now. Here, we can see that unique Chinese deification process through popular faith very clearly, as the title is attributed directly to the master craftsmen of the region.

You may very well have come across, or indeed own, some porcelain from Jing De Zhen in Jiang Xi, which is the home of the world-famous blue and white Chinese porcelain. Antiques of this porcelain are found in private collections and museums all over the globe. Recently, a bronze statue was erected there of Tong Bin, a local craftsman during the Ming Dynasty, depicting him as Yao Shen, making him a mascot of the country's major tourist and heritage sites. The people of Hua Ning, in Yun Nan, hold annual ceremonies in which they make offerings to the shrine of Che Peng, the founder of their 600-year-old Kai Long Kiln. In Taiwan, pottery and porcelain ware are used alongside incense and food as offerings to Yao Shen. These ceremonies are still performed in traditional outfits with emphasis placed on accurately performing the ancient rituals.

Rarely does even Chinese culture have an actual living god, but there is a living person who bears the title of Yao Shen. He is Hu Wu Qiang, from the town of Tong Guan in Chang Sha, Hu Nan. He was taught by his father from the age of twelve, and pottery became the love of his life. Fired from his job due to his obsession, Hu persevered for the next thirty years, through many failed trials, to set up his own kiln. At last, he created an award-winning work, "The Fire Phoenix," using a high-temperature technique from the Tang Dynasty to achieve the "blood crimson" glaze effect. Once known by the nickname "the mad potter," Hu was elevated to Yao Shen by his fellow villagers.

Contemporary worship of the Yao Shen can take many forms, from the purchase of Chinese porcelain and pottery online and from shops that are occasionally found in big Western cities, to taking lessons in the craft at a location near you, to a visit to Jing De Zhen. Potters from all over the world now flock to this town, some even setting up studios there. There, they consult with local craftsmen to whom pottery-making is as natural as living and breathing, in an attempt to make their designs come to life. English ceramics artist Roger Law, who infuses his Chinese-style giant teapots with an English sense of the whimsical, is just one of these. The powers of Yao Shen are strong there.

More adventurous travelers can try the town of Shen Hu in He Nan, the home of Diao Ci porcelain and one of China's five major kilns. Apart from a temple ornamented with examples of this craft, you can browse contemporary wares in fairs in the town's ancient streets. Or you can simply spend some time appreciating the beauty of pottery bowls and porcelain teapots you have in your possession, and marvel at the quintessence of China—the soul of the craftsman, distilled over centuries, into an object you can hold in your hand.

As pottery and porcelain are molded by fire, dramatizations inspired by Yao Shen have tended to feature "baptism by fire" stories. The TV series *Yao Shen* tells the tale of a child who becomes hunchbacked due to an accident. He grows up to become a master potter and is able to transcend the pains of his life through the fires of his kiln. The Yao Shen have also inspired online fantasy novels, one of which is based on the concept that the hero is the last of his tribe.

For hard-core devotees, Master Hu of Tong Guan, now in his seventies, is anxiously seeking apprentices who will continue his rare craft. To this day, he still uses only wood fires to produce his pottery. He offers free tuition and his contact information can be found online. If you're interested in learning the craft and perhaps becoming the next Yao Shen, reach out to him!

BAI MEI SHEN, GUARDIAN OF SEX WORKERS

白眉神

The gods of the old trades are a major feature in the pantheons of Chinese gods. Workers in each trade prayed to the appropriate gods for skill in their work, reward for their labors, and protection from occupational hazards. Craftsmen have Lu Ban, cloth merchants have the Mei Ge Sages, and pottery makers have Yao Shen. It's not surprising that the "oldest trade" would also have a deity. When a trade puts you at the mercy of your clients' basest whims, you definitely pray to some god for protection. In fact, the sex workers of ancient China prayed to several.

The first set of deities are the guardians of the brothels, in the form of Wu Da Xian (五大仙, the Five Spirits). These are five animal spirits: the hedgehog, the turtle, the weasel, the snake, and the rat. Some brothels even put aside secret chambers for the veneration of these animals, which were believed to hold spiritual powers that control the rise and fall of the business as well as the personal safety of the women who worked there.

For fiscal success, sex workers prayed to Guan Zhong (725–645 BCE), a politician of the Warring States era who, before courtesans appeared in ancient Greece or other Eastern civilizations, introduced sex workers into the Chinese court, to be employed by the emperor, officials, and the imperial army. Many courtesans viewed Guan as the patron god of their trade. He is, to some extent, the founder of the Chinese sex industry, setting up imperial brothels around the country. While this can be seen as a very negative thing, these measures gave sex workers recognition as legitimate employees protected by the state, vastly improving their status and safety.

For skill and prowess, working girls turned to Bai Mei Shen (literally, "god of the silver eyebrows"), who gained a devout following during the Ming Dynasty. He sports a long beard and crimson eyes, and is often depicted on horseback carrying a knife. Originally a Persian figure, he was transferred to China with the silks and spices brought along the Silk Road during the Wei Dynasty. Trade with Persia and central Asia not only introduced new goods and new faiths; it also brought a taste for the exotic. These bolder foreign cultures were perceived by the Chinese as provocative and alluring. The Han Chinese were dazzled by dancers of traveling troupes, and attracted to those who promised fresh delights. It is no wonder that the escorts and courtesans of ancient China turned to Bai Mei Shen for access to these exotic skills of seduction. It was a sign of China quite literally embracing new cultures. Over time, Bai Mei Shen took on the classic image of a Chinese sage, with white eyebrows and long beard.

Bai Mei Shen was particularly venerated by sex workers in northern China because of the legends surrounding his earthly incarnation, Dao Zhi. Dao Zhi was a famous criminal mastermind, as well as the leader of slave uprisings during the Warring States. He once hid in a brothel to escape capture and was cared for there by the girls. Just before he died, his eyebrows turned silver, hence the name by which he is known. Some Ming and Qing brothels had Bai Mei temples within their establishments and, in some parts of the north, asked that their clients bow to the god before proceeding. Others chose to worship alone in anticipation of their next clients.

In modern times, these temples have fallen into disuse as social tastes and trends changed. Today, the sex industry thrives in China, although its members are still socially ostracized, especially on the Mainland. Even with charitable organizations like Zi Teng (Wisteria) and Midnight Blue, which provide help and support to sex workers, they still live in fear of attack or incarceration. Because they ply their trade "underground," so to speak, it is difficult to document their beliefs and customs. It is probably safe to assume, however, that there are still devotees of Bai Mei and Guan Zhong in China, even if these gods are only called upon in times of need.

Guan Zhong and the protective spirit animals have yet to have an impact on popular culture, but Bai Mei Shen—or, more correctly, his human incarnation as Dao Zhi—has a persona that lends itself to the fantasy sword-fighting genre of Wu Xia, and the roguish, flirtatious bandit has found his way into many films, novels, and TV shows—most notably the 2014 *Legend of Qin*. In this animated series, he is Wen Shi Ren, a master thief, but he is still the favorite of ladies of the night.

Kong Fu Zi, Confucius

Chapter 13

Immortal Sages

Ever since the beginning of their civilization, the Chinese have had great reverence for knowledge, learning, and wisdom. In fact, the many excellent branches of indigenous sciences and philosophy grew out of observation and self-learning. It follows that sages, people who embody these qualities, are highly venerated in China.

KONG FU ZI, CONFUCIUS
孔夫子

It's a common misconception that there are three co-existing faiths in China—Buddhism, Daoism, and Confucianism. Reality is a lot less neat. There is a fourth area of faith, folk religion. However, most people in China tend to be not just one of these, but a combination of at least two. I have written about many Buddhist, Daoist, and folk deities. This section is dedicated to the eponymous founder of Confucianism, the school of thought that has had the most profound impact on the Chinese state, on politics, and on society—on so much, in fact, that it has become a kind of faith in itself.

Kong Fu Zi—shortened to Kong Zi and best known around the world by his latinized name, Confucius—was born in 522 BCE in the state of Lu, in Shan Dong. He spent years traveling before finally return-ing to Lu, where he wrote his famous classics. It is not entirely certain whether or not he ever held ministerial posts.

There are many reasons given for why Kong Zi left his native state, all of them involving dancing girls. One is that Lu grew strong under his guidance, until neighboring states felt threatened and sent a group of dancing girls to distract its pious prince. The prince succumbed, and Kong Zi left in disgust.

Another well-known tale tells of two brothers, one a sage and one a brigand. Having failed to convince the sage brother to convert his brig-and sibling, Kong Zi ventured to attempt it himself. Prostrating himself before the brigand, Kong praised him as a champion of morality, where-upon the brigand proceeded to lampoon the scholar for the rigidity of his appearance, his ineffectual jabbering, his self-conscious morality, and his ingratiating behavior with the landed gentry.

Kong Zi was also berated by Communist China, which associated him with the traditionalism and conservatism standing in the way of progress. Considering the principles for which he is now known—unquestioning fil-ial piety, the treatment of women as chattel, the subordination of feelings, and the supremacy of social order and hierarchy—it is difficult for con-temporary liberal and progressive minds to relate to his views. To make sense of them, we must remember that certain Confucian principles were hand-picked by leaders throughout history to establish and reinforce their power and control. Good examples of this occurred during the reign of Ming emperor Zhu Yuan Zhang and under the Manchu, who enforced the Confucian ethical framework as law, thus insinuating themselves into the indigenous society as quintessentially Chinese leaders.

But there is much more than this to Kong Zi's philosophy.

Kong Zi lived in a time of lawlessness and instability, when feu-dal states warred with each other and were growing in power, size, and complexity. The philosopher offered leaders models for governance and administration to help ease the rising political and social chaos. He advo-cated a bureaucratic meritocracy in which offices were granted to those with the wisdom and intelligence required for the job, rather than to those with family ties to leadership.

Like any other individual, Kong Zi had a complex mind. His father had a son from his first marriage who was crippled. Tradition declared that only those who were physically whole could conduct sacrifices to ancestors. So the seventy-year-old father remarried and sired Kong Zi so he could fulfill his filial duty. Since his entire existence derived from a need to honor ancestors, it is understandable that Kong Zi was extremely sentimental about filial piety and traditional ceremonies. It was rather unfortunate, however, that these ultra-conservative views have overshadowed his very enlightened ideas of government. Kong Zi was not anti-pleasure. In fact, he was particularly fond of music. He just wanted pleasure to facilitate the harmony of the state.

Some may dispute the association of Kong Zi with religion, for spiritual beings were one of the topics on which he refused to speak. However, the way he achieved god-like status after his death provides a prime example of how real Chinese people became deities. When he died in 479 BCE, a shrine was erected in Kong Zi's memory where he was venerated by his followers and his family. This veneration remained much like any other ancestral cult until an emperor came to pay his respects in 159 BCE. After that, the Kong family was ennobled and, in 59 CE, the Han emperor Ming Di decreed that sacrifices should be made to Kong Zi in all schools. Over 400 years after his death, Kong Zi's status had grown from that of a local earth god who was venerated by devotees exclusively from his own region, to that of a national deity elevated by imperial leaders.

The Han state ordered temples built for Confucius in every administrative district. In these temples, the central shrines of the sage are surrounded by statues of his disciples. Through the years, the number of statues surrounding the shrines has been increased by state edict, right up until 1919. Among the many high titles granted Kong Zi is Sheng, of which the closest Western equivalent is "Holy One." During the Northern Song Dynasty, through the philosopher Zhu Xi, the neo-Confucian concepts of Dao Xue and Li Xue (teachings of methods and principles) continued to influence the running of the country—not only in politics, but also in the arts and medicine—eventually entering the curriculum for the imperial civil service. During the Ming era, thinker Wang Yang Ming added his branch of Xin Xue (cultivation of the mind-heart) to neo-Confucianism. Through all its variations, however, Confucianism has always emphasized the importance of the self-cultivation of morality that must accompany the acquisition of knowledge.

In more recent times, neo-Confucianism has become a movement in Japan, Korea, and Vietnam. In the 20th century, it has engaged in dialogue with Western philosophy. Even in the 21st century, the Chinese, both at home and abroad, still revere this sage. Yu Dan, professor of Media Studies at Beijing Normal University, stressed the importance of philosophy in everyday life in her book *Confucius from the Heart*, which aimed at bringing the sage's teachings to a broader audience. Readers loved her highly personal interpretation of Kong Zi's philosophy, with tips on attaining spiritual happiness and finding a place in China's bewildering modernity. The book sold 10 million copies worldwide.

The Confucius Institute, founded in 2004, is a non-profit organization under the auspices of China's ministry of education that has been working to promote Chinese language and learning, and the understanding of Chinese culture. It now has over 500 branches around the world and has made Kong Zi a symbol of Chinese learning in an age when China's language and culture are embracing the world. Perhaps there is some similarity between the instability of Confucius's own times and the accelerated economic development of today that threatens to bring social chaos to contemporary China. People in these turbulent modern times are once again turning to the comfort and order of Confucian ideas. In his 2017 speech in Geneva, President Xi emphasized the importance of harmony between nations of the world. It is an encouraging sign that, this time around, some of the positive aspects of the sage's philosophy are being channeled by those in power.

LAO ZI, THE OLD SAGE

老子

As mentioned before, there is a prevalent misconception that there are three religions in China that co-exist separately. In fact, these three systems of philosophies and belief have constantly interacted with the country's sprawling folk beliefs. And most people have a set of beliefs that are a mixture of these. The sage associated with Daoism is Lao Zi, whose evolution as a deity clearly demonstrates how each of the different faiths in China contributed to the development of the others.

Lao Zi was once a real person—Li Er or Li Dan—a thinker who lived during the Spring and Autumn period in the kingdom of Chu (He Nan). His life is recorded in Si Ma Qian's famous *Historical Records*. Li Er was exceptionally well-read and knowledgeable, and worked as head of the national library and archives during the Zhou Dynasty. When the dynasty went into decline, he resigned and went away to live as a hermit. At the city gates, he was treated as a guest by the Daoist guard, who implored him to write a book. The sage produced a work called

Lao Zi, the Old Sage

the *Five Thousand Words*—and then vanished. Li was older than Confucius and was revered by him for his wisdom and learning. He is said to have lived to be 160 years old. This, along with his mysterious disappearance, assured that his image would come to be surrounded by a certain mysticism.

The life of Li Er had little to do with religion until he was turned into the "face" of Daoism by Zhang Dao Ling, who founded this organized religion during the Han Dynasty. Facing fierce competition from Buddhism and Confucianism, Zhang needed a powerful ancestral figure who was already venerated by the public for his intellect and endorsed and respected by other sages—a figure with the same status as the Buddha. Li Dan was the perfect candidate. His philosophy of the mystical force of the Dao was also just the thing to form a central tenet of the new faith. Zhang began to attribute all his own teachings to transcriptions of the wise words of Lao Zi, whose *Five Thousand Words* became the now world-famous *Dao De Jing*. *The Book of Wei* was one of the earliest texts to refer to Lao Zi by his granted title of Tai Shang Lao Jun—Tai Shang being a term usually applied to royalty meaning "highest" and "most honored," and Lao Jun meaning "elderly gentleman."

Lao Zi the deity was super-human in every way. He was said to have been born out of the primeval element of Yuan Qi (元气), a foundation of Daoist faith and philosopy, the cosmic force or energy from which all things, including the Dao, emerged—the essential way of nature, the way that all things are, and how all things move and change. Legend tells us that a female Immortal swallowed an elixir made from the essence of Yuan Qi and, after eighty-one years of gestation, the sage emerged from her left armpit, his hair already silver—hence the name Lao Zi, which means "The Old Sage."

The Daoists enveloped this sage in ever more wondrous stories. His body was not of flesh and blood, and he came from a time before our star system was born. He was nine feet tall, with eyebrows five inches long and ears seven inches long. His eyebrows and eyes were green and purple. Purple celestial mist emanated from his nostrils. Clothed in colorful clouds, he lived in a palace of gold, silver, and jade, and was attended by over 200 Immortals. He slept on the back of a giant celestial turtle.

Lao Zi's principle of the Dao was an enormous one that encompassed life, the universe, and all things—mental and physical, material and immaterial. It is a concept that allegedly can not be explained, only perceived. A second key figure of Daoism, Zhuang Zi, brought followers closer to the Dao by providing the faith with existential goals that had first been introduced in Lao Zi's work—the quest for immortality, the importance of a lifestyle of quiet seclusion and simplicity, and the need to be free from desires. These practices came to be referred to as Xiu Lian, and were adopted as an essential part of the training of anyone seeking the Way of Dao. The veneration of the Dao had a profound impact on ancient Chinese civilization.

Eventually, a triad of highest deities—the Three Pure Ones—came to preside over a Daoist pantheon of celestial Immortals, earth deities, and demons. This pantheon grew to be vast and diverse. In their intense competition, Buddhism and Daoism each claimed that their leaders were ancestors to the other. Daoists documented their "victories" in this competition in a book of scriptures that gave accounts of Lao Zi traveling to and teaching in India, and his encounters with Mani, the Persian prophet who founded Manichaeism, a gnostic religion[24] that spread to China in the 6th century via Xin Jiang.

It is clear that Lao Zi and Daoism were powerful tools in the hands of whoever exploited them. The emperors of the Tang and Song Dynasties were enamored of this faith, especially the Tang imperial clan of Li, who were keen to tie their ancestry to the now divine Li Er. The Tang emperor Li Yuan was engaged in a difficult battle at Huo Shan when an old man in white appeared and offered a strategy that ensured his victory. The emperor informed his people that Tai Shang Lao Jun—Lao Zi— had come to his aid. In 666 CE, the Tang emperor Gao Zong ordered that the *Dao De Jing* be studied by court officials as part of their preparation for office. Another Tang emperor, Li Long Ji, made a more frivolous use of Daoism, ordering his daughter-in-law to become a Daoist nun so he could smuggle her into his quarters for his own pleasure.

There are Lao Jun temples dedicated to Lao Zi all over China, the most famous being the magnificent Tai Qing Temple in Lao Zi's hometown of Lu Hu, He Nan. There, you'll find Lao Zi with his two major disciples. The forum where Lao Zi first expounded his work to the gatekeeper Yi Xi lies at the foot of the Zhong Nan Mountains in Shaan Xi. Although many gods are honored by large sculptures that have been erected in modern times to supplement their effigies in temples, Lao Zi already had one made of him during the Song Dynasty. It still stands in the foothills of the Qing Yuan Mountains in Quan Zhou, Fu Jian. The sculpture is as tall as three grown men. Judging by the deity's declared mythical stature, it is probably life-sized!

The *Dao De Jing* was first translated into English by the missionary John Chalmers in 1868. One of Lao Zi's most famous appearances in Chinese pop culture occurs in a comical episode in *Journey to the West*, in which

Sun Wu Kong breaks into the preparations for Xi Wang Mu's splendid Pan Tao Banquet and gets blind drunk. He steals into Tai Shang Lao Jun's (Lao Zi) quarters, where he swallows all of the priceless elixir in his gourd. As a punishment, the god locks him into his stove to burn him. Wo Kong not only emerges in one piece, however; he also acquires metal bones and golden eyes.

The best way to venerate Lao Zi is to live by his teachings and philosophy. Some of the main principles advocated by the great sage include the need to meet aggression with mildness and attacks with softness; it is inner strength that will endure in the end. Only those who are kind and tolerant have the strength of morality. Go with the flow; allow all things to take their natural course. Let kindness and beauty spring from within, not from prescribed conventions. Maintain a mood of tranquility; do not force others to do what they do not want to do. Be kind as water, for it nurtures all things and never resists. Keep your mind unclouded by the multitude of desires. Remember that all things will take their natural cause. Whatever your path in life, you can benefit from this wisdom.

LU YU, THE TEA SAGE

陆羽

If, at the end of a very busy day, you sit down with a cup of tea and think "Thank god," the god you're thanking is Lu Yu, the Tea Sage. Lu Yu, who is also known as Cha Sheng (茶圣), created Cha Dao (茶道), the way of drinking Chinese tea as a ceremony in its own right. Tea was originally taken as a medicinal herb in ancient China. Lu Yu transformed it into something more profound in his work Cha Jing (茶经), The Book of Tea. From its first appearance, this work has been widely regarded as the ultimate source of knowledge for Cha Dao in its purest form. Despite his great legacy, however, Lu Yu's life began like a piece of discarded, unhewn jade.

As a baby, Lu Yu was left on a riverbank in Jing Ling, Hu Bei. Rescued and adopted by a monk from the nearby Long Gai Temple, he either took the monk's surname or was named after a water bird. Here, he first came into contact with *camellia sinensis*, the tea plant, which was originally cultivated in temples and taken by monks to help them meditate. Lu Yu tired of living in hardship at the temple, however, so he escaped and joined a traveling theater troop.

Lu Yu led an adventurous and fulfilled life playing the roles of clowns and fools on the stage while becoming an accomplished scholar. As he educated himself, however, one topic remained his life-long obsession. As he traveled all over the country, he studied and investigated varieties of tea and methods of tea-making in different regions. Inspired by Lu Yu's scholarly excellence, poems about tea were written by literati like Su Dong Po and Bai Ju Yi (772–846).[25] Huang

Lu Yu, the Tea Sage, by Haruki Nanmei, 1841

Pu even dedicated poems on tea-picking to Lu Yu. The imperial court granted him the role of Master of Ceremonies, although he refused the post and went to live as a recluse in Shao Xi, Zhe Jiang, where he wrote his masterpiece. Tang historical records of a god painting on the wall of an official's quarters show that, not long after his death, Lu Yu was already on his way to deification.

Tea-drinking in China today, although still elaborate by Western standards, is a very pared-down version of traditional practices, which you must understand in order to have an idea of the scope of Lu Yu's achievement. Lu Yu set out the parameters for leaf-picking, grading each leaf by where it was grown and the part of the plant from which it was plucked. He created the whole process of preparing tea leaves, prescribing a wide range of tools and utensils for picking, preparing, making, and drinking tea. On his travels, he investigated the distinct tastes of different varieties of tea and evaluated all kinds of water sources, setting up a grading system to rate their quality for making tea. He even specified materials to be used for making the fire for boiling tea (the ancient Chinese ground the leaves into powder before boiling it in water) and laid out precise temperature guidelines.

Ultimately, Lu Yu put forth thousands of other details that made tea-drinking into an art form, arriving at what he called the "nine challenges to tea drinking": preparing the leaves, discerning the leaves, using the instruments, managing the fire, controlling the water, regulating the heat, observing the foam, boiling the tea, and drinking the tea. During Lu Yu's time, tea-drinking became common and tea was transported all over the country. The Tang notable Yuan Zhen (779–831),[26] a key literary figure of the Tang Dynasty, described tea-drinking as one of the seven most important things in a Chinese household, along with wood (for fire), rice, cooking oil, salt, soy sauce, and vinegar. Royalty, nobility, and intellectuals alike held Cha Dao ceremonies. In the Song Dynasty, elaborate outdoor events for tea-drinking were held at scenic spots that boasted good water sources. These sometimes involved the reading of poetry and competitions for making the most beautiful tea foam.

During the Song and Yuan eras, as trade developed throughout the country and urbanization changed the social landscape, tea gained wider appeal with the growth of teahouses and popular storytelling entertainments. Due to the curtailing of the literati's involvement in politics during the Ming era and their association with tea-drinking, the activity then retreated indoors. The process became more compact and the direct infusion of leaves became common. While this was a departure from Lu Yu's methods, the purity of mind and spirit associated with tea, which he represented, was emphasized even more.

Both tea merchants and owners of teahouses have built shrines and made offerings to Lu Yu through the ages. Today, tea is still as integral to modern Chinese life as flavoring is to its cuisine. For Lu Yu, the teapot is a temple and the leaves the offerings. Of course, there are plenty of temples to visit to venerate Lu Yu and many places of pilgrimage around China, like the Guang Xiao Temple in Jiang Xi, where he once lived.

There is still a tea plantation there and you can see his cottage and the spring known as the "fourteenth best spring under heaven." But the best way to practice devotion to Lu Yu is to sip a cup of tea.

The oriental tea trade in the West has really developed over the last few decades. At first, Chinese teas were sold as luxury items or alongside herbal medicines in traditional medicine shops. Today, a wide variety of Chinese teas are available at reasonable prices, including at least four of the six major varieties and herbal leaves. Many new merchants based in Europe or America offer tea grown in China, but served in their own tearooms or offered through convenient online delivery services. You can also purchase teaware online—everything from pots, to trays, to strainers.

The essence of Chinese tea-drinking is enjoying the scent of the tea leaves, appreciating their beauty and the beauty of the infused liquid, savoring the taste of the tea, and letting it transport you to a state of mind that is calm, clear, at one with nature, and at peace with yourself. So take a contemplative moment out of your busy day to replenish your spirit. The motions of making the tea will help transport you, just as music or a plant or flower might do, whether you prepare a simple cup or opt to perform a full ceremony. Tea helps you focus your mind during scholarly pursuits or business meetings. Catch up with friends over a cup of tea and let it fuel the conversation. Whenever you perform any of these acts, you are summoning the spirit of the tea sage, epitomized by this poem he wrote:

> I envy not vessels of jade,
> I envy not piles of gold.
> I envy not the Court, nor Office.
> I envy ten thousand folds the Xi Jiang water that flows past Jing Ling.

Lu Yu would not have approved of tea bags, however. To increase the chance of a successful manifestation, please avoid using this modern "convenience."

The Eight Immortals crossing the sea (anonymous, Ming Dynasty c. 14th-15th centuries).
Clockwise in the boat starting from the stern: He Xian Gu, Han Xiang Zi, Lan Cai He,
Tie Guai Li, Lü Dong Bin, Han Zhong Li, Cao Guo Jiu and outside the boat is Zhang Guo Lao.
(from Myths and Legends of China, 1922, by E. T. C. Werner.)

Chapter 14

The Eight Immortals

Ba Xian (八仙), the Eight Immortals, are by far the most famous and popular group of Chinese gods, both domestically and around the world. They are best known as Tie Guai Li, Han Zhong Li, Zhang Guo Lao, He Xian Gu, Lan Cai He, Lü Dong Bin, Han Xiang Zi, and Cao Guo Jiu. These important gods were all supposedly real living people who became Immortals. They lived among the people and their deeds were closely linked to the human world. Because of this, they have become a Daoist vehicle for demonstrating to the laity that they, too, have a chance at immortal life.

The stories of these Immortals are a mixture of folklore, myth, and religion that have won over the populace through the ages. In China, they hold high enough status to have whole films and TV series dedicated to them. Since the 1970s, their stories have been retold at least once every decade, starting with film and gravitating toward television more recently. The Eight Immortals are also a favorite subject in Chinese folk arts like embroidery and pottery.

TIE GUAI LI, IRON CRUTCH LI

铁拐李

The first of the Eight Immortals is Tie Guai Li, also known as Iron Crutch Li, who is often depicted as a dirty, disheveled cripple begging for alms on the streets. Legend claims that he once lived as a very handsome Daoist scholar named Li Xuan whose appearance was in every way pleasing to the eye. One day, Li thought it was time to separate his soul from his body so it could roam the skies and meet with the great Lao Zi. So he instructed his disciples to cremate his body if his soul did not return in seven days. When seven days had passed with no news from their master, the disciples obediently carried out his command.

Later, Li Xuan's soul returned to find its body gone. So it wandered the forest in search of a new one. It found a dead man and attached itself to his body, but Li soon found that he was limping. He swallowed an elixir he received from Lao Zi, which, despite his now ugly appearance and crippled state, made him immortal.

The man whose body Li Xuan found lived in a village in the Zhen Dang Mountains during the Zhou Dynasty (1046–256 BCE)—a village that was exceptionally poor and plagued by natural disasters. Because of this, it gained a reputation as "the beggars' village." Here, there lived a beggar named Cripple Zhang whose whole family had died of starvation, leaving him behind. Cripple Zhang, who was always seen carrying his crutch and water gourd, was a kind and honorable man. No matter how scarce the food and drink in the village became, he always shared his with other beggars. This gained him the nickname of the Beggar King. But even his strong constitution and sturdy frame eventually gave way to hunger, and he breathed his last while looking for wild vegetables. The soul of an enlightened scholar like Li Xuan finding and inhabiting the body of an honorable dead beggar was too much of a coincidence for the gods to ignore, and Li's deification seemed inevitable—although there is no indication that the story of Zhang preceded that of Li.

Another version of Li Xuan's deification tells of a squire who lived at the foot of the Lao Shan Mountains. At the age of fifty, the squire's earnest prayers to Kuan Yin for a son were answered. He named the child Li Xuan (Xuan meaning "mysterious"). Fifteen years later, on a visit to the temple, Kuan Yin recognized the boy as an attendant she had exiled to earth for punishment of a misdeed and decided it was time to recall him. So Li Xuan slipped, fell into a ravine, and died. His soul was guided to heaven. Centuries passed as Li Xuan served Kuan Yin, but he never forgot his time on earth. As his mistress attended Xi Wang Mu's Heavenly Banquet, Li Xuan snuck back to earth. Though his family home was long gone, somehow he could not bring himself to leave. So he found a dead beggar at a derelict temple and inhabited his body so he could remain in the living world.

Unlike many deities whose stories culminate in their ascension, Li Xuan was much enamored of the human world and returned to it with special powers and clarity of vision to do good. Also unlike many mythical deities who start off rather malformed and become more comely as they evolve, Tie Guai Li's path is precisely the reverse. What he lost in external beauty and grace, however, he gained in wisdom and power. He is the embodiment of Lao Zi's doctrine that appearance has no influence over the cultivation of the Dao. The message to the populace was loud and clear. Those who are not gifted with good looks and physical abilities suffer no handicap when it comes to attaining immortality, as long as they have faith.

Stories of Tie Guai Li's powers as a healer—and of him testing and rewarding good deeds—were widespread during the late Ming period. He is never seen without his medicine gourd. One story tells of two doctors named Cai and Gao who worked tirelessly to heal the poor, never once accepting payment. By the roadside, they came across an old man with a badly injured leg and proceeded to help him, despite his incessant curses and discourtesy. After they dressed the wound, the old man stood up and moved as if his leg were totally fine. As he walked away, he told the doctors that he couldn't pay them money, but that, in 300 years' time, their grandchildren would be landed and wealthy.

Another story tells of a traveling doctor who specialized in healing minor external wounds with herbal poultices. Undeterred by the complicated preparations required of different herbs and the cloth required for the poultice, he treated the rich and poor without ever taking a penny from the latter. Tie Guai Li visited him anonymously to test him, claiming that his leg was badly hurt and that he had no money. When Li asked to be treated, the doctor did so, but, on the second day, his leg seemed to get worse. The doctor felt guilty and brought his patient home to feed him some nourishing meat soup. The old man took some animal flesh that was still hot from cooking and smeared some of the doctor's medicine on it, then plastered it over his wound—the deity's famous "animal-skin poultice." When the worried doctor rushed to remove the skin, the wound was healed. He was too shocked to notice that the old man disappeared into thin air.

It is clear that sincerity of heart is important in the veneration of Tie Guai Li. He is a beacon of hope for the disabled and those misjudged due to their appearance. This deity teaches that you must know that you have worth and that your beauty lies within.

The temple to visit for Tie Guai Li is Yao Wang Miao, Temple of the Medicine King, in He Fei. Built during the Yuan era and rebuilt during the Ming period, it is the largest temple dedicated to the deity in the country. The Eight Immortals also have a massive following in Southeast Asian countries like Malaysia, where elaborate street processions are held on Li's feast day, and also in Taiwan, where you'll find many temples to him, the greatest of which is Xian Gong Temple in Tai Nan. Li can often be found on the rooftops of temples carrying his iron crutch and gourd, and leaning against his medicine stove.

Tie Guai Li's contemporary presence extends to the stage in works like *The Immortal of Penglai*, a recent Gei Zai Xi musical, a form of traditional theater that originated in Fu Jian and spread to Taiwan. Because of Li Xuan's famously handsome looks as a man and his famously hideous form as an Immortal, he is sometimes played by two actors, the former often being a woman.

You can collect Tie Guai Li as a puppet in the 2013 set by the Samadhi Tang Creative Puppet Group, an organization that creates props for Bu Dai Xi, a form of puppetry that originated in 17th-century Fu Jian and Guang Dong and has now been revived in Taiwan. Bu Dai Xi, which means "cloth bag theater," tells its stories using glove puppets that are made of cloth attached to sculpted wooden heads and hands. These extremely detailed lifelike designs are great items to collect. Convenient stage costumes of Tie Guai Li can be found online, and are also suitable for cosplay.

HAN ZHONG LI, THE MAD DAOIST
汉钟离

Some believe that Han Zhong Li, not Iron Crutch Li, was the first of the Eight Immortals. This god's name was originally Zhong Li Quan. Legends of him as the scion of a Han Dynasty warrior family are told in collections like *Deities Through the Ages*, which include mystical accounts of his birth. In these stories, his birth chamber was submerged in celestial mists and a giant appeared to proclaim that a great god was about to be born. The god made his entrance into the world as a three-year-old with striking features. He did not cry and seemed to have a sense of justice straight away. So his father named him Zhong Li Quan, "quan" being a word for the weights used on a set of balance scales.

Zhong Li Quan grew up to be tall, strong, handsome, and intelligent, and eventually became the Master of Debates at court. He was sent to quell the rebellion of the Turfan people. His rival, Liang Ji, prevented him from succeeding by assigning him a troop of 20,000 weak and old soldiers. His army was defeated and, during its retreat, Zhong got lost in the mountains. He ran into a beggar monk who led him to the great celestial Wang Xuan Pu, a leading founder of Daoism, who taught him a rare sword technique and the secrets of immortality. Another celestial, Hua Yang Zhen Ren, trained him in yet more techniques and taught him recipes for elixirs. Eventually, Zhong was granted a post by the Jade Emperor.

Zhong Li Quan became known in history as Han Zhong Li. The first syllable of his name came from generations of misinterpretation of his famous words upon becoming a Daoist master. His phrase of self-mockery which, correctly punctuated, meant "Zhong Li, the idlest man under heaven" was misread as the more laudatory but incorrect "all under heaven shall know the name of Han Zhong Li." This is probably one of the most famous cases of grammatical error in Chinese history.

Han Zhong Li does indeed seem to pass into history as a beacon for the failed, the idle, and the unrestrained, representing quite an unconventional way of life. Another legend of his life has him appointed the General of the Borders during the Wei and Jin eras (386–535 CE and 265–420 CE respectively). But here again he lost in battle. During the Tang period, he was romanticized in poetry as the drunken, dissolute Mad Daoist. To this day, he is considered the second founder of Daoism, preceding his fellow Immortal Lü Dong Bin, who is in third place. Perhaps this deity is a way in which Daoism reaches out to hearten those who encounter repeated failures in life, or provides representation for the few and far between who prefer to indulge and enjoy rather than prosper and succeed. This deity certainly illustrates that even an Immortal can be very human.

Han Zhong Li's traditional representation makes for an unlikely warrior. He is portrayed as a very fat deity with his hair trussed up into two buns, which emphasizes his enormous eyes, bright red face, and great curling beard. Baring his upper body to expose an enormous belly, he carries a palm-leaf fan and sometimes rides a Qi Lin (a portentous mythical beast). In modern pop culture, his appearance falls into two broad categories that signify the duality of his deified persona— a cute version of his traditional fat form and a fiercer version of a slender warrior. His representation by Pi Li Bu Dai Xi, a form of theater made for television begun in the 1980s by the Taiwanese media group Pi Li, is an example of the latter, but nevertheless retains a remarkable similarlity to the original deity's striking appearance.

Tales of Han Zhong Li slaying monsters have appeared in many children's books and Xiao Ren Shu (traditional Chinese comics). He also appears alongside his seven fellow Immortals in computer games like The Way of Dao, including one that portrays him as a demon of the sea. His image has found its way onto lottery artwork and embroidery patterns as well. His dramatic depictions include the 2013 TV series The Swordsman and the 2009 series Legend of the Ba Xian, in which he dons a beret and a mustard-colored tunic reminiscent of Sandy, the pig spirit in the Toho series *Monkey*.

You are likely to find sculptures of Han Zhong Li among the Eight Immortals in temples across the country, and at old mansions featuring folk or regional architectural elements, like the rooftops of the Chen Clan Ancestral Temple in Guang Zhou. Collectors may want to check out the exquisite Eight Immortals series created by Samadhitang Creative. And if you are into cosplay, you can order costumes online from sellers in China. A traditional Han Zhong Li cosplay offers opportunities for diverse body shapes.

Zhang Guo Lao, Immortal Trickster

张果老

Zhang Guo Lao is one of the most colorful characters among the Eight Immortals. It is widely accepted that he may have been a highly skillful con artist who promoted his so-called powers for his own benefit, but stories about him illustrate the power of the popular imagination and are still much loved today.

Anecdotes of Zhang Guo Lao were recorded in historical texts of the Tang and Ming Dynasties. There was a real Daoist monk who lived during the Tang period who was named Zhang Guo. He claimed to have mastered the secret of immortality and served under King Rao, meaning that he was at least 3,000 years old. The character for Lao (meaning "senior" in this context) was added to his title as a term of respect and in recognition of how old he claimed to be. Ming novels depict Zhang as a hermit in the Zhong Tiao mountains in Shan Xi, where he met Immortals like Tie Guai Li who showed him the way. Riding a donkey backward, he traveled hundreds of thousands of miles each day. At the end of his journey, he flattened his donkey, folded it up like paper, and put it in his pocket. When he was ready to travel again, he simply unfolded the donkey and animated it with a splash of water, then went on his way.

Many Tang emperors wanted Zhang Guo as part of their royal court, but their emissaries invariably had their invitations declined or were tricked into turning back without completing their mission. It took four emperors and an emissary who, unlike the others, showed him respect despite Zhang's apparent lack of teeth and withered hair to accomplish this feat. When Zhang arrived at the palace, the emperor Xuan Zong remarked on his decrepitude, whereupon Zhang proceeded to pull out what little hair was left on his head, along with the remainder of his teeth. These bloody acts caused great alarm. The emperor hastened to assure Zhang that he believed in his powers. Zhang turned away and swayed his body a few times. When he turned back, his hair was jet black and his teeth gleaming.

Zhang Guo Lao went hunting with the emperor, and they caught a deer. The deer was about to be slaughtered when Zhang revealed that the animal was, in fact, the 852-year-old celestial deer that had been released by the emperor Wu Di of the Han Dynasty. He knew this because the emperor had tied a coin on the deer's left antler. Xuan Zong ordered his servant to check and indeed found a Han coin tied where Zhang had said it would be.

Even great fortune-tellers could not tell Zhang's fortune. Although Xuan Zong and his court were immensely impressed and revered him highly, Zhang stuck with his eccentric ways, declining the daughter offered to him as bride by the emperor himself. Intrigued, the emperor asked the Daoist master Ye Jing Neng about him. Ye confessed that he was terrified to share what he knew. Once given the emperor's absolute guarantee of his safety, he revealed that Zhang was a white-bat spirit from the beginning of time! As soon as Ye mouthed these words, blood spewed from all seven orifices of his head, and he fell over dead. When confronted, Zhang explained that he just couldn't stand a loudmouth. After the emperor repeatedly begged him to revive Ye, Zhang spat on his face and he returned to life.

As with the other great moments of his legendary life, Zhang Guo Lao went out in style. Toward the end of his life, he requested permission to return to the mountains, and the emperor dispatched an entourage of several hundred messengers laden with gifts to accompany him. On the way, the great master collapsed and passed away. He was buried by his disciples, but they later discovered his coffin to be empty. His body had undergone the Jie Shi (解尸), a Daoist term for a process whereby the body of someone about to become immortal dissolves into thin air. After hearing this, Xuan Zong ordered the construction of Xi Xia Temple, which was dedicated to Zhang.

Leading a life of celibacy, Zhang Guo Lao traveled the country riding his donkey backward and helping those in need. He also converted them to Daoism using the Yu Gu, a folk instrument consisting of a narrow bamboo cylinder with a drum on one end and a pair of long bamboo clappers on the other. This is why, traditionally, Zhang is always seen riding his donkey backward, with his Yu Gu slung over his back. You can find tutorials on how to play this instrument on YouTube and download Yu Gu scores from the Internet. Sometimes Zhang resorted to Dao Qing Opera, an art form enjoyed across China, particularly in Shan Bei, Si Chuan, Hu Bei, and Zhe Jiang. This traditional form has recently been adapted to pop music by numerous TV programs.

Zhang Guo Lao's contemporary image has remained largely the same as his traditional persona. Because he is immortal and indestructible, he is a very powerful character to have available to you in computer games. He is also still very much a part of everyday life. He was said to have been a keen gardener and a great cook during his human life. If you visit the mountains named after him in Xing Tai, He Bei, Zhang Guo's hometown, try the chive buns and dumplings made there, or some of the other dishes named after him—pancake wraps (a pun on his name), donkey buns, and donkey meat bakes. And be sure to visit the caves and the temple. One Chinese bicycle company is now producing the ninth model of its Zhang Guo Lao series, the first of which was a bike with two sets of handlebars and two seats, so that you can ride it either frontward or backward.

Zhang Guo Lao is a perfect demonstration of the rambunctious nature of the Eight Immortals. Although it is common knowledge that he may have been a trickster, Chinese devotees can not resist a deity who stood up to social hypocrisy; dared to defy fortune-tellers; religious leaders, and even emperors; and lived on his own terms.

LÜ DONG BIN,
CELESTIAL SWORDSMAN
吕洞宾

The most influential of the Eight Immortals is Lü Dong Bin, who has the most temples, ancestral halls, and pagodas dedicated to him alone across the country, in addition to those that commemorate all eight as a group.

An abundance of versions of Lü Dong Bin's origins have been explored in a mixture of Daoist texts, regional histories, novels, poems, and biographies. These all claim that a man named Lü Yan was born during the Tang Dynasty and later adopted the name of Dong Bin. His family fled from political persecution and went into hiding in the mountains. Lü was a scholar and well educated from birth. Some say that he passed the Jin Shi exams before becoming an Immortal; many say that he persisted for twenty years, without success. It was on his way to a round of these exams at the age of forty (some say sixty) that he met Han Zhong Li, the leader of the Ba Xian, and became an Immortal under his guidance.

Fictional and stage dramatizations of Lü Dong Bin's encounter with Han, some by well-known writers like Ma Zhi Yuan, enjoyed great popularity during the Song Dynasty, leading to even more works about him during the Yuan and Ming eras. One famous episode is the *Yellow Millet Dream*. Upon meeting Han Zhong Li, whom he took for a Daoist priest, Lü was impressed with his remarkable appearance and poetic prowess. The two drank to their hearts' content at an inn in the capital and engaged in some poetic repartee. As Han cooked yellow millet on a small stove, Lü fell asleep. He dreamed of passing the imperial exams, of gaining riches and success, and then of his own eventual downfall. When he woke, Han pointed out to him that his spirit was still worldly and was not yet ready for the celestial world. He told him he would have to undergo further trials to become an Immortal.

Daoist canon intervened at this point in the story and created the famous ten trials, which could really only have been endured by someone with a religious degree of indifference to worldly affairs. These ten trials caused Lü to lose his family, his wealth, and his life to demons

Lu Dong Bin, Celestial Swordsman, from Gudai yijia huaxiang,
created by Lin Zhong (*Qing period, 1644-1911*)

and natural disasters; tempted him with greed, avarice, and desires of
the flesh; and challenged the genuineness of his bravery, kindness, and
honor. Lü faced them all with equanimity, constancy, and acceptance.
Satisfied, Han Zhong Li taught him the secret art of procuring the elixir
of immortality. Lü also gained a pair of Yin Yang swords and learned
inner alchemy and the Dun Tian (Heaven Concealing) Sword Technique.
When stories spread across the country of Lü helping the disadvantaged,
fighting tyrants, slaying tigers, taming snakes, and subduing flood dragons, he was granted the title of Jian Xian (Celestial Swordsman).

Lü Dong Bin's legendary drunkenness also earned him the title of Jiu Xian (Drunken Celestial). It is said that he travels on the backs of cranes and that wine is his only sustenance. The novel *Legend of the Eight Immortals* (*Dong You Ji*) by Ming novelist Wu Yuan Tai tells the story of Lü helping a poor old lady to attain great riches by sprinkling some rice into her well and turning water into wine. You can also venerate this deity by reading his poems, seventy-nine of which are published in *Complete Tang Poems*.

There used to be temples dedicated to Lü Dong Bin in every major city. Today, the best one to visit—and perhaps the most magnificent—is Yong Le Temple in Rui Cheng, Shaan Xi, birthplace of the deity. This temple, also famous for its murals, was constructed during the Yuan Dynasty. The palatial buildings and murals, which span 1,000 square meters, took 110 years to complete and are one of China's most treasured large-scale artworks. They depict over 290 personages, with an entire room of fifty-two pieces telling the legend of Lü from birth to immortality.

Most of these murals are accompanied by a cartouche that tells the story of Lü from man to Immortal. A lot of the text on these cards comes from Daoist canon. The differences between what is drawn from the texts and what is drawn on the walls by artisans who were more influenced by the pop culture of the time show an interesting contrast between Lü's Daoist image as the master of inner alchemy and his popular image as an attractive and powerful exorcist, healer, and wonderworker. Neither the texts nor the paintings deemed it proper to feature Lü's alleged romantic and sexual encounters with prostitutes, an aspect that has been picked up and explored in modern interpretations like the 1984 comic strip in a popular Shaan Xi literary journal.

Because Lü Dong Bin is skilled in the art of making elixirs, he is also a good deity for devotees seeking cures for themselves or for loved ones. You can also visit other sites in Shaan Xi, like the Jin Temple, where you can cast divination sticks from six separate holders, choosing the one you will use according to the type of illness you are seeking to cure. To increase your chances of success, you can bring home a bag of Sheng Hui (sacred ashes) from the incense burned at the temple.

Lü Dong Bin's origins have always been shrouded in mysticism. It was said that his mother was impregnated by a celestial and that he was born more than eight feet tall with tortoise patterns on his feet. He was described as a tiger, with dragon jaws, phoenix eyes, and eyebrows so long that they merged with his hair. According to one collection of stories about the gods, he was born at the precise time when all the dates associated with his birth were filled with Yang energy—hence his Daoist title of Chun Yang (Pure Yang).

What has been passed down to posterity is a mixture of representations of Lü Dong Bin by the Quan Zhen school of Daoism, and through folklore. Canonical representations have Lü disguising himself as an ugly and filthy beggar. But his popular image as a celestial-looking, very comely Daoist priest is the one that has survived in contemporary artwork. It is not surprising that his sword has gained prominence in computer games, where it is often depicted as bigger than the deity himself. In one of these, he uses five swords at once.

Although Daoism gifted the Immortals with their godly status, outside the temples and scripture, it was popular belief that influenced the plays and operas that depicted them. Lü is likely the most conventional and least rambunctious of the Eight Immortals and perhaps the most accomplished of the group. He achieved great heights, both as a warrior defender of the people and as a deity of intellectual genius who was also blessed with a very impressive appearance. However, a lot of Lü's appeal lies in his fallibility. In his human life, he was a scholar who failed to succeed in the world for most of his career, and who came to realize the emptiness of the dreams he had been chasing. So he let them go and thereby gained more power than he had ever imagined.

HE XIAN GU, CELESTIAL HEALER

何仙姑

Despite being the only female Immortal, He Xian Gu's following far outstrips some of her male counterparts. She is likely to have originated as a real woman who lived during the Tang Dynasty. The two prevalent versions of this goddess are He Qiong, from Yong Zhou in Hu Nan, and He Xiu Gu, daughter of a Dou Fu maker (bean curd, more popularly known as tofu) from Zeng Cheng in Guang Dong. At the time of her birth, an auspicious purple mist surrounded the He family hut, and cranes flew around it. As a child, He Xian Gu loved to play among the luscious mountains and crystalline rivers of her homeland, which was rich in minerals and vegetation. It was on such an occasion when she was around fourteen that she ran into an old man. In exchange for some of her knowledge about the local terrain, the old man presented her with a Pan Tao, the celestial peach grown by Xi Wang Mu that grants those who eat it thousands of years of life. Then the man vanished into the clouds. He Xian Gu ate the peach and began to feel her energy and vitality growing daily. In fact, she no longer needed food. Many versions of this story identify the old man as Lü Dong Bin, another key figure in the Eight Immortals.

Lü returned to teach He the secrets of gathering natural ingredients—particularly minerals and making them into medicine.[27] He Xian Gu went gathering every day and learned to distinguish different plants and herbs and their properties, producing remedies to cure the local inhabitants of their ailments. Those who saw her in the mountains with her basket said that her movements were as light as a swallow's, almost resembling flight. Even before she formally entered the Daoist pantheon, He Xian Gu had already gained the title of Xian Gu, the Daoist term for a female Immortal who remains on earth to help the living. Her abilities as a witch healer are by far the most enduring of her powers, and have survived until today. The local people built a stone bungalow for her to live in, which is now part of the temple in Zeng Cheng. When she died, her body dissolved into the air. Her spirit cast off its corporeal form and she became an Immortal.

Variations on He Xian Gu's origins give different locations for her birthplace, and different versions of who granted her her powers and what she consumed to gain them—an elixir, a peach, a mineral? In addition to Yong Zhou and Zeng Cheng, Fu Jian, Zhe Jiang, An Hui, and Guang Xi are all given as possibilities for her hometown, and each of these places has its own version of the goddess's story. She has a huge

He Xian Gu, Celestial Healer, by Zhang Lu (1464–1538)

following in South China. An alternative version of the myth claims that Xi Wang Mu herself manifested before her and granted her the Pan Tao, or perhaps a celestial date.

He Xian Gu's function as a deity is threefold. As a Daoist nun, she once taught Daoist wisdom to state leaders like Wu Ze Tian (624–705), a Tang Dynasty empress who remains the only female ruler in imperial Chinese history. She taught Wu to be free of earthly desires, to give up the pursuit of fame and fortune, and to perform acts of benevolence. Wu also sought her aid as a shamaness, as have others in history. In his youth, the great Song general Di Qing was worried about his southern military campaign. As he passed the hometown of He Xian Gu, he heard that she could divine the future. Though not convinced, he still made inquiries and was told that he had nothing to fear. Later, the Song fought the army of Zhi Gao, which fled in defeat. The law courts of Song are said to have engaged He Xian Gu's foresight to expose several cases of corruption.

For contemporary devotees of He Xian Gu, there are two important dates to note—the seventh day of the third lunar month, her birthday, and the eighth day of the eighth lunar month, when she became an Immortal. Both of these are great days to visit her temples for festivities, which are attended by thousands. She is honored through formal Daoist ceremonies, as well as by theatrical perfomances that fictionalize her life and deeds. The ultimate place for pilgrimage is the Ming Dynasty temple in Zeng Cheng, Guang Dong, with its exquisite sculptural Ling Nan architecture that reflects the art and culture of the region. There you will find the bungalow where He Xian Gu is said to have lived, her ancestral hall, and the temple itself. A peach tree grows miraculously between the roof tiles of one of the buildings. If you're an invalid, or have a sick friend or relative, be sure to visit the 1,000-year-old well within the temple grounds.

He Xian Gu was a woman of unusual beauty who led a revolutionary life, devoting herself solely to her medicinal practices. Fed up with the nagging of her family and the ceaseless pursuit of suitors, legend says that she leaped into a well to free herself from her earthly form. Another version of the legend says that one of her embroidered shoes fell into the well as she was summoned to the skies by her fellow Immortals. The water from this well is said have healing properties. The thought of drinking corpse marinade or shoe water doesn't particularly appeal, but devotion and faith are not such without some testing. You'll be glad to know that while the local water has a slightly salty taste, the water from the well is said to taste clear and sweet.

Today, He Xian Gu also enjoys substantial popularity in other Southeast Asian countries like Singapore, where you can visit Xian Gu Dian, and Malaysia, where a variety of temples are available, among them the Taiping He Xian Gu Temple, the Ipoh Menglembu He Xian Gu Temple, and the Ho See Koo Miao Temple.

He Xian Gu is a powerful goddess even today, her tale propagated by countless period drama films and TV series, both live action and animated. In traditional art, she is more often portrayed as a beautiful, ethereal young maiden in flowing robes who floats among the clouds. Less often, she is portrayed as a portly matron. She carries a branch of lotus flower, which seems to have little to do with her characteristics other than as a homonym for her surname and the plant's association with Chinese spirituality. He Xian Gu is best known in the West through Japan's Capcom, which presents her as Hsien-Ko or Lei Lei, most famously in

Night Warriors: Darkstalker's Revenge (1995), a fighting game with an element of gothic horror. Here, Lei Lei is doomed to roam the earth with her twin sister hunting Darkstalkers in order to free their mother's soul. She has the special power to turn into a powerful Jiang Shi (僵尸, literally "stiff corpse"), a hopping Chinese zombie that is popularly mistaken for a vampire. Her iconic image in this form—in feminized Qing official uniform dress—is heavily influenced by Hong Kong horror movies of the 1980s. Apart from her Chinese origin, her name, and her use of Bonsai as a weapon, this version has little to do with the Chinese deity. Nevertheless, it was one of the early introductions of the deity into computer games and global pop culture.

Contemporary worship of this Immortal takes place at different kinds of temples and altars. And if China is too far for you to travel, you can play as He Xian Gu in hundreds of Chinese online and mobile computer games that are actually set in the proper Daoist fantasy world. She appears as a mature lady in red with a lotus-inspired dress in Legend of the Eight Immortals, an MMORPG (Massive Multi-player Online Role-Playing Game) developed by Hong Yang that combines exciting boss fights—battles with a significant computer-controlled enemy—with visual novel elements. She is a coy young water maiden wearing a traditionally inspired blue bikini in Leiting's The Search For Dao (Wen Dao), a turn-based strategy game where players take turns. In another, she is a staff-wielding plant magus. As a wizard type, her healing abilities and powers of foresight are sure to stand you in good stead. And if you have a penchant for slapstick comedy games, you can play as the wide-eyed flower sprite in Sohu's Legends of the Eastern Seas, a Meng-style game.[28] Playing some of these games may involve a certain knowledge of Chinese.

A very simple way in which to worship He Xian Gu is to make offerings of lychees to her on her festival dates—the seventh day of the third lunar month and the eighth day of the eighth lunar month. It is important to consume your offerings in order to complete your veneration and ensure its efficacy. Lychees are a tropical speciality of Guang Dong province, and Zeng Cheng produces the rare Gua Lü (literally, "hanging green") variety, which has a slim thread of green running all around the crimson skin of the fruit. Legend says that, during a gathering of Immortals in the celestial world, He Xian Gu once decorated some lychees with a green ribbon. The Gua Lü are very rare and very expensive, so if you happen to find one in a bunch you purchase, it is considered exceptionally lucky!

LAN CAI HE, IMMORTAL SONGSTER

蓝采和

Another of the more graceful of the Eight Immortals is Lan Cai He, a mysterious vagrant who captivated people with his music and charisma, and his kindness to the poor. Lan Cai He seems to exist only in legend, and his origins and history are as elusive as his whereabouts.

Sequel to Biographies of Immortals (*Xu Xian Zhuan*), written by Shen Fen during the Song Dynasty, gave this Immortal his definitive eccentric image. Dressed in a tattered blue gown with a black waistband, he wears a boot on one foot, but his other is bare. In the summer, he wears a cotton-padded gown; in the winter, he sleeps on ice, his breath rising in puffs of steam. In these depictions, whenever he busked on the streets, he struck his three-inch clappers and beat his foot to the music. When he sang, he was always drunk. Wherever he went, people followed him and asked him questions, because, when he answered, he impressed them and made them laugh with his replies. When given money, he hung the coins on a string and pulled it along. He either gave his money to the poor, or spent it on drink. When old people saw him, he seemed to look exactly as he had when they were children.

Lan Cai He's transformation into an Immortal was rather abrupt. One day, he was drinking at an inn when a flock of cranes descended from the sky and celestial music sounded in the air. Lan Cai He simply threw down his clappers, climbed onto a crane, and ascended to the heavens.

Lan Cai He had a big repertoire of songs with mainly philosophical lyrics that encouraged his listeners to think. His most famous was the Ta Ge, or Thumping Song, featured in *The Book of Nan Tang* by Song poet Lu

You (1125–1210 CE) and in *Legend of the Eight Immortals (Dong You Ji)* by Ming novelist Wu Yuan Tai. The song was supposedly written by a hermit called Chen Tao, which the poet Lu believed was Lan Cai He's true identity. Others suggest that Lan Cai He was a pseudonym for Xu Jian, a musician who was brutally beaten after he offended an official. Xu Jian gave up worldly affairs, became a wanderer, and ultimately an Immortal after running into Han Zhong Li. He acquired the name of Lan (meaning blue) because of his blue robes.

Lan Cai He's popularity stems from a combination of mysterious earthly presence, eccentric deportment, and utter indifference to the world while still remaining exceptionally sociable and unpretentious with the people. A very interesting aspect of this deity is his gender fluidity. In fact, it has never been entirely clear whether Lan Cai He is male or female. In male form, he is the most effeminate of the male Immortals. Some Ming and Qing plays, on the other hand, have portrayed this deity as an Immortal maiden, while yet others have depicted a male character in female clothes. Some legends even go as far as to say that the deity was born without any sexual organs.

This gender ambiguity has carried over into his modern incarnations. In most dramatic representations today, Lan Cai He is played by a female actress. However, the gender roles are not clear-cut opposites. The *School of Immortals* film series put a male actor, playing a male character, in female clothes. The 2013 TV series *Complete Legend of the Immortals (Ba Xian Quan Zhuan)* casts Lan Cai He as a male actor in male clothes, but gives that actor the direction to act androgynously. In another series, the deity is played by a woman in female clothes, who nevertheless acts like a man. It is evident that Lan Cai He is a suitable patron for transgender devotees and those interested in cross-dressing and gender fluidity. A popular cosplay of the deity comes from *Guo: Ba Xian*, a series of fantasy novels by Cang Kui. This version retains the deity's original association with blue by portraying him in an embroidered blue gown with wide sleeves and bright blue hair. You can buy the entire costume online.

Han Xiang Zi, Green-Fingered God of Gardening

韩湘子

The Eight Immortals have enjoyed astonishing popularity through the ages. It seems as if people take to them for their earthiness and closeness to the affairs of the human world. Some say the Immortals were created as examples for people so that they too can acquire the way of Dao and become immortal. On closer examination, however, we find that the Eight are actually a group of misfits and eccentrics, more so than any of the other deities in China. Consider, for instance, Tie Guai Li, the acerbic and mal-formed healer, He Xian Gu, the female herbalist who shunned matrimony, and Han Zhong Li, the fat warrior with a bizarre fashion sense. But it is in this very eccentricity that the root of their popularity lies.

Another misfit in the group is Han Xiang Zi, whose original name was Han Xiang. He came from a prestigious literary family and was a great-nephew of the great Tang Dynasty writer and minister of the Department of Justice, Han Yu. Han Xiang Zi, however, exhibited no academic talent whatsoever—at least not in the conventional sense. The Tang collection of legends and hearsay known as *You Yang Miscellany* by Duan Cheng Shi tells of how Han, having been informed that he was disruptive in class, was sent by his great uncle to a temple where the monks complained of his refusal to follow routines. Upon being chided for being useless, the youth proclaimed that he did indeed have a talent or two—he could grow peonies in any color under the sun.

Han Xiang covered up the temple's purple peonies and demanded that no one look at them for seven days. At the end of seven days, the covers were removed and, to Han Yu's astonishment, the peonies had transformed into tri-colored blossoms of red, white, and green, with a couplet of poetry written in purple on the petals.

Looking back at Chang'an, overcast, you cannot see your home.
Danger lies ahead, in snow-filled Lan Guan, your horse stands immobile.

Wise as he was, Han Yu could not comprehend the meaning of the couplet. On another occasion, Han Yu was giving a banquet when his great-nephew managed to pour every single guest a cup of wine from one tiny flagon, and instantaneously grew a tree from a pot of soil by spraying water into it with his mouth.

Han Xiang's wondrous feats resembled magic, and earned him the name of Han Xiang Zi even before he became an Immortal. Song Dynasty author Liu Fu wrote about Han confounding his exasperated great-uncle with a mixture of poetic prowess and horticultural wizardry. This time, green blossoms appeared in the blink of an eye, with the same mysterious couplet written in gold.

Han Yu later urged the emperor to put a stop to the veneration of fake relics known as Buddha's Bones. The furious emperor exiled him to a post in the remote southernmost regions. On his journey there, he found himself marooned in the snow and it was his great-nephew who came to his aid. At last, Han Yu understood the meaning of the mysterious couplet and its reference to snow-covered Lan Guan, where he was stranded. At his post in the south, Han Yu encountered crocodiles. When the poem he apparently composed to appease the predatory carnivores proved ineffective, his great-nephew again came to his aid and subdued the crocodiles. Nonetheless, Han Yu remained bitter toward Han Xiang and indifferent to his kindness throughout his life.

The deeds of Han Xiang Zi teach us that everyone has a talent or skill, even if it may not be one that is considered valuable by others. We must all use our talents and skills, whatever they may be, to benefit those around us, even if our efforts are not always appreciated.

Ever since the Yuan era, Han Xiang Zi has been written into Chinese literature. These dramatizations often feature a metamorphosis akin to the Immortal's transformational powers. *The Tale of Han Xiang Zi* by Ming novelist Yang Er is set in the earlier time of the Han Dynasty. In the story, the emperor wants the beautiful and talented young daughter of his prime minister, An Fu, as a bride for his nephew. An Fu refuses and is stripped of his post. The daughter, Ling Ling, pines her life away. After her death, her soul transforms into a crane and meets with two other members of the Eight Immortals, Lü Dong Bin and Han Zhong Li. The Immortals guide her reincarnation as the son of Han Hui of Chang Li county. Orphaned at an early age, the boy is purchased by his uncle, Han Yu. As a young man, he is chastised for learning the way of Dao, and runs away to the Zhong Nan Mountains to get away from his harsh uncle. Eventually, he becames Immortal.

Han Xiang Zi is also known as the patron god of musicians. His contemporary guise remains consistent with his traditional image as an elegantly dressed scholar with flowing hair who is always playing a Xiao (bamboo flute). This Xiao was given to him as a gift and was very dear to him, as told in a Chinese version of *The Mermaid's Tale*. On his travels, Han heard that the daughter of the dragon king of the eastern sea was exceptionally musical. So he often went to the shore to play his flute for her. The princess, who was mesmerized by his music, appeared before him as a dancing eel. Eventually, she revealed her true form. Han returned time after time, hoping to see her again, but she never reappeared. Eventually, a fisherwoman told the dejected Han that the princess's father had locked her in a cave at the bottom of the sea and that she had been asked to give Han a Xiao made from the mystical purple bamboo of the southern sea.

Han Xiang Zi was clearly the "heartthrob" among the Eight Immortals. Popular stories tell of a romance between Han Xiang Zi and He Xian Gu—for instance, in the TV series *The Legend and Immortalization of He Xian Gu* (*Xiu Xian Ji Zhi He Xian Gu Zhuan*). As a scholarly character, Han displays an interesting duality, being at once genteel and carefree. He has appeared in various screen productions from the 1970s on, as well as a range of computer games. Sometimes he is portrayed as an erudite delinquent; sometimes as a well-bred gentleman who embraces freedom, music, and justice; and sometimes as a rather nerdy and painfully sincere scholar. In role-playing games, he is often a good supporting wizard type to have when you're battling a big boss.

Cao Guo Jiu, Immortal Statesman

曹国舅

The last to join the Immortals was Cao Guo Jiu—Duke Cao. Relatively little is known about this deity, although there are three generally accepted versions of his origins. He is believed to be Cao Jing Xiu, brother to the wife of Emperor Ren Zong of the Song Dynasty, hence the title by which he is known.

Ming works including *Legend of the Eight Immortals* describe Cao as a naturally quiet and frugal man. Ashamed of the debauchery of his younger brother, he went into hiding in the mountains, fasting and meditating in rags. One day, he met the Immortals Lü Dong Bin and Chun Yang, who showed him the way of the Dao, and he became Immortal.

Other Ming works, like the *Cases of Bao Gong* (a celebrated judge of the time), present a less savory portrait. In them, a scholar named Yuan Sheng travels to the capital with his wife, Zhang, to attend the examinations. Cao's younger brother, Jing Zhi, sees her and covets her for himself. He arranges for Yuan to be strangled and tries to force himself on Zhang. When she refuses, she is locked away. Yuan's spirit informs Judge Bao of his murder, but Cao Jing Xiu hears of this and warns his brother to release Zhang immediately, whereupon the younger Cao pushes Zhang down a well. She is rescued by an Immortal, but runs into the older Cao, who beats her violently and leaves her for dead in an alley. She nevertheless regains consciousness and manages to get to the judge and inform him of the truth. Bao refuses to free the Cao brothers, even at the behest of their royal relatives. Just before their execution, however, the emperor declares a universal pardon for all criminals. Having come so close to death's door, the older Cao sees the error of his ways and goes into the mountains to live a life of abstinence and repentance, eventually meeting Immortals who show him the way.

The third version of the legend identifies the deity as Cao Yi, brother to a different Song empress. The empress was renowned as one of the most intelligent and resourceful women ever to have held this title, single-handedly rescuing her husband from death in an inner palace coup by her wits alone. Her brother was an even-tempered scholar who was talented in many arts, and was a great musician, poet, and archer. Cao Yi became a distinguished politician and lived to the ripe old age of seventy-two, allegedly by adhering to his own way of life. He never discussed politics outside of the imperial court.

Although legend describes Cao Yi as wearing common, rough-hewn hermit's hemps—the attire in which he became Immortal—plays, paintings, and contemporary costumes that appear at temple fairs and banquets tend to dress him in an official's red robes. His character is often shown as a parody and, in theater and opera, he is often portrayed as a clown. His image as comic relief among the Eight Immortals has ensured his longevity in modern society, lending itself to new media like emojis used in chat and communication apps, as well as boxed-lunch designs, animated entertainment, and even thermometer designs. This satiric representation seems to hinge on a plot twist found in the second version of his origin myth where the widow Zhang, escaping near-death, mistakes Cao for Judge Bao. This twist makes a parody of his official role in the figure of justice. In some recent dramatic interpretations, however, Cao seems to have been redeemed as a genuine figure of justice.

Again, we can see Cao Guo Jiu as a deity who deviates from the norm, whether as a ruthless criminal who hardly deserves to be made immortal, or as an eccentric who manages to live among the mainstream population while sticking to his own philosophy. This further demonstrates the Chinese fascination with outcasts or flawed characters who violate the accepted conventions of social behavior. This is one of the factors that make Chinese religion very compatible with the contemporary liberal Western outlook. It confirms that there is a model of behavior and a way to godliness for everyone, not just for good citizens on the straight and narrow path, but for reformed criminals as well.

Chapter 15

Tian Long Ba Bu

天龙八部

Daoism is not the only religion with many different gods in charge of different matters. Buddhism has its own array of gods known as the Tian Long Ba Bu, a large group of demigods who populate the heavens that are separated into eight types.

The Buddhist universe is divided into three realms: the realm of sensuous desire, which includes the human world, the underworlds, and six planes of existence; the realm of form; and the realm of formlessness, which are the heavens. In turn, the heavens are split into twenty-two levels. The Tian Zhong—literally, the "multitude of gods"—are the deities who inhabit these places. They include major gods like Yan Wang and all the heavenly guardians.

All the dragon gods belong to a type called the Long Zhong, literally "multitude of dragon gods." They are in charge of bringing rainfall to the world below, and making sure the land is free from drought. Dragon kings, who are found in both Daoism and Buddhism, have long been a staple element in Chinese pop culture.

Another group called the Yecha, or Yaksha, are the fierce and nimble protector gods who devour ghosts and demons. Some of them are assigned to protect the human world; others live in the heavens. Due to their fierce appearance, their name has often been used to refer to minor demons. The Yaksha are very much alive in the imagination of the modern Chinese, their name and image borrowed by contemporary artists and performers to create new works of fiction and art—for instance, Yaksa, the Sichuanese metal band that formed in 1995, a pioneer of Chinese punk and metal. Their music and lyrics reflect the nature of the Yaksha, ferocious and yet a corrective guardian spirit, rendering a shock to the system that causes listeners to awaken and change things. Other contemporary creators draw from the still darker version of these beings as ghosts that haunt the wilderness and eat waylaid travelers, as seen in science fiction writer Xia Jia's work.

Another group is called the Gan Da Po, or Gandharva, of whom there are 6333. These are the heavenly bards who make music to worship and honor the Buddha. They live on the scent of incense and emit a special fragrance that mesmerizes listeners, adding an illusory and hallucinogenic quality to their music. This is why the Chinese often refer to desert mirages as "Gan Da Po cities." A second group of musicians, the Jin Na Luo, or Kimnara, are human-shaped deities with horned heads. These are great singers as well as dancers. While the Gan Da Po can be likened to pop musicians, the Jin Na Luo are court musicians who specifically compose Buddhist music.

There are a few quite impressive individual demigods among the Tian Long Ba Bu as well. The rather grotesque-looking Ah Xiu Luo, or Asura, is an evil spirit from Indian mythology who entered the Chinese Buddhist pantheon as a guardian deity. This being makes frequent appearances in Asian pop culture, portrayed in comics and other literary forms. Jia Lu Luo, or Garuda, is a golden-winged Peng, a large mythical Chinese bird with a wingspan of millions of miles. Surviving on a diet of snakes, this bird is regarded as a protector of crops and a guardian against pests. It appears as one of three demon kings encountered by the pilgrims at Lion Camel Ridge in *Journey to the West*, a novel that shows major influences from both Buddhism and Daoism. The Peng lures in

The golden-winged Peng

victims with its Yin Yang Flask and then takes their essence, leaving a bloody pulp behind. This demon is so powerful that it took the Buddha himself to subdue it. Another of these demigods is the Mo Ho Jia Luo, or Moharaga, a python, also known as the earth dragon to differentiate it from its counterpart, the sky dragon.

If you mention Tian Long Ba Bu to the Chinese, a considerable number will think of the great Jin Yong's Wuxia novel series of the same name. Although this work has nothing to do with these demigods, it dramatizes the tensions between societies under different rulers in northern and western China during the time of emperor Zhe Zong of the Song, and makes evident the author's intent to portray all manner of men, monsters, eccentrics, and outlaws in that universe.

A 19th century engraving of the dragon Long (artist unknown)

Chapter 16

Dragons Everywhere

What book on Chinese deities would be complete without a chapter on dragons? Some European nations have a tradition of fire-breathing dragons, like the blue dragon of Wales. Some other Asian countries also feature dragons in their myths. But rarely has a nation been so closely associated with a creature as China has been with the dragon.

The dragon is known and recognized around the world as the totem of China. In fact, the Chinese consider themselves to be Long De Chuan Ren, descendants of the dragon. Images of the Chinese dragon adorn Chinese life—from books to films and artwork, from clothing design to furniture, from housewares to tattoos. If you want to make something look exotic, put a dragon on it. It's not a good fantasy story unless it has a dragon in it. The dragon saves the day. Unwittingly or not, we all venerate the dragon. But what is there about the Chinese dragon that makes it unique?

The Chinese dragon, Long (龙), is a creature unlike any other. It possesses the features of nine animals—nine (九) being the most powerful number in Chinese tradition and a homonym for long-lasting (久). Long has the head of a camel, the horns of a stag, the ears of a bull, the eyes of a rabbit, the neck of a snake, the body of a sea monster, the scales of a carp, the paws of a tiger, and the claws of an eagle. Dragons were sacred to the ancient Chinese, their use forbidden to all under heaven except the emperor. Even on official attire adorned with figures that resembled dragons, the creature had only four claws instead of five and so these were technically known as Mang Pao, or python robes.

The element associated with the Chinese dragon is water. The Long control rainfall, and water in streams, lakes, rivers, and seas. They are divided into five broad categories—heavenly, imperial, spiritual, and earthly dragons, and dragons who are guardians of hidden treasures. Dragons represent the Yang energy (as opposed to phoenixes, which represent the Yin) and usually hold kingly status. They frequently appear in human form and there are different dragon myths from regions all over China.

Early myths in the *Book of Mountains and Seas* record 138 supernatural beings with dragon or serpentine features. There were twenty-three mountains where immortals with human heads and dragon bodies roamed. Offerings of livestock, rice, and wine were made to them, and shamanic dances were performed to petition their protection. Descriptions of Zhu Long, who controlled day, night, and the seasons, show just what great powers were associated with dragons. The world changed from day to night when he closed his eyes; when he breathed in, summer began; when he breathed out, winter fell.

The single most unique feature of the Chinese dragon is that it stands as a symbol of wisdom, power, and good fortune. Unlike the covetous, dangerous, and destructive creatures in Western dragon lore, Chinese dragons are generally well intentioned. They like to have treasure, but will share it with mortals who come to their aid. And they will go to the aid of mortals if they are asked nicely—a trait picked up by the iconic manga *Dragon Ball*, which spawned the hugely popular *Dragon Ball Z* anime and all its offshoots. There are dragons, like the Jiao Long, the flood dragon, that causes trouble in the land, but good dragons like the winged Ying Long would come to people's aid. Ying Long helped Huang Di stop the floods during his battle with Chi You.

In northeasternmost China lives the legend of Tu Wei Ba Li Hei, Tailess Black Li, a black dragon and banisher of floods. It is said that this black dragon was born as a boy into a family with the name of Li. When he turned into a dragon, many feared him as a monster. They cut off his tail. But Li Hei still loved his homeland very much. When the white dragon brought on the floods, he subdued them. The villagers severely regretted how they had treated Li Hei, so they named their province Hei Long Jiang (Black Dragon River). The Bai minority in Yunnan have a similar myth that involves a dragon pearl and a little yellow dragon.

The Chinese myth of the scholar and the dragon king reflects the benevolence of the Long. It tells of a scholar in the Tang Dynasty called Liu Yi who was returning home after passing his exams in the capital. He walked past the lakes and saw a beautiful woman herding some sheep. She looked very distressed, so he spoke to her. She revealed that she was the daughter of the dragon king of Lake Dong Ting. Her father had married her to the son of the River Jing, who neglected and mistreated her. The dragon king knew nothing of her sufferings, as she was not allowed to leave her married home. She entreated Liu to carry a message to her father. Arriving at the northern banks of Lake Dong Ting, Liu found the sacred tangerine tree and, as instructed, tied his belt around it and knocked on the trunk three times. The dragon's servant asked Liu to close his eyes. When he re-opened them, he found he had been transported to the magical underwater palace of the dragon king.

Everyone in the palace wept when they heard the news of the daughter's distress. Qian Tang, the king's younger brother—whose territory, the Qian Tang River, is famous for being turbulent—flew into a rage, bringing down thunder, lightning, hail, and sleet before he stormed off. Soon Qian Tang returned with his niece, but only after causing thousands of deaths, damaging hundreds of acres of crops, and eating his treacherous nephew-in-law.

The scholar Liu Yi, who had been kind, was wined and dined and heaped with precious pearls. He was even offered the dragon king's daughter as a reward but declined, knowing the heartache the union between mortals and gods often brought. With much regret, Liu returned to live in the human world. He married twice, was widowed twice, and then was married a third time to a genteel woman who bore a remarkable resemblance to the dragon king's daughter. She later admitted that she was indeed that goddess. They lived on land happily until Liu got old, then went to live happily ever after in the fantastical palace under Lake Dong Ting.

What this story tells us is not only that the Long can be exceptionally kind, but also that you should never get on the wrong side of a dragon. The myth of Peking and Gao Liang demonstrates just what happens if you do.

In Chinese geomancy, dragon lines (like ley lines) are believed to be the earth's veins and arteries through which its energy flows. If this flow is obstructed, disaster will fall. Once upon a time, on the desolate salt marshes of You Zhou, where several dragon lines crossed, a very powerful dragon lived with his family. A Ming emperor wanted to build his capital there, and was encouraged to do so by the mischievous god, Ne Zha (see chapter 10). He built his city and named it Peking. Upset at this interloper building in his kingdom, the dragon turned into an old man and entered the emperor's dreams. He asked imperial permission to empty two jars of water into the sea—one filled with sweet water and one filled with bitter water. Little did the emperor know that he had been tricked into consenting to have all the water in Peking removed. He awoke from his dream to find all the springs and wells had dried up.

Ne Zha sent a dream to the imperial architect, Liu Bo Wen, informing him of what had happened. The architect ordered a report of traffic in the city, and heard that an old man and his wife had left with two heavy jars of water. Liu devised a plan in which a capable soldier would ride up to the couple and pierce the jars with a spear, returning all the water to the city before they reached the sea. Only one brave soul, a soldier named Gao Liang, volunteered. Liu made him promise not to look back after piercing the jars, only to ride home at top speed. All went according to plan, until Gao Liang pierced one jar and was pushed back by the force of the water. The furious dragon-in-disguise assumed his natural form and Gao had no choice but to ride away. He refrained from looking back despite the raging waves, noise, and confusion. Of course, in myths like this, where characters are told they must never break a taboo, they always do. Gao Liang was almost to the gates of Peking when he saw Liu and felt he was safe. As he took one look back, a giant wave fell on him and he drowned.

The water that was returned to Peking was from the jar from the wells, which supposedly explains why the city's drinking water now tastes slightly bitter. The jar Gao Liang failed to pierce contained sweet spring water, which remained in the mountains and has become the Jade Spring Hill of today. Sixteen gardens were built on the hill, but they were sadly destroyed during wartime. You can still visit there, however, to enjoy the gushing spring water and the natural scenery. To commemorate the brave Gao Liang, a bridge was built outside the city that still exists today on the borders of Hai Dian and Xi Cheng.

Dragons are well worth venerating because, apart from their amazing and sometimes terrifying appearance, they can bring a lot of good luck. For example, you may chance upon a dragon pearl. These are exceptionally precious to dragons, and they usually keep them in their mouths or under their chins. The radiant light from these pearls never fades and anything in proximity to them is sure to multiply. In a tale set in Si Chuan, a poor young boy lived with his mother on the banks of the River Min. He made a living by cutting grass to sell as animal fodder. Upon seeing a patch of grass that seemed to renew itself repeatedly, he dug it up to move it to his front garden. In the process, he discovered a mislaid dragon pearl. Learning of the pearl's properties, he was able to live in comfort with his mother while helping others in need.

When less kind neighbors figured out the source of the boy's good fortune, they came seeking the treasure. In a desperate attempt to keep it from falling into the wrong hands, the young man put the pearl into his mouth and accidentally swallowed it. The boy felt a burning sensation inside him and, no matter how much water he drank, he could not quench his thirst. The earth shook, great flashes rent the sky, and the heavens shook with thunder. The trembling young man saw scales grow from his legs and horns grow from his head. He was turning into a dragon. It may be lucky to find a dragon pearl. But don't, under any circumstances, swallow it.

Long, the Chinese dragon, continues to inspire amazing fantasy stories. In China, it recently appeared in new genres like silk-punk stories that look at historical China along alternative technological timelines. And in Western fantasy, Chinese myths of dragons are often combined with other Asian dragon myths to create unique worlds.

Chairman Mao

Chapter 17

Chairman Mao, Benefactor of the East

毛主席

Many of the gods I have written about here have their origins in ancient rituals. They have evolved out of the deification of heroes and artisans born hundreds, if not thousands, of years ago. Because of this, it is easy to assume that the creation of gods is something isolated to our ancient past. But this is not quite so.

In modern China—that is, post-imperial China—one figure has towered above any other warrior, leader, or craftsman. Although many politicians, revolutionaries, and pioneers have been influential in China, none has achieved the god-like status of this one man—Mao Ze Dong, whose name means "luster" or "benefactor of the East."

As a modern figure, Mao has not yet been categorized as a hero or villain. To millions, he fulfilled his destiny, bringing China into the 20th century. Millions more berate his legacy, remembering those who died in the name of "progress." Here, I do not seek either to endorse or vilify his life, only to explain his greatness from a devotee's point of view, and to investigate how his deification is occurring even today.

Communism is not a native Chinese school of thought, but modern China is associated with it around the world due to the acts of Chairman Mao, whose greatness is all the more remarkable considering his very humble beginnings. Mao was born in 1893 into a peasant family in Xiang Tan, Hu Nan. Privately taught from an early age, he won places at the province's top institutions on the strength of his own talent. In 1911, the eighteen-year-old joined the Xin Hai Revolution, which established China as a republic founded on socialist-democratic principles. After graduating, he worked as a librarian at Peking University, where he learned about Marxism and the October Revolution from China's leading politicians.

In 1919, the twenty-six-year-old returned home and led the May Fourth movement in Hu Nan, part of a nationwide student response to the government's concessions to decisions made at the Versailles Peace Conference. The following year, he founded a small Communist group in his hometown, which would later become the famous Chinese Communist Party (CCP).

For the generations who lived through the turmoil of the last years of imperial China and the subsequent decades of lawlessness, during which some political factions colluded with occupying foreign forces to carve up the country—not to mention the Japanese encroachment, invasion, and occupation that lasted on and off for half a century—Mao Ze Dong was the savior who hauled China out of years of infighting and colonial occupation. He was instrumental in creating a united national war for independence against Japanese occupation. He founded military bases in rural areas across north China, and inspired and trained workers and peasants across the country in highly effective guerilla warfare. It is safe to say that, without Mao, China would not have gained its independence in 1949, and might have remained a colony of invading forces indefinitely.

Above and beyond his military success, Mao was a great reformer. After the formation of the People's Republic of China in 1949, he carried out a series of reforms over two years against waste, bureaucracy, tax evasion, bribery, gross negligence, and embezzlement within the government. He instigated policies regarding equality for women, education for rural workers, and investment in science and industry. Mao was a visionary, with ideals for a socialist state.

Mao Ze Dong's mistake lay in his implementation of this ideal. His Great Leap Forward, which depleted the nation's resources to fill impossible quotas artificially, led to the Great Famine. His incitement of a proletariat class struggle led to an anti-rightest movement that was spurred on by factions, resulting in the notorious Cultural Revolution, which brought a decade of destruction upon China's heritage and intellectual talent. Although he realized his mistakes, Mao could not stop the train wreck. The error of his ways was officially recognized by the CCP five years after his death, and by the people. However, this has not stopped the nation from revering him as its great savior.

What was it about Mao that led to him become the image of the party and achieve god-like veneration?

Mao, as a person, had qualities beyond those of his fellow party leaders. He was outspoken, charismatic, and studious by nature, a trait that embodies the Chinese reverence for knowledge and learning, and places him naturally in a pantheon of scholarly gods. This was doubly remarkable because of his humble beginnings, validating the idea that, if one lowly villager can succeed, then so can you.

Mao was a poet. His use of language was exceptional, which explains why his collected works, which were once read by every Chinese citizen and have been read by millions around the world, are called *The Analects of Chairman Mao*. This work became the *de facto* book of unity within China, rather than the much drier manifesto of the CCP.

Mao's physical attributes lent themselves to being photographed and painted. In his iconic portraits, he was presented as a revolutionary and military leader, but also as a classical scholar in a cheongsam, gazing out at the beautiful landscape of his homeland. When the youth of the rest of the world went wild for the Beatles and the Rolling Stones, China's teenagers went crazy for Mao. My own family and friends of my parents' generation recounted to me their experiences attending Mao's huge rallies as Red Guards. After much overcrowding, shouting, cheering, and waving of their Little Red Books, some of them even fainted and had to be carried out, just like any overly enthusiastic groupie at a rock concert.

As an individual face among the ruling body, Mao filled a cultural void that had been evident since the days of Pu Yi, the last emperor of China. Because of this, he found himself in a position closely tied to godhood, a role that was reinforced after his death. Mao's mummified remains were placed in a tomb that is still open for public visitation in Tian'men Square directly outside the Forbidden City, the imperial palace of the last imperial dynasty of China.

In the case of other Chinese gods, long periods passed between a person's life and deeds and the moment when they were truly distinguished as gods. The faith of their devotees grew slowly over time. But this was not so for Mao. He was recognized, even in life, as a savior and a god. Many decades after his death, this faith in Mao Ze Dong has continued unabated, if not actively grown. In myriad temples and parks across the country that house shrines for national or local deities, you can find sellers of talismans, statues, and other artifacts and totems of worship of Mao, along with those for local deities and popular "guest" deities like Kuan Yin. The thoughtful face of Mao Ze Dong is presented in exactly the same way, often surrounded by brass charms or resin-sealed icons showing him as the leader of the Red Army. His *Analects* are sold side by side with sutras and Confucian texts. And in many houses, his portraits are placed reverently on the household shrines.

Whether or not you feel that Mao's achievements merit his elevation to the position of a deity, his memory now enjoys all the trappings of religious worship and demonstrates that the court of heaven is yet to be fully staffed.

Ma Shen, Horse Gods

马神

In early civilizations, humans lived more closely to animals, who provided support or inspired fear and awe. The *Book of Mountains and Seas* documents many mythical beings that arose in the Chinese imagination that seemed to be related to livestock, including creatures with human heads and horse bodies, or dragon heads and horse bodies. They are known as the Ma Shen.

For the Chinese, as for many other cultures, horses were vital to many aspects of life—agriculture, transport, and warfare—and even occasionally as part of the diet in times of hunger and need. Horses were so important to the Chinese that they were also used in the earliest animal sacrifices. This is why, to this day, some paper offerings are still horse-shaped and horse statues are believed to bring good luck.

The powerful capabilities of the horse were so admired that they eventually became legendary. There was a mythical horse named Ma Si who was assigned the task of transporting the moon to and fro each

Long Ma Si

day. So amazing was its flight that Ma Si was deified. This legend is still alive in parts of north China, where Ma Si images are still hung on walls. From this celestial horse, the idiom Tian Ma Xing Kong ("as the celestial horse crosses the sky") was derived, referring to a powerful and unrestrained imagination.

As early as the Zhou Dynasty, seasonal worship of the horse gods was decreed by the emperor. In springtime, Ma Zu, the ancestral horse god (not to be confused with Ma Zu, goddess of the sea), is venerated. The ancient Chinese believed that the ancestor of all horses is Long Ma, the mythical dragon horse. In the summer, Ma Mu Shen, the god of horse herds, tamer of wild horses, and deity for livestock farming, receives offerings. In the autumn, respect is paid to Ma She Shen, horse god of the land; in winter, Ma Bu Shen, the protector of horses, is petitioned to prevent the animals from catching diseases. Through the Sui, Tang, and Song Dynasties, veneration of the horse gods remained part of state rituals.

Horse gods were particularly popular during the reign of the founder of the Ming, Zhu Yuan Zhang, who ordered that their veneration fall under the care of the Tai Bu, one of his nine ministers. Temples flourished all over the country, with Tai Bu temples and committees specifically set up for horse-breeding and care. The trades of horse breeder and horse merchant blossomed, bringing these gods even more devotees. An official date of veneration was established during the Qing Dynasty— the twenty-third day of the sixth lunar month—with horse merchants offering rock-bottom prices to their customers on this day.

With advanced mobile weapons and automobiles, Ma Shen have lost some of their relevance in today's urban China, although Tian Ma, or Sky Horse, remains a very popular name for all types of companies—from those in the technology business, to couriers and clothing firms. Horse imagery is still closely associated with vitality in the Chinese psyche, with the idiom Long Ma Jing Shen ("as strong as a stallion") being a common wish on the new year and birthdays. Horse-themed pottery and bronze statues are still popular ornaments for the home or office.

There seem to be opportunities for Ma Shen to acquire a following in the West, where horseback riding and horse racing are popular pastimes. Ma Shen usually appear in the form of a majestic looking horse. If you own or ride a horse, acquire a statue for your shrine at home and make offerings to the Ma Bu Shen for the protection of your horse or pony from illness and accidents. With horseback riding becoming more popular with a certain strata of Chinese society, we may yet see this god revived in China as well.

CALENDAR OF CHINESE FESTIVALS

Chun Jie (Spring Festival, Chinese New Year)—Lunar New Year's Eve to the fifteenth day of the first lunar month.

Yuan Xiao Jie (Lantern Festival)—fifteenth day of the first lunar month

Qing Ming Jie (Qing Ming Festival, Festival of Pure Brightness, Tomb Sweeping Day)—fourth or fifth day of the fourth lunar month

Duan Wu Jie (Dragon Boat Festival)—fifth day of the fifth lunar month

Xia Zhi (Summer Solstice)—twentieth through the twenty-second day of June (Roman calendar)

Qi Xi (Qi Qiao, Double Seventh)—seventh day of the seventh lunar month

Zhong Yuan (Ghost Month, Hungary Ghost Festival)—fifteenth day of the seventh lunar month to the fourteenth day of the eighth lunar month

Zhong Qiu Jie (Mid-Autumn Festival, Moon Festival)—fifteenth day of the eighth lunar month

Chong Yang (Double Ninth)—ninth day of the ninth lunar month

Xia Yuan—fifteenth day of the tenth lunar month

Dong Zhi (Winter Solstice)—twentieth through the twenty-third day of December (Roman calendar)

La Ba Jie (La Yue Festival)—eighth day of the twelfth lunar month

Xiao Nian (Little New Year)—twenty-third or twenty-fourth day of the last lunar month until New Year's Eve

Timeline of Chinese Dynasties and Periods

China's Prehistory

1,000,000–12,000 BCE: Paleolithic Age

12,000–2000 BCE: Neolithic Age

    8000–5000 BCE: Beginning of agriculture

    5000–3000 BCE: Yang Shao civilization

    3000–2200 BCE: Long Shan civilization

2200–500 BCE: Bronze Age

    2200–1750 BCE: Xia Dynasty

    1750–1040 BCE: Shang Dynasty

    1100–256 BCE: Zhou Dynasty

    600–500 BCE: Beginning of Iron Age

Imperial China

    771–256 BCE: Eastern Zhou Dynasty

    403–221 BCE: Warring States (Spring and Autumn)

221–206 BCE: Qin Dynasty

206 BCE–8 CE: Western Han Dynasty

25–220 CE: Eastern Han Dynasty

220–589 CE: Period of North-South disunion (Northern and Southern Dynasties)

265–420 CE: Jin Dynasty

386–535 CE: Northern Wei Dynasty

589–618 CE: Sui Dynasty

618–907 CE: Tang Dynasty

960–1279 CE: Song Dynasty (Liao Empire of Northern Song, followed by Jin Empire of Southern Song)

1279–1368 CE: Yuan Dynasty (Mongol Empire)

1368–1644 CE: Ming Dynasty

1644–1911 CE: Qing (Manchurian Empire)

1840–1842: First Opium War

1850–1864: Taiping Rebellion

1856–1860: Second Opium War

1883–1885: Sino-French War

1894–1895 CE: Sino-Japanese War (Japanese begin occupation of Manchuria and Taiwan)

1900–1901 CE: Eight-Nation Alliance

Modern China

1911: Xin Hai (Republican) Revolution

1912: Presidency of Sun Zhong Shan (Sun Yat-Sen)

1912–1916: Presidency of Yuan Shi Kai

1916–1927: Warlord Era

1919: May Fourth Movement

1921: Founding of Chinese Communist Party

1927–1949: Guo Min Dang (Kuomintang) and Chinese Communist Party wrestle for power, known as the Chinese Civil War

1934–1936: Long March

1937–1945: Sino-Japanese Second War

1949: Birth of People's Republic of China

1957: Anti-Rightist Campaign

1958: Great Leap Forward

1959–1961: Great Famine

1966–1976: Cultural Revolution

BIBLIOGRAPHY

China: A New History, John King Fairbank and Merle Goldman, The Belknap Press of Harvard University Press, Cambridge (Massachusetts), 1992.

Chinese Gods: An Introduction to Chinese Folk Religion, Jonathan Chamberlain, Blacksmith Books, Hong Kong, 2009.

Chinese Gods and Myths, Grange Books, Kent, 1998.

Chinese Gods: the Unseen World of Spirits and Demons, Keith Stevens, 1998.

Chinese Whispers: Why Everything You've Heard About China Is Wrong, Ben Chu, Weidenfeld and Nicolson, London, 2013.

A Dictionary of Chinese Mythology, E. T. C. Werner, Kelly & Walsh, Shanghai, 1932.

Encyclopaedia Britannica (britannica.com)

Essential Chinese Mythology, Martin Palmer and Zhao Xiao Min, Thorsons, HarperCollins, London, 1997.

Feng Shen Yan Yi (*Investiture of the Gods*), Xu Zhong Lin, Yue Lu Press, Hu Nan, 2010 edition.

Handbook of Chinese Mythology, Li Hui Yang and De Ming An with Jessica Anderson Turner, Oxford University Press, New York, 2005.

Hua Xia Zhu Shen, Ma Shu Tian, Yan Shan Publishing, Beijing, 1990.

Liao Zhai Zhi Yi (*Strange Tales From a Chinese Studio*), Pu Song Ling, first published 1765, based on 1962 Zhang You He edition, Zhong Hua Shu Jü, Beijing, 2008.

Materialising Magic Power: Chinese Popular Religion in Villages and Cities, Wei-Ping Lin, Harvard University Asia Center, Harvard University Press, Cambridge (Massachusetts) and London, 2015.

Monkey, Wu Cheng-En, translated by Arthur Waley, Penguin Books, Middlesex (UK), 1961.

The Origin of Chinese Deities, Cheng Man Chao, translated by Chen De Zhen, Fang Zhi Yun, and Feng Hua Xiu, Foreign Language Press, Beijing, 1995.

Patron Gods of Popular Chinese Trades, Wu Jing Yu, illustrated by Chan Kok Sing, Asiapac Books, Singapore, 1997.

Shan Hai Jing (Book of Mountains and Seas), original text based on Qing Dynasty Hao Yi Xing edition and annotations on various Ming and Qing versions, Yue Lu Press, Hu Nan, 2006 edition.

Sou Shen Ji (In Search of Supernaturals), Gan Bao, based on the Ming Dynasty Wan Li edition, Foreign Language Press, Beijing, 2004.

Unruly Gods: Divinity and Society in China, edited by Meir Shahar and Robert P. Weller, University of Hawai'i Press, Honolulu, 1996.

Xi You Ji (Journey to the West), Wu Cheng-En, based on 1592 Jin Ling Shi De Tang edition, People's Literature Press, Beijing, 1955.

ENDNOTES

Introduction

1   A prosperous district, also rich in cultural heritage, in the city of Foshan, Guang Dong province; renowned for its chefs and its cuisine, the best of the best Cantonese food.

Chapter 1

2   An account of events in China up to the end of the 2nd century CE that is considered one of the most important texts of early Chinese history.

3   A collection of tales based on the Buddhist monk Xuan Zang's 7th-century journey to India that evolved in the folk and Buddhist oral traditions. Wu builds on and embellishes the traditional stories with poetry and song to create over 100 chapters that combine adventure, Buddhist teachings, and very readable prose of great literary beauty.

Chapter 2

4   Historians believe that Chinese legends and myths may have been propagated orally for about 1000 years before the earliest written record of them appeared in the 12th century BCE in books like *Shan Hai Jing*. The *Book of Mountains and Seas*, the popular name for *Shan Hai Jing*, describes in great detail not only the witchcraft, myths, and religion of ancient China, but also its geography, diverse regional customs, medicine, history, and ethnicity.

5   Qi Xi is also known and celebrated as Qi Qiao, the Festival of Skills, in honor of the goddess' time on earth as a weaver.

6   Gan Bao was an imperial historian of the Jin Dynasty who compiled stories about the supernatural in the form of a unique Chinese literary genre Zhi Guai, in which tales of the strange are recorded as if they were historical records.

Chapter 4

7   These included rheumatoid arthritis, infection, inflammation, boils and fever, and skin diseases. It is sometimes even used as a male contraceptive.

Chapter 5

8   This celebration emerged during the Han Dynasty and became a popular tradition during the Tang Dynasty. While the Chinese Moon Festival shares similarities with Western harvest festivals in which families re-unite and give offerings and thanks to the gods, in China, the festival is also a time when people gather to enjoy their union with nature and with each other.

9   A compilation of 2nd-century BCE texts on metaphysics, cosmology, and matters of the state assembled under the patronage of Liu An, nobleman of Huai Nan. A key Daoist text that partially inspired the emergence of Neo-Daoism.

10   Rebels of the Yuan Dynasty, like Zhang Shi Cheng, were said to have inserted secret messages into the filling of these cakes to be passed around as part of the resistance effort.

Chapter 7

11   The Chinese python resembles a dragon but has one fewer claw, which distinguishes the garments from imperial robes. The term "Yuan Bao" originally referred to early metal coins, but during the Yuan Dynasty became associated with taels, a form of Chinese currency.

12   Zheng He, born into a Chinese Muslim family as Ma San Bao, entered the court at a young age and served as a eunuch under the Ming Emperor Yong Le. He was a diplomat, warrior, explorer, and mariner who led his Great Armada on seven famous sea voyages, charting lands like Africa and South America nearly a century before European explorers. Little is known about Zheng's voyages due to the destruction of historical records. But recent publications by writers like Gavin Menzes have begun to shed light on his life and accomplishments.

Chapter 8

13   These twenty-four climate-based agricultural seasons (two per month) were originally devised to indicate stages in the cycles of planting and crop cultivation, and are therefore often closely associated with traditional festivities and customs.

14   These optimistically themed designs—usually of fairs, household gods, women, and children—are printed in bright colors using woodblocks, a technique later used in political art. He is especially popular in Fu Zi Tu (fortune paintings), typographical designs based on the Chinese character for fortune (福) that are similar to the decorated letters found in Western illuminated manuscripts.

Chapter 9

15   These lugubrious ghouls were featured in early Chinese horror movies and were made familiar around the world by Hong Kong Jiang Shi films of the 1980s and early 1990s, which have enjoyed a recent revival on mainland China. Due to an error in translation and representation, however, the Jiang Shi have been remembered as vampires rather than monsters in their own right that are far closer to zombies. This is hopefully being corrected by their continued evolution in the recent trend of grave-robbing adventure films. Whether vampire or zombie, however, these ghouls can not stand up to the magical powers of spells invested in the Zi.

16   There, a peach tree that can grant immortality grows and, in Chinese fantasy literature, it's a place where characters go as a last resort—usually to seek the power to save the world or to bring a loved one back to life. Don't confuse this mythical mountain with the real Kun Lun mountain range in west China and central Asia.

Chapter 10

17   One of the major endeavors of Daoism is to attain immortality by conditioning the body and mind, and by making and consuming elixirs—alchemical mixtures of metals and minerals refined by heat. These experiments often led to explosions, however. Indeed, it was in the process of making one of these concoctions that gunpowder was first discovered. The actual practice has been immensely mythologized in the deification of may Daoist supernatural beings.

18   A self-educated painter, poet, and calligrapher who was one of the last great masters of traditional Chinese painting. Known for his portraits of small things in nature such as fish, shrimps, crabs, and frogs rendered in fresh and lively ways, he won the 1955 International Peace Award.

19   Also known as Su Shi, this brilliant scholar held many official positions in various provinces. He was never afraid to critize the policies of ministers if they were detrimental to the people. Despite his repeated banishments, he remained optimistic throughout his long life. He was master of nearly all literary forms and founder of the Hao Fang ("heroic abandon") school of writing that emphasized spontaneity and expressiveness. Many of his greatest works were written in exile.

Chapter 11

20   One of the Si Xiang, or Four Symbols, mythological creatures in the Chinese constellation. Also, owing to the long lifespan of some tortoises, a symbol of longevity.

21   This semi-autobiographical novel about the decline of a large powerful family, also known as *The Dream of the Red Mansion*, famously documented a lot of traditional Chinese culture in its detailed descriptions and is considered one of the four cornerstones of Chinese literature, along with *Journey to the West*, *Outlaws of the Marsh*, and *Romance of the Three Kingdoms*.

Chapter 12

22   Statesman of the Qin kingdom who died in 235 BCE.

23   One of the five classics of Confucian literature that focuses on the moral principles behind imperial and scholarly rituals, etiquette, and decorum.

Chapter 13

24   Gnosticism, which grew out of the Jewish tradition and flourished in the Mediterranean region in the 2nd century CE, taught that the material world was created by an emanation of the highest God, trapping a divine spark within the human body that could be liberated by gnosis, which means "knowledge." This tradition thus blended well with the wisdom-based teachings of the Dao.

25   The great Tang poet known for rejecting courtly literary styles in favor of more elegant and simple verse based on old folk ballads, and for his protest of social ills like corruption and militarism.

26   Yuan was an advocate of literature as an instrument of ethical and social improvement and was known for his short fiction and the revival of Gu Wen, an ancient literary style.

Chapter 14

27   Daoists believed that ingesting certain minerals like mica would prolong life, and they sought to attain immortality making elixirs from these ingredients.

28   "Meng" is the Chinese term derived from the popular Japanese slang term "Moe," referring to a pretty, cute, and sweet female character archetype in manga, anime, and video games that generate strong feelings of affection from players.

ABOUT THE AUTHOR

Xueting Christine Ni was born in Guangzhou, during China's "reopening to the West." Having lived in cities across China, she emigrated with her family to England at the age of eleven, where she continued to be immersed in Chinese culture alongside her British education. She ultimately realized that this gave her a unique cultural perspective, bridging her Eastern and Western experiences. After graduating from the University of London with a degree in English Literature, Xueting began a career in the publishing industry, while also translating works of Chinese fiction. She returned to China in 2008 to continue her research at Central University of Nationalities, Beijing. Since 2010, Xueting has written extensively on Chinese culture and China's place in Western pop media, presenting publicly in collaboration with companies, theaters, institutions, and festivals. Having worked on manhua, poetry, documentaries, and science fiction, she continues her literary translation of China to the West, with a mission to help improve understanding of Chinese heritage, culture, and innovation, and introduce its wonders to new audiences. Xueting currently lives in the suburbs of London with her partner and their cat, both of whom are learning Chinese.

To Our Readers

Weiser Books, an imprint of Red Wheel/Weiser, publishes books across the entire spectrum of occult, esoteric, speculative, and New Age subjects. Our mission is to publish quality books that will make a difference in people's lives without advocating any one particular path or field of study. We value the integrity, originality, and depth of knowledge of our authors.

Our readers are our most important resource, and we appreciate your input, suggestions, and ideas about what you would like to see published.

Visit our website at *www.redwheelweiser.com* to learn about our upcoming books and free downloads, and be sure to go to *www.redwheelweiser.com /newsletter* to sign up for newsletters and exclusive offers.

You can also contact us at *info@rwwbooks.com* or at

Red Wheel/Weiser, LLC
65 Parker Street, Suite 7
Newburyport, MA 01950